Here is a link to the past

Anyone who fixes up an old house understands. . . .

Here was where someone had built a life, and as far as anyone knew this was all that remained—their contribution to the enterprise in which we were somehow all engaged. That made the house a precious thing, a window on an age that had otherwise slipped away. It brought out your inner archaeologist. Just when you were fed up with leaky roofs and sclerotic pipes and at the point of calling in the bulldozers, you'd haul up on some dusty artifact from days long past, and instantly your mind would be as afroth with questions as if you'd found a fragment of cuneiform in some *tel* in the Mideast: *What was it for? What did it mean? What were these people* thinking? And sometimes, seeing as this was a house in the city: *What went wrong?*

—from *The Barn House*

"A lively, often funny, sometimes startling, occasionally surreal account of the rehabbing process, from getting the mortgage to choosing the architect to balancing dreams with reality. It's the perfect book for armchair or would-be renovators." —*Booklist*

"Enlightening. And entertaining. [Zotti's] humor brings to mind Dave Barry." —*St. Louis Post-Dispatch*

"If you are a do-it-yourselfer with a compulsion to fix up a house, this will be a fun read, and you can laugh along as Ed hires a homeless trumpeter to guard the open house, forgets to wish his wife a happy Mother's Day, and single-handedly tames ancient radiators, forcing their rusted bushings to yield to his will. . . . I have no idea what a bushing is, either, but I read all forty pages about that incident, a classic tale of Man vs. Rusty Widget. It was just that amusing." —*Chicago Sun-Times*

VIEW FROM STREET   3·19·93

The

BARN HOUSE

Confessions of an Urban Rehabber

Ed Zotti

 NEW AMERICAN LIBRARY

New American Library
Published by New American Library, a division of Penguin Group (USA) Inc., 375 Hudson Street, New York, New York 10014, USA • Penguin Group (Canada), 90 Eglinton Avenue East, Suite 700, Toronto, Ontario M4P 2Y3, Canada (a division of Pearson Penguin Canada Inc.) • Penguin Books Ltd., 80 Strand, London WC2R 0RL, England • Penguin Ireland, 25 St. Stephen's Green, Dublin 2, Ireland (a division of Penguin Books Ltd.) • Penguin Group (Australia), 250 Camberwell Road, Camberwell, Victoria 3124, Australia (a division of Pearson Australia Group Pty. Ltd.) • Penguin Books India Pvt. Ltd., 11 Community Centre, Panchsheel Park, New Delhi - 110 017, India • Penguin Group (NZ), 67 Apollo Drive, Rosedale, North Shore 0632, New Zealand (a division of Pearson New Zealand Ltd.) • Penguin Books (South Africa) (Pty.) Ltd., 24 Sturdee Avenue, Rosebank, Johannesburg 2196, South Africa

Penguin Books Ltd., Registered Offices:
80 Strand, London WC2R 0RL, England

Published by New American Library, a division of Penguin Group (USA) Inc. Previously published in a New American Library hardcover edition.

First New American Library Trade Paperback Printing, September 2009
10 9 8 7 6 5 4 3 2 1

Copyright © Ed Zotti, 2008
All rights reserved
Illustrations by Charlie Friedlander
Frontispiece by Bruce Bondy

NAL REGISTERED TRADEMARK—MARCA REGISTRADA

New American Library Trade Paperback ISBN: 978-0-451-22787-4

The Library of Congress has cataloged the hardcover edition of this title as follows:
Zotti, Ed.
    The barn house: confessions of an urban rehabber/Ed Zotti; illustrations by Charlie Friedlander.
        p. cm.
    ISBN 978-0-451-22557-3
    1. Dwellings—Remodeling—Illinois—Chicago. 2. urban beautification—Illinois—Chicago. 3. Zotti, Ed—Homes and haunts. I. Title.
TH4816.Z68 2008
690'.837—dc22   2008009397

Set in Adobe Garamond
Designed by Jessica Shatan Heslin/Studio Shatan, Inc.

Printed in the United States of America

Penguin is committed to publishing works of quality and integrity.
In that sprit, we are proud to offer this book to our readers;
however, the story, the experiences, and the words
are the author's alone.

To my wife Mary,
and my children Ryan, Ani, and Andrew,
without whom I'd have had no story to tell

Acknowledgments

My thanks first of all to Charlie Friedlander, a good friend and fine architect, who contributed most of the illustrations. I also acknowledge with gratitude the encouragement and good counsel of those who read the manuscript at various stages, among them Bob Bruegmann, my editor Mark Chait of New American Library, the Chief, Howard Decker, Charlie again, Ann and Jim Kepler, Ruth Knack, Ann LaFarge, my agent Dave Larabell, my wife Mary Lubben, Irene Macauley, Mike Miner and Betsy Nore, Jim Shapiro (especially Jim Shapiro), Sue Sharrock, and Bob Yovovich. If you think this book is a mess now, you should have seen it before. Thanks also to Bruce Bondy, Gabe Burgos, Ned Coe, Tony Czupryna, Diane and James Fitzhugh, Lisa Hoffer, Fran Markwardt, Kendall Mallette, Pat O'Neil, Ned Reece, Jane and John Santogrossi, Carol Sills, Mike Waechter, and the Rev. Jack Wall for their valuable contributions. Finally, my deepest appreciation to the workers too numerous to name who helped rebuild the Barn House, including my friends and relatives who volunteered—they proved craftsmanship isn't dead, it merely awaits summoning.

THE BARN HOUSE

PROLOGUE

Around noon on what was surely the worst day of his life, my friend Mike got a call from a neighbor telling him that smoke was pouring out of the chimney of his house on the north side of Chicago. It wasn't the usual sort of smoke. The house was on fire.

Mike hurried home to find his house surrounded by fire engines, policemen, and curious bystanders. Up on the roof of the front porch a fireman in a black raincoat stepped out of a window and came down a ladder carrying Mike's ten-month-old daughter, Joanna. Her eyes were rolled up and she was covered with soot. "She's alive," the fireman told Mike as he put the baby in an ambulance. "What about the woman who was in there?" Mike asked. His housekeeper, Nina, had been in the house watching Joanna while he and his wife worked. "She's dead," a cop said. "We think she's been murdered."

Nina had been beaten and choked and her body submerged in a running bathtub on the second floor of the house. Joanna had been lying only a few feet away. Apparently the killer then went down to the basement and set a fire in another bathroom. The bathroom was destroyed and most of the house suffered smoke damage.

A few days later Mike asked several people, including my friend Mary and me, to help him sort through his family's belongings and make an inventory for the insurance adjusters. I worked in the disheveled basement; Mary went upstairs with Mike's wife, Betsy. We didn't speak much that I remember. I didn't ask Mike whether he and his family planned to stay in the house; probably at that point he didn't know. In the end they stayed. Mike wrote a column about the experience for the newspaper both of us worked for. Joanna recovered uneventfully.

Sometime later the police arrested a man in connection with another murder and a rape, and, in the interest of closing the books on Mike's case, decided the fellow had killed Nina, too. Mike had his doubts, but the police didn't pursue the matter further. The evidence in the other cases was persuasive enough to earn the man a life sentence; he was never formally charged with Nina's murder.

As time went on I saw less of Mike. By the time Mary and I started looking for a house—we were married now, with two kids and a third planned—it had been years since I'd been down his street.

Mary and I (well, I) wanted to stay in the city. But the prices in the most popular neighborhoods were well beyond our reach, even for fixer-uppers. We started looking farther out, in areas that were still a little rough. One winter's day Mary drove by a place that struck her, in what presumably was dim light, as promising. We both went back to see it.

Yowsah, I thought as I peered out the car window. The house was the kind of place that the neighborhood kids probably held their breath and crossed their fingers when walking past. The front porch pillars splayed out and the porch roof seemed on the point of collapse. The steps and railings sagged. The paint, an ugly yellow and brown, was peeling in birch-bark-sized flakes. Some of the window sashes had rotted; pieces hung at odd angles. The roof had a misshapen appearance that bespoke weekend remodelers with too little patience and too much beer. The entire building was covered with enormous weather-beaten cedar shakes installed by someone whose architectural goals had pretty much been limited to keeping out the rain. Still, it was big and cheap compared to other places we had seen, and sat on a lot that for the city was unusually large. We called the real estate broker and arranged a walk-through.

That night I looked again at the address on the real estate listing. "You know," I said to Mary, "this place is two doors up from Mike and Betsy's. You remember. We went there one time."

"I remember," she said after a moment.

Two weeks later, in February 1993, we signed a contract to buy the Barn House, as the kids, and then we, called it. This is the story of that house.

1

I don't remember when I decided I wanted to fix up an old house, but it must have occurred at an early age. The fixing-up part I came by naturally. My parents had started renovating their first house (of two) in 1952, a few months after I was born. I spent much of my childhood holding up objects (boards, pipes, screen doors) that my father was working on the other end of. My father was an irascible perfectionist in all things. I shivered in the cold for hours while he fussed with storm windows and chimney caps and asphalt siding. The experience taught me several things: *Life is hard. Things take a long time. There is no job that, with advance planning, can't be made twice as complicated.* But also: *There's a right way to do everything.*

I became the family electrician at the age of fourteen, shortly after my parents bought their second house. This was partly by default and partly by design. The design arose from my determination to avoid plaster-mixing duty, the fate of my younger brothers, which I found tedious beyond description. The default part stemmed from the fact that all my father knew about electricity was that you weren't supposed to connect the black and white wires together. I, on the other hand, had played with electric trains as a child and had owned Remco Thinking Boys' Toys— men of a certain age will recall these as small cardboard canisters containing bits of plastic and wire that could be assembled into electric motors and telegraphs and such—and on the basis of this rigorous technical training had learned how to wire a three-way switch. In addition, I had a certain rough-and-ready ability to figure things out, although I claim no special gift in this regard.

The key thing, and you'll forgive my bragging a bit, was that I was dogged—again, not a unique gift, but an indispensable one for grappling with life's more intractable tasks, of which home renovation was certainly one. Take the matter of three-way switches. As it turned out, there are actually two ways to wire a three-way switch, the way every electrician knows and another way that I've never seen before or since.[1] This second way, I discovered one afternoon, had been used to wire the lights in the front hall of my parents' home. The lights had manifestly worked at one time, but in trying to change the switches (they were the old-fashioned push-button kind, which my parents found unseemly in their updated house), I'd mixed up the wires. Now, examining the grimy interior of the switchbox, I discovered to my alarm that the available wires didn't lend themselves to any combination that in my limited experience was likely to produce the desired result. It was like a third-year medical student opening up a patient on the operating table and finding a kidney where he expects to see a lung. I had no idea how to get the lights to work.

Thoroughly confused and a little panicky lest my parents find out, I sat down with a piece of paper and a stubby pencil to draw wiring diagrams in an attempt to parse the matter out. It was a

[1] Those having an interest in such things will find a diagram in Appendix A.

long afternoon, made longer by the fact that I had connected the wires incorrectly at one point, shorting out the switches and rendering them irreparable even if I'd been Thomas Edison. (They were the silent type, which used mercury as a conductor, and in shorting them I had apparently vaporized the mercury.) But by suppertime, by God, I'd figured the thing out.

"Took you a while," said my father, as I flicked the lights on and off at last.

"Eh," I said, "bastards didn't use travelers." My father had no idea what a traveler was, which wasn't surprising since I myself had learned the term not three hours previously from a book I'd consulted in hopes of clarifying matters. But he was suitably impressed.

My parents' second house, in the Chicago suburb of Oak Park, had been built in 1890; they purchased it in 1966. It had been reasonably well maintained, but no substantial work had been done on it in the seventy-six years since its construction. The kitchen was tiny and primitive; there was no family room. My parents proposed to remedy these defects by building an addition. They hired a contractor to dig out the basement, pour the foundation, frame the walls, and put on the roof. Most of the interior work we did ourselves. This included replacing the plumbing and much of the wiring, and then plastering the walls.

My father's principal assistant and consultant in this work was his friend George, a sheet-metal worker. George and my father had their hands full with the plumbing. One afternoon after hooking up the supply lines for the second-floor bathroom they signaled my mother to open the main valve. Water squirted from every joint—they'd used threaded steel pipe. The bathroom looked like the fountains of Rome. "Jesus Christ, Mare! Shut it off!" my father shouted from the top of the basement stairs. I was in stitches, of course. The old man was less amused.

Preoccupied as they were, George and my father didn't have much time to hassle me about the electrical work, which was fine by me. George didn't know much more about electricity than my father, but he presented me with an electrician's manual that he thought might help me out. It had been published by Sears, Roebuck—probably, as I think back on it now, in the wake of the Rural Electrification Act of 1936. I remember there was something in there about how to wire up your egg incubator. The basic principles were universally applicable, though, and what I couldn't get from the book I picked up by trial and error.

There was a great deal of entertainment value in this process. I remember once I was connecting overhead lights in the kitchen. It was late in the evening; I was tired; I wanted to finish up and go to bed. My mother was providing assistance, which consisted of throwing switches on the main panel in the basement when instructed.

I twisted one last wire nut. "Okay, Ma," I shouted down the stairs. "Switch it on."

There was a moment of silence, then a loud pop. A shower of sparks shot out of the ceiling box. (I don't remember what I had done—probably connected the black and white wires together.)

Whoa, I thought. *Being an electrician is* fun.

It was, too. Three things could happen during a wiring job. First, it worked. You had gloom and powerlessness before; now you had light. This was always cool. Second, you could be killed. The chances of this were small, luckily, but the possibility lent a daredevil edge to the proceedings that you didn't get from mixing plaster. Third, you had a spectacular failure, which might involve a loud noise, destruction of tools, blackening of surprisingly large areas on exposed metal parts, loss of power to much of the premises, and alarmed expressions on the faces of those nominally in charge, none of which was likely to strike the average teenager, and certainly didn't strike me, as problematic. (I'd long since gotten over the harrowing uncertainty associated with anomalous three-way switches.)

Once, while working as a summer helper for an electrical contractor a couple years later, I was given the job of cutting the wires that powered the portable cloth cutters at a factory that made men's suits. (We were replacing the old wiring with new.) The cutters used "three-phase," a specialized type of high-voltage power. I was supposed to pull the plug out of the power source in the ceiling, yank the other end of the wire out of a retractor suspended below, then clip off the connector on the end. Pull, yank, clip. Pull, yank, clip. There were dozens of cutters, the work was repetitious, and it was a warm summer's day. My attention began to wander. Pull, yank, clip. Pull, yank, clip. Yank, clip—*pop!* There was a blinding flash, a pencil-lead-sized hole appeared in my wire clippers, and all work on the assembly line involving cloth cutters came to an abrupt halt. The foreman ran over and chewed me out. I looked suitably abashed and promised I would never do it again. But I considered it a day well spent.

Being the electrician gave one a certain basic life confidence. On one occasion while wiring my parents' house I was trying to hook up two lights in different locations that were to be operated by the same switch. Not knowing any better, and thinking I might economize on wire, I connected the lights in series rather than in parallel. When I flipped the switch, the lights shone at half intensity. I puzzled for a moment, realized my mistake—I'd had this problem with Remco Thinking Boys' Toys once—then corrected the wiring. When I flipped the switch again, the lights shone at normal intensity.

My father, who'd been observing this procedure, asked me what I'd done. I explained. He was mystified. I provided a more detailed explanation using my stubby pencil on a scrap of gypsum board. He still didn't get it. I hammered away at the subject for a good twenty minutes. At length my father leaned back and said with a resigned expression, "Well, at least *you* understand it."[2]

[2]Those believing they're better equipped to handle this than my old man may inspect the diagram in Appendix B.

You can appreciate the position this puts one in. I was just short of fifteen years old. Like all adolescents I affected to believe my parents were morons while secretly clinging to the belief that if things really went off the rails I could get my dad to put things right. Now that pleasant sense of security had been swept away. I was in effect being told: *It's all up to you, schmuck.* At some point in life everyone comes to such a realization. Prior to it he is a child; afterward, whatever profound mental, physical, and moral deficiencies he may have—I'm thinking of my brother here—he's an adult.

So it was with me. I spent the rest of the summer wiring the house and can say with some assurance that everyone was satisfied with the result, which is to say the lights all operated and the house didn't burn down, to my mind the acid test of quality electrical work. To be sure, I made my share of mistakes, some of which didn't become apparent until later. There was the business of the soffit lights[3] in the kitchen, for example, where, having packed the maximum number of conductors into a conduit run and not having any more wire anyway, I decided to hook a switch into the neutral side of a circuit. The lights seemed to work fine and I considered the project a job well done till some years later, when I got an anxious call from my mother: There was something wrong with the soffit lights. It wasn't that she couldn't turn them on; she couldn't turn them *off*. They were fluorescent lights, you see, and one of the ballasts had melted and shorted to the frame. Normally this failure would have tripped the circuit breaker, but, owing to the inopportune siting of the switch, it instead provided an alternative path to ground for the balance of the lights on the line.

---

[3]To a carpenter, a soffit is a boxlike piece of framing hung from the ceiling, commonly found above kitchen cabinets. (Another frequent use is to conceal air-conditioning ducts.) Soffit lights are built into the soffit to provide task lighting for the counters below.

Obvious, no?[4] It took me a couple minutes, too. I was able to repair things for the time being, but—I tell you this truly—for the ensuing thirty-one years it bothered me that someday long after my time the ballast would fail again, the lights wouldn't shut off, and some electrician called in to deal with the mess would think: *What horse's ass did* this? Which is why one day at age forty-six, with my own house far from finished, I went out to my parents' home with several spools of wire and, while my flabbergasted family watched (I had timed this to coincide with a reunion), pulled all the wiring out of the kitchen ceiling, ran new, and hooked up the lights correctly, thereby, in my view, getting right with God at last.

You may think I digress. Not so. I speak for a class of person that is little heralded in this day and age—the class that says: *I will get this right or die.* And for another class also, to a considerable extent coinciding with the first, that says: *It's all up to me*, and (I suppose this class is somewhat larger, since it includes Frank Sinatra): *I'm going to do it my way.* It's largely these people who have rebuilt cities in our time, and if they recognize themselves in this book, the effort will have been well spent.

That brings me to a second point I want to address before taking up my story. It wasn't enough for me to fix up an old house; I wanted to fix up an old house in the city. I'm not sure exactly when or why I fastened on this idea. My family's first home had been in the city, but my brothers and sisters had lived there without in consequence forming the opinion that they needed to reside in cities ever after. Just the opposite—the city was something they were happy to leave behind. I was different. I was a city guy.

It may be presumptuous to say so, but it seems to me that being a city guy is a little like being gay. There's nothing inherently good or bad about it; it's just what you are. You may try to

[4]Maybe not. See Appendix C.

live in the suburbs like other people, and for a time you may succeed. But one day your primal impulses will reassert themselves,
and you'll find yourself prowling the streets looking for Italian
beef or cheese steaks[5] or some other low commodity; or riding the
subway doing the crossword (or I suppose nowadays the sudoku)
puzzle;[6] or sitting at a rickety café table adjacent to whatever
grand promenade your town may have, ostensibly reading the
newspaper while surreptitiously checking out the *boulevardiers*; or
bicycling along the waterfront on a warm summer evening with
the lake (ocean, river, whatever) on one side, purple clouds coil-
ing behind the tall buildings on the other, and the human pag-

---

[5]An Italian beef is a sandwich made of spicy sliced beef on Italian bread
drenched in juice. Having eaten this delicacy most of my life and assumed it
was a staple of Italian national cuisine, I was surprised to learn in college that
it was available only in Chicago. This was like finding out Chicago was the
only place that had girls. Why Italian beef hasn't found a wider audience is
an abiding mystery. The cheese steak, as I suppose most inhabitants of the
East Coast know, is a sandwich consisting of chopped grilled steak with
melted cheese on Italian bread, which originated at a place I know only as
Pat's in Philadelphia. Like Italian beef it's exceedingly tasty, but, also like Italian beef, will kill you if consumed in excess, meaning oftener than maybe
once a year. However, I venture to say anyone departing this vale of tears as a
result of Italian beef or cheese steak overdose will die with a smile.
[6]I include this recognizing that even among confirmed city dwellers mass
transit is more tolerated than enjoyed, but it remains one of the quintessential
urban experiences, and riding it is not without, shall we say, opportunities for
personal growth. One night during freshman year at college I and my room-
mate Mike (a different Mike) were riding the L, as the rapid transit system in
Chicago is known, when a large middle-aged man across the aisle began addressing us in a loud but incomprehensible voice, owing to the fact that he
was stone drunk. Growing agitated at his evident failure to communicate, the
man restated his proposition several times in a progressively more belligerent
tone. Still no go. Mike, a nice Jewish boy from suburban Philadelphia, looked
completely terrified, and I felt a little anxious myself. On the third or fourth
iteration, however, it dawned on me what the man was saying. "Right!" I
shouted back. "Joe Louis! Joe Louis was the world's greatest fighter!" Delighted at having made himself understood, the man broke into a grin, shook
our hands, and staggered off at the next stop.

eant all around; and you'll think: *Who am I trying to kid? I'm a city guy. This is where I live.*

A city guy doesn't live in the city because he has to, or because it's more convenient, or because all his buddies live there, or because the rent is cheaper, or because he has a better chance of getting laid, although all of these things may be true, rent by and large being the exception. He lives there because it's where he's happiest.

A city guy isn't necessarily smarter or hipper or more virtuous or better-looking than suburban people, not that it would take much. He's merely, shall we say, a little less risk-averse.

The city guy isn't necessarily male, although it must be said there are significant attitudinal differences between male and female city folk. The city girl worries about the children. The city boy figures they're small and quick and can dodge the bullets.

The city guy has an unshakable optimism. Once I telephoned a couple I knew to get some comments for a magazine article I was writing about the neighborhood they were living in, a gentrifying but not then gentrified section of Chicago called Bucktown. The wife wasn't sold on it. "Last year there was a drive-by shooting," she fretted. Her husband, whom I spoke to separately, had more of a city-guy take on the situation. "It's been a year since we had a drive-by shooting," he said.

City people turned up in unexpected quarters. When our children were small we hired a young woman from Switzerland to help care for them. Her name was Petra. She had been raised on a farm near a tiny village outside Lucerne. Made no difference. Upon moving in with us she discovered she was a city person and spent most of her spare time out on the town. After she had been with us a while she accompanied us on a vacation to my in-laws' in Tennessee. Petra wasn't impressed with the Smoky Mountains—she had lived in the Alps. She was a good sport during the trip, but you could tell she was bored. Heading home at last, we turned off the interstate at the first city exit past the steel mills, wound through a park past a museum, then drove up Lake Shore Drive. The weather was cool—May in Chicago can be like that—but there were boats on the lake and joggers, bicyclists, and picnickers in the park, and ahead of us in the blue haze you could see the tall buildings downtown. As soon as all this came into view Petra brightened noticeably—it's little exaggeration to say she glowed. She was far from her native land; she'd lived in the city for just eight months. But she was home.

The city guy is accustomed to being thought a little odd, an impression he is (well, I was) happy to encourage. Once while I was at a business dinner a fellow at my table was holding forth on the glories of the house he owned in, I think, rural Indiana. "I'm surrounded on three sides by forest!" he exclaimed. I leaned over to the woman next to me, another city dweller, and stage-whispered, "I'm surrounded on three sides by the Latin Kings."[7] The woman laughed. The suburbanites at the table stared. Other city folk may form their own judgments, but I thought: *Nicely done.*

Non-city people are often baffled by the desire to live in the city and bring up numerous objections to it. In the suburbs, they say, crime is lower; the schools better; the gasoline (and a great many other goods and services) cheaper; the shopping opportunities greater (assuming your idea of shopping is going to Wal-Mart); the houses bigger and generally, although this varies with the neighborhood, less costly on a square-foot basis; the streets wider; the parking easier; the air cleaner; the park space more abundant; the traffic less congested; the neighborhood quieter;

---

[7]I hasten to say this wasn't literally the case. So far as I knew, the kids in what was known in the neighborhood as the "bad building" behind us weren't affiliated with the Latin Kings street gang; they were freelance delinquents. Even that may be putting it too strongly. While staving in my neighbor's garage door with a truck couldn't be dismissed as youthful hijinks, experience suggested that many of the balls, toy cars, and like items that went missing were carried off by five-year-olds unclear on the concept of private property. I still wonder what happened to those four plastic lawn chairs, though.

the locals less likely to have (or deserve) criminal records; the government bureaucracy more responsive; the public services better; the police politer; the incidence of drive-by shootings lower; the potholes fewer; the graffiti less prevalent; the public utilities in better repair.

"Perhaps so," the city guy will concede grudgingly. "But the city has better coffee."[8] The city guy isn't about to get drawn into a discussion of practicalities, because he knows that the practical advantages of urban life make for a short list. Better bus service, which to a suburbanite is like boasting that you've got cleaner jails. More restaurants, in some cities anyway. Easier access to drugs, and we're not talking about the kind sold at Walgreens. You see my point.[9]

The city guy knows that if he can nudge the discussion into intangibles, things even up a bit. "Cities are dirty fun," my non-city-guy brother Bob once acknowledged. Bob being Bob, I imagine he was thinking of how he and Kevin McGuire used to throw flaming model airplanes off the back of the third-floor porch. But surely his comment applies in a more general sense: Cities are entertaining.

One December when I was very young, probably no more than four or five, my mother took Bob and me downtown to go Christmas shopping. Chicagoans often reminisce about looking in the display windows of the Marshall Field's department store,[10] which

[8]One recognizes that with the funguslike spread of Starbucks to the suburbs this isn't as true as it used to be.

[9]Some city people, it must be said, are in denial about this. No disrespect, but New Yorkers are by far the worst offenders. I talked once with a fellow who had moved from Chicago to Brooklyn for career purposes, and who was having a hard time making the adjustment. "People come up with the weirdest rationalizations for living here," he said. "I wanted to buy a frying pan, and a guy told me, 'Well, one thing about New York, you can always find a frying pan.' And I thought, *I should hope to God.*"

[10]Although there is still a large retail establishment located in the building formerly occupied by Marshall Field's, the store itself, alas, is no more, having been sold to another company. I forget the name of it.

were elaborately decorated for the holidays. I suppose we did that, but it's not what I remember. Rather, it was the return trip home on the bus. It was evening; the weather was cold; the bus was crowded. Somehow my mother got a seat for us. She was a gregarious woman who could get into a twenty-minute conversation with a wrong number; the other passengers were in good spirits. Soon a general discussion was under way. The other passengers began fussing over my brother and me. A stout man in a heavy coat asked us in a conspiratorial tone: *Want to see something?* Of course we did. He pulled out a handkerchief, stuck it in his left ear, fished for a moment, then pulled it out of his right. My brother and I watched with our mouths open. The crowd laughed and applauded. The idea formed in my mind: *A city was a place where strangers would take it upon themselves to amuse you.* Long afterward I realized, as all city dwellers eventually do, that we'd been not so much spectators as the show. But the seed of city-guyness had been well planted.

It's the rare non-city guy who's completely immune to the attractions of urban life. I once lived in an apartment building that stood beside the Chicago River. One day I had my family over for dinner on the rooftop deck. One could hear the clanking of painters on cleats as boats tugged against their moorings in the marina below. Other craft cruised up and down the waterway; waves splashed against the pilings in their wakes. A few blocks away the towers of the city glinted in the sunset. You would have had to be in a coma to be oblivious to the charm of such a scene. My brother-in-law Dave, a suburbanite so committed he refused to allow me to lock the car doors when I accompanied him to a suburban strip mall, gazed around, drink in hand. "I have to admit," he said. "The river. The boats. The buildings. This is cool."

Just so. Cities were cool. Things happened in them that weren't likely to happen anywhere else. I remember an event that occurred when Jane Byrne was mayor of Chicago during the early 1980s. Ms. Byrne's tenure isn't now remembered as one of the bright spots of Chicago history, but she had a sort of bread-and-circuses approach to municipal administration that, while probably unhealthy as a regular thing, could be entertaining in small doses. One year she or someone in her administration decided that there should be fireworks on New Year's Eve. Official fireworks displays in Chicago are normally held on the lakefront, where there's plenty of room. This time, through some decision-making process the details of which are mercifully obscure, it was determined that the fireworks should be held downtown, near the Michigan Avenue bridge, which crosses the Chicago River. The Chicago River isn't especially wide, and is lined with tall buildings. The reader can guess what a fireworks display in such a confined space was like. A cherry bomb in a garbage can gives a pretty close approximation.

Mary and I went to see the celebration. It was the most spectacular display of pyrotechnics I ever expect to witness not involving an act of war. Rockets bounced off buildings. Bursting incendiaries filled one's entire field of vision. Bits of scorched paper rained down; the air was filled with acrid smoke. Planets have surely been spawned with less noise.

It lasted fifteen minutes, more or less. Our reaction, and I venture to say I speak for everyone in attendance, could be summarized as: *holy shit.* We stumbled home completely shell-shocked. The event was never held again. Ms. Byrne wasn't reelected for reasons unrelated to fireworks—New Year's Eve fireworks, anyway. But I bet even now there are nights when she stares out her apartment window at the city lights and thinks: *Let's see those bastards in the suburbs top* that.

So okay, life in the city had its points. One still faced the question of the vantage from which best to enjoy it. Apartments were all very well when you were in your twenties. At a certain stage of life, however—city dwellers were no different from suburbanites in this respect—one entertained thoughts of a house. Thus do we arrive at the subject of this book.

City guys tend to like old houses, which is good, because in the city that's mostly what there are. In years past the city guy was obliged to become a rehabber whether he wanted to or not, mainly because the city houses he could afford to buy were in such a dilapidated state that emergency repairs were often required to achieve basic livability. (In some ways things aren't so different now, but that's a topic we'll explore in greater depth later.)

Not every city guy likes to fix up old houses, and not everyone who fixes up old houses is a city guy, but the two tend to go hand in hand. To the city guy, or at least a large subclass of city guys—and here I include myself—the city is an old house writ large. Give him a house or an old neighborhood, and his first thought is: *This will be really nice when it gets fixed up.* Never mind that right now it looked like Dogpatch. One took the long view.

Fixing up an old house in the city is nothing like fixing up an old house anywhere else. It's not that the process of construction is so much different. In the city as in the suburbs, one uses nails, hassles with contractors, and gasps at how much faucets cost. It's true that the scale of an urban project is often greater, since city houses are so frequently neglected; you get used to working in close quarters and worrying about things like subsidence and equipment clearances and where you're going to park the Dumpster.

The more important difference, however, is that the city guy working on an old house must contend with, how shall I say, sociological considerations, by which I mean everything from rats in the alley to the local crime rate.[11] A suburbanite faced with such

[11]Crime and neglect by no means exhaust the list of urban perils. In 1992, the year before we bought the Barn House, gas utility workers in a gentrifying Chicago neighborhood called River West opened a valve on a pressure regulator they were overhauling, inadvertently sending a surge of high-pressure gas through the mains serving the surrounding neighborhood. Within a short time eighteen buildings had blown up, killing four people. Although it soon dawned on the gas workers that the howling sirens, explosions, fires, and

problems has a relatively easy out—move. For a city guy, however, living in the city is the point. It's not enough, therefore, to fix up the house; sometimes you have to fix up the neighborhood, too.

In pursuit of that goal the city guy will endure extraordinary hardships. About the time we began work on the Barn House, I interviewed a couple who lived on the south side of Chicago for a magazine story. James was black; Diane was white; they had one child. They were both teachers. They lived in an area called North Kenwood/Oakland. Kenwood had once been one of the wealthiest sections of the city—Julius Rosenwald, the president of Sears, Roebuck, had built a mansion there in the 1920s. Starting in the late 1940s, black people began moving in and the neighborhood became poorer. The University of Chicago, which was close by, decided that it would try to shore up the portion of Kenwood nearer to the campus through interventions of various kinds (some of which generated considerable controversy). But it lacked the resources to preserve everything, and North Kenwood was left to fend for itself.

---

chaos surrounding them were quite likely their fault, they didn't shut off the gas for forty minutes pending instructions from their superiors. A few months later, only a few blocks away, a disused freight tunnel passing beneath the Chicago River collapsed, allowing hundreds of millions of gallons of water to flood into the city's extensive freight-tunnel network, which had formerly been used for deliveries, ash removal, and so on, and connected with the basements of most larger pre–World War II buildings in downtown Chicago. The flood knocked out several electrical substations, caused losses of nearly $2 billion, and rendered a portion of the city's subway system unusable for three and a half weeks. An investigation determined that the tunnel roof had been damaged almost two years previously by a contractor driving pilings into the riverbed near a bridge. Although an inspector had detected the damage almost immediately and recognized the danger, the city bureaucracy didn't consider the matter urgent and the tunnel had gone unrepaired. My point isn't that the people in charge of the municipal infrastructure in Chicago are unusually incompetent—hey, we all make mistakes—but that when things go wrong in an urban context, it's not just those immediately involved who feel the heat.

The dividing line between the two halves of the community had been 47th Street. Forty years later the difference between the two sections was immediately apparent. The neighborhood south of 47th was intact and the buildings were in good repair; north of 47th there were vacant lots, which became more numerous the farther north you went.

James and Diane's house (which was actually half of a duplex) was at 40th Street. It was a formidable-looking edifice, with a Romanesque masonry façade, eight fireplaces, an ornate full-height mirror in the parlor, and oak wainscoting and other fancy woodwork throughout.

It was also one of the few remaining structures on the block. The couple had seen many of the others demolished. A few doors up the street, for example, there had been a six-flat apartment building owned by an old woman. She hadn't been able to maintain it and her tenants moved out. When she was hospitalized, scavengers moved in to pilfer the bricks.[12] Eventually so many bricks were removed that the rear of the building collapsed. A wrecking crew had to be called in to finish the job.

James and Diane's house hadn't been spared. In the entry hall there was a window with a large pane of clear glass. The clear pane was a replacement; the original window had been made of stained glass. The previous owner of the house had come downstairs one day to find thieves trying to jimmy the window out of its frame. He chased them off, but soon after removed the window himself and sold it. Better he should get the money than thieves.

James took me to his rear door. A few years previously, he told me, you could see the El Rukn temple from where we stood. The

---

[12]Most masonry buildings constructed in Chicago prior to 1975 used a type of brick variously known as "Chicago pink" or "Chicago common." These bricks, which are basically beige but have an attractive reddish cast to the clay from which they were made, haven't been manufactured since the closing of the old brickyards. They remain highly prized, however, and command a substantial premium at salvage yards—as of 2003, according to *Crain's Chicago Business*, it was two and a half cents a brick.

El Rukns at one time had been one of the largest street gangs in Chicago. While in prison the gang's leaders had adopted the trappings of Islam in order to shield themselves from the authorities. The tactic had been successful for a time. The Rukns had purchased an old movie theater for their headquarters and converted it into a fortress decorated with pseudoreligious symbols and protected by massive steel doors. In 1988, federal agents and Chicago police had raided the building and used heavy equipment to punch holes in the walls looking for weapons and drugs. In 1989, the building was seized by the government and the following year it was demolished.

All of this had happened two blocks from James's house. I could do little but mumble: *Wow. No kidding. Unbelievable.* It was always tough to top a good El Rukn story. Whatever difficulties I might have in my comparatively tranquil part of town were nothing compared to what James and his wife had seen. Yet by his own lights he was an ordinary fellow, neither beaten nor bitter, who was merely trying to lead an ordinary middle-class life.

I asked James why he stayed. He offered practical reasons at first. He and Diane liked old houses; the neighborhood was near the lake; the purchase price had been laughably low; he felt certain the neighborhood would turn around soon.

None of this seemed very convincing. Surely there were easier ways to make money than buying a house in a free-fire zone. I pressed him a bit.

Eventually he came clean. It was as I suspected: The house was part of his personal crusade. "Chicago doesn't have many substantial black communities," he said. "If only black people could recognize what they had and try to develop it. By our sacrifice in living here we're showing it could be done." He was going to reclaim the south side, starting with his own house. A mad hope, I thought then (it seems less so now). As I prepared to leave he spoke confidently about getting up on the roof to fix the leaky slate. He was, it seems hardly necessary to say, a city guy.

You see the pattern. City guys had a mission. It wasn't a mission that necessarily made a lot of sense to anybody else. Considered objectively, in fact, a reasonable person might say it was completely stupid, quixotic, dangerous . . . I could go on for quite a while. But it was what they wanted to do, and by God they were going to do it. These are my people, and when I tell my story, it's their story, too.

2

Some insight into Mary's and my relationship may be gleaned from the fact that it took me a good two weeks to realize she was gorgeous. I had hired her in the spring of 1978 to work as night supervisor at the little company I ran that produced the student publications at Northwestern University. I had no ulterior motives; she was well qualified. A short time later I mentioned the fact that I'd signed her up to one of the guys on the production crew.

"Is she cute?" he asked.

"Not really," I said.

Incredulous laughter erupts at this point whenever I tell the story. Mary then jumps in with her side: "I knew I had a tendency to fall for authority figures, so I was relieved when I met Ed. I thought, *I'm not going to have a problem with* this *guy.*"

A week or so after she started, the student newspaper went on hiatus with the approach of finals and Mary began working days. One afternoon I sent her on an errand to a local print shop.

About a half hour after she left I got a call from the printer, whom I'd known for a long time.

"So who's your friend?" he asked.

"That's Mary," I said.

"Man, she's a *knockout*."

"Yeah?" I resolved to pay more attention. This wasn't all that difficult. Mary was, in fact, a strikingly attractive woman. The immediate impact, it must be said, stemmed from the fact that she had a killer figure, but it was the details that sealed the deal. In those days her hair was long and blond (it's darker now), and she wore it up in a French braid; tendrils invariably worked loose and framed her face. The effect was enchanting. She had, in addition, a cheerful if somewhat mercurial disposition and a musical laugh, plus at times a rueful little smile that would melt the hardest heart. Mary, for her part, says her opinion of me shifted when I began wearing shorts to the office—we were pioneers in business casual. I think it's also fair to say she found me amusing. One thing led to another; by July we were a couple.

We didn't get married till nine years later. We must have broken up and gotten back together twenty times. The problem was that temperamentally we were opposites. She was organized, assertive, and quick; I was scatterbrained, diffident, and slow. She could multitask; I would get absorbed in the job in front of me and ignore all else. She was acutely aware of her surroundings and the feelings of others; as may be evident, I was often in a fog. What she found particularly maddening, I think, was that I could be plenty observant when I wanted to be—I noticed, for example, when the *Chicago Tribune* redesigned the serifs on its headline font—but for the longest time couldn't remember what she liked on her hot dog. (For the record, it's lettuce, tomato, and celery salt.)

What kept us together, I think, was the realization that, notwithstanding our differences, we made a good team, and that however unhappy we sometimes were together, we'd be unhappier apart. We were both stubborn perfectionists. For all her organizational skills, Mary didn't have a clear idea of what she wanted to do in life; for all my absentmindedness, I did. She felt I would take her places she wouldn't go herself; I knew the trip would be vastly easier with her along. Somewhere around year eight of our relationship we wallpapered a bathroom together, commonly considered a litmus test of compatibility; it came out fine. I proposed to her on a boat in Lake Michigan. After the wedding we moved into a newly built town house on the near west side with a magnificent view of downtown; I liked it well enough but considered it just a staging area. We decided to have a third child in December 1992, bought the Barn House soon after, and embarked on the great adventure of our lives.

"The house defeats people," our friend Mike had told us when we came to visit that frosty morning following our first walk-through. The Barn House lent itself to cheery pronouncements of this sort, most of them, as in this case, well founded. We found a door with the paint half stripped off, a handful of fancy glass doorknobs in a box in the basement—tokens of projects bravely if a bit cluelessly begun (normally one took the door down first), then abandoned once the magnitude of the task sank in. The house's history, to the extent we could piece it together, reinforced the impression of doomed struggle. We learned of great plans come to nothing, and hopes that had gone unfulfilled.

The current owners, an older couple, had gotten married shortly before buying the house. As a young man the husband had been a trombonist with Gene Krupa's band[1] (Krupa was a legendary jazz drummer from Chicago); at the time they bought

---

[1] I learned about the Krupa connection from Charlie the architect, about whom we will hear more later. Charlie was a jazz buff—I learned *that* when I inquired why it was taking him so long to prepare baseline drawings of the Barn House. Turned out Charlie was spending long afternoons at the house discussing jazz with the previous owner. Charlie assured me I wasn't being charged by the hour for these colloquia. Whether his firm was paying him by the hour I didn't ask.

the house he was employed by a printer. The wife had a job with an insurance company. They'd intended to renovate the house, but her company went bankrupt soon after they completed the purchase and his income didn't permit any but emergency repairs—which began, moreover, even before they moved in, when the furnace failed and a radiator cracked during a bitterly cold December, filling the back of the house with three inches of ice. The furnace having been replaced and the radiator disconnected, for a time they continued to entertain hopes of doing some of the simpler restoration work; at one point they'd had some balusters made to replace those missing from the elegant front staircase. But he'd never worked up the nerve to install them, and from what I could tell (I found them in a stack on the landing), they wouldn't have fit anyway. No further progress had been made. Mary glanced at the wife during a lull in the closing at the lawyer's office. She was crying.

The owners prior to the older couple had been Paul and Carol Sills. Paul, among other things, had been one of the founders of The Second City, the improvisational comedy troupe. Like many latter-day occupants of the Barn House, the Sillses had had some notion of fixing it up, a task made more urgent by the guy from whom they'd bought it, who'd pulled down the plaster in the living and dining rooms and gotten as far as hanging drywall, but not taping or painting it, before halting the project and selling the house in the wake of getting divorced. The Sillses had finished the job and in addition had undertaken numerous repairs in an effort to stabilize matters—Carol told me the list ran to nine single-spaced pages. The house needed more than repairs, though; it needed to be rebuilt, which was beyond their means. After a few years the Sillses relocated to California and rented the house to boarders—the neighbors remembered those days as the time the hippies lived there. It was the Sillses, I learned, who'd removed the house's fancy doorknobs in preparation for a never-completed refinishing project. The ones I found, plus a few others elsewhere on the premises, were apparently just the leftovers. Someone had stolen the rest.

As the preceding may suggest, fixing up an old city house wasn't the sort of project you undertook if your goal was immediate, or possibly any, gratification. Two kinds of problem arose. I've already mentioned the exogenous issues, as it were—crime, neighborhood neglect, and so on. Often equally trying, however, were the difficulties for which one could thank the previous owners of the house.

A gentle word needs to be said here. Virtually everyone who purchases an old house is certain the previous occupants were idiots who performed critical repairs with duct tape, vandalized desirable features during harebrained remodelings, and generally let the place go to hell. I myself entertained such thoughts once or twice. At these times I reminded myself that my predecessors had done enough right to keep the place from getting torn down, which, judging from the condition of some Chicago neighborhoods, where you half expected to see tumbleweeds, was a considerable achievement. Still, come on. When the Great Building Inspector called the ex-owners of the Barn House before the bar of judgment, his first question was going to be: *So, guys. Whose bright idea was the beam?*

The beam was the first thing you noticed when you walked into the kitchen at the rear of the house. It was a massive unfinished timber extending across the ceiling, perhaps fifteen feet long and eight inches wide by a foot deep, with heavy wooden posts supporting it on either end. It gave the kitchen the appearance of a hunting lodge. To judge from the patch marks on the floor, someone had removed a load-bearing wall in the kitchen and replaced it with the beam.

Idiosyncratic construction methods always invited suspicion, however. A few weeks after taking possession we asked a structural engineer named Bob to inspect the house. Bob was a large, soft-spoken man with the unflappable air one prizes in an engineer. He regarded the beam with the expression of mild interest you see in a doctor who's just found a suspicious lump. He made a few measurements and asked to be taken to the basement. The basement was divided into a warren of small, scrofulous rooms such as might have been used to torture prisoners in some ghastly Balkan republic. After a brief exploration Bob found the room he wanted, took more measurements, then waved his hands in midair.

"There's nothing here," he said.

He had me there. But I didn't follow him—you could find nothing lots of places.

Bob pointed to a spot on the basement ceiling. One of the posts in the kitchen, he explained, came down immediately above. If it were to be of any use as a structural support, there needed to be a corresponding post in the basement to carry the weight of the building down to the ground. No such post had been provided. All that was keeping the top of the house from collapsing into the basement was the kitchen floor planking.

"Oh," I said. It was always the way. A suburban design faux pas might mean that the previous owners had bequeathed you purple toilet fixtures; in a city house you had to solve the problem with structural steel. I added another item to what was already a long list: *Fix beam.*

The house bore traces of many such dubious improvements. The owner prior to the Sills family, we learned, had been the proprietor of an auto repair shop. He'd poured a large concrete slab in the backyard to build a garage for his business. How he expected to get this venture past the zoning inspectors was unknown, but then again it was Chicago—with a few pesetas in the right pockets he could probably have gotten permission to build a rendering plant. Unfortunately for him, though no doubt to the relief of the neighbors, he'd had to sell the house before he could bring this scheme to fruition. But the slab was still there, with bolts still sticking up around the perimeter for walls that had never been built.

We decided, mainly because all the other owners we heard from denied responsibility, that the auto repair guy had also installed the second-floor deck that now hung off the back of the house. Whoever had done it had nailed the supports to the roof of the one-story addition immediately below without sealing up the holes. On the scale of inadvisable things to do in a house, this was one notch below checking for gas leaks with a match. By the time we saw it, water had been leaking in for the better part of fifteen years. A corner of the ceiling had fallen in and the floor below was sagging—the framing had rotted. The back of the house stank of mildew.

Still, the auto repair man had done one other thing that, while it hardly redeemed him, at least inclined me to cut him some slack. One day, we learned, he'd noticed a brass memorial star for a fallen U.S. serviceman in a sidewalk that was being torn up some blocks away. The star commemorated Sgt. Carl T—, U.S. Marine. I have no idea who Sgt. T— was, apart from the fact that he had died in Okinawa in 1945, and probably neither did the auto repair man. However, he felt it was his duty to preserve the sergeant's memorial and had made it his business to do so, setting the star neatly into the concrete in his backyard—one of the odder sights in a house crammed with oddities. Nonetheless, I thought I knew what the auto repair man had been up to. No doubt patriotism and so on had been part of it. But in the back of his mind I suspected he had nurtured the thought: *Here is a link to the past, lost but for me.*

Anyone who fixes up an old house understands that impulse. It wasn't that some famous person had necessarily lived there, the occasional brush with celebrity notwithstanding. Mostly it was just the opposite: Here was where someone had built a life, and as far as anyone knew this was all that remained—their contribution to the enterprise in which we were somehow all engaged. That made the house a precious thing, a window on an age that had otherwise slipped away. It brought out your inner archaeologist. Just when you were fed up with leaky roofs and sclerotic pipes and at the point of calling in the bulldozers, you'd haul up on some dusty artifact from days long past, and instantly your mind would be as afroth with questions as if you'd found a fragment of cuneiform in some *tel* in the Mideast: *What was it for? What did it mean? What were these people* thinking? And sometimes, seeing as this was a house in the city: *What went wrong?*

The Barn House frequently provoked speculations of this sort. Despite its dilapidated state, you could see it had once been an impressive home. We decided after studying the architectural guidebooks that it was a conservative Queen Anne—lacking the wraparound porch (arguably the lot was too narrow), but having the asymmetrical façade and busy massing.[2] There were two projecting bays, one in the front and one on the side. The peaked roof was in the form of a T, with the ridgeline in the rear running the length of the house, the one in the front running laterally and intercepting the rear one at right angles, like the transept of a church. It must have been a helluva job to frame.

The Barn House, we found out at the local public library (the house was part of a historic district and the submittal documents were on file), had been built in 1891 for a woman named Georgianna Carr, about whom nothing more was known, at any rate by us. I imagined her to be a wealthy widow of somewhat eccentric tastes, although I grant you eccentricity at a hundred

---

[2]No one knows why a Queen Anne house is so called, nor does there seem to be a consensus on what its defining features are. There was a queen of England named Anne, who ruled from 1702 to 1714; her reign saw the introduction of a style of furniture characterized by (a) walnut construction, (b) cabriole legs (that is, legs shaped like an elongated S, usually having a paw foot or claw-and-ball foot at the bottom), and (c) intricate decoration. I learn this from the *Encyclopedia Britannica*. The *Britannica* goes on to say, with reference to houses, that the Queen Anne was also a "red brick architectural style of the 1870s in Great Britain and the United States [having] no real connection with the original Queen Anne period." Red brick was confined strictly to the chimneys in the Barn House, which was otherwise of frame construction, as are most Queen Anne houses I've seen, including the

years' remove can be a difficult thing to judge. Take the front hall. Certain components of the stairs excepted, the hall was finished entirely in pine. From there the visitor passed into a parlor finished in maple and then to a dining room finished in oak—a natural progression in terms of grandeur, I suppose. But it seemed to me Mrs. Carr had taken things a bit far. The parlor was separated from the dining room by a massive pocket door four and a half feet wide by three inches thick. You could stop a bullet with such a door, or anyway with the rails and stiles that framed it, but that wasn't the remarkable thing, in my opinion. Rather, it was the fact that the door was maple on one side, oak on the other, to match the rooms. Likewise the door between the dining room and the front hall, two inches thick, was oak on one side, pine on the reverse. This had been accomplished by applying a three-eighths-inch veneer of one wood to a solid door made of the second one. Even in 1891, I think it's safe to say, that would have been an expensive proposition. Completing the ensemble were heavy brass hinges and knobs of intricate design. Had I been on hand at the time of construction, I might have made sniffy remarks about this display when there were children starving in the Crimea. However, I have to say that a hundred years later it looked pretty cool.

---

majority of those thus described in every reference book other than the *Britannica*. The *American Heritage History of Notable American Houses* (1971) observes that American interest in the so-called Queen Anne style was apparently inspired by certain English buildings seen at the Philadelphia Centennial Exhibition of 1876, but notes that the open halls and large fireplaces of those structures recalled the Elizabethan and Jacobean eras, not that of Queen Anne. The *History* further says that "the style was soon transformed into an American vernacular characterized by light frame construction, irregular outlines, verandas and balconies, steep-pitched roofs, and large, open interior spaces [plus] the inevitable porches covered by sloping eaves," which, as far as the Barn House is concerned, is a little more like it. I mention all this merely to suggest the difficulties faced by architectural historians when confronted by the work of uneducated vernacular carpenters with no sense of system.

It's possible Mrs. Carr had gotten her ideas about design from her neighbor two lots up the street. The builder of that house had had such an infatuation with Victorian splendor that he installed a stained-glass window in the pantry. I was shown this by Ned, the owner, who gave me a tour. He also showed me an odd porch that opened off the dining room. The porch was perhaps ten feet long but only three feet deep. There was scarcely room for a chair—anyone proposing to take the air there had to stand. That was the idea, Ned said. It was a smoking porch, where the men would retire with their after-dinner tobacco lest they stink up the house.

We found an equally inscrutable gesture in the Barn House—a small window on the rear wall of the closet under the front stairs. At first we thought this was evidence of another visit from the stained-glass-window salesman. But an architect who visited the house said no: The little pane provided natural illumination in the days when one couldn't rely on electric lights.

One of the many curious features of the Barn House was its two staircases—not an unusual thing in itself, but these were side by side. There was the fancy front staircase already mentioned, plus a narrower rear stairway immediately adjacent, the latter rising the height of the building. My brother-in-law asked about it one day as we descended the narrow back steps. "The other one's for the white people," I said—not the most sensitive remark I ever made, but probably the truth. The Barn House had been divided into two distinct zones, one for the menials and one for the gentry.[3] Mrs. Carr no doubt spent much of her time in the parlor and

---

[3] A house owned by some friends showed an even more extreme division. It was a beautiful old place in Chicago's north suburbs—a mansion really, with dark wooden wainscoting, stained-glass windows, a massive fireplace, and enormous rooms clearly intended for entertaining on a grand scale. But the house was oddly designed. If you walked up one staircase, you found yourself in a large bedroom suite—but it didn't connect to the rest of the second floor, except through a concealed door at the back of a closet. The other half of the

dining room, retiring at night via the imposing front stairs to the master suite at the front of the second floor. The master suite was—well, luxurious probably overstates matters, but certainly comfortable, consisting of a bedroom with a fireplace plus an adjacent sitting room, the two connected by a pocket door. Meanwhile the lower classes confined themselves to the kitchen and pantry at the rear of the house, reaching the second floor (and if need be the basement or attic) via the servants' stairs. The dining room and one of the bedrooms had separate entries for the lady of the house and her employees. There was a small room with no other obvious purpose at the back of the second floor; we guessed it had been the maid's. If the maid had been discreet, Mrs. Carr might have gone without seeing her for days.[4]

Okay, so Mrs. Carr had probably not gone on to vote for Eugene Debs and the Social Democrats. At least she'd had the work on her house done properly. That was more than you could say about her successors.

Back to the front hall. It was by far the most striking interior feature of the house, dominated by an ornate staircase rising to the second floor. The staircase was of elaborate design, with a carved oak banister and newel posts and turned oak balusters. At some point prior to our arrival an occupant of the house had decided that the beauty of the staircase would be enhanced by

---

second floor had its own staircase. Downstairs, we learned, a large pocket door made it possible to divide the first floor into two halves, each with its own door into the kitchen. Our friends had been told that the house had originally been owned by two spinster sisters. They could only guess that the two loathed each other, each living separately in her own half of the house, joining the two halves of the first floor only when they entertained.

[4]How many households had servants in the 1890s isn't precisely known. One book I read claimed the number was only 20–25 percent, implying that this fraction was small. But it seems to me that, assuming you had roughly equal numbers of servers and served, the theoretical maximum had to be in the neighborhood of 50 percent, making 25 percent a pretty impressive total. Then again, the fact that a house was equipped for servants didn't mean there

painting the risers red and the balusters brown. This belief was without foundation. In all likelihood this same person—I refused to believe the house had been in the possession of two such bozos—had gone on to paint the oak flooring in the upstairs bedrooms red, white, and blue. The color scheme was less patriotic than it sounds; the red was a sort of maroon, the white more or less cream, and the blue somewhere between turquoise and teal.

To give the painter his due, however, he'd left us something to work with. That wasn't the case in the second-floor hall, where the balustrade at the top of the front stairs was missing altogether. It appeared to have been broken off—one could see the place where the banister, a formidable piece of hardwood, had splintered. We imagined a bar fight with the brawlers crashing through the railing; they must have been the size of sumo wrestlers. The Sillses, finding the railing missing at the time they acquired the house, had repaired the damage with construction two-by-fours pending the day when they could do the job right. That day hadn't dawned during their tenure; now it was up to us.

Some parts of the house had deteriorated simply because of age. Overlooking the front staircase was a tall nine-paneled window, the top six panels of which, arranged three wide by two high, used an unusual sort of decorative glass called bottle glass. Each panel

---

actually were any. My parents' house in Oak Park, for example, had a butler's pantry in the dining room that backed up on the regular pantry in the kitchen. The two were separated by a small sliding panel at counter height. The idea apparently was that the cook would place dishes of food on the counter in the kitchen pantry, whereupon the butler would enter the dining room pantry, slide open the panel, extract the dishes, and serve the guests. This was in a house of perhaps eighteen hundred square feet as originally constructed, hardly large enough for one servant, let alone two, and in any case there were no servants' stairs, maid's room, and so on. My guess was that the butler's pantry enabled you to *pretend* you had servants, only you had given them the night off. Conceivably you might go through the motions of passing dishes through the pantry a few times, but undoubtedly you'd eventually concede it was simpler just to walk through the door.

consisted of glass circles, thickened in the center and similar in size and appearance to the bottom of a wine bottle, arranged in a four-by-four grid. In description it sounds a little weird, but I assure you it was a pretty thing to see, or at any rate had been in 1891. Now the glass was grimy and sagging—the panels would need to be cleaned and releaded.

The abundance of such details brought to mind an obvious question: What was this house *doing* here? It wasn't a typical city house. It was incongruously large, for one thing. Its fine finishes, what was left of them, suggested it had been designed for an upper-middle-class suburb. Yet here it was in a thoroughly urban section of the north side.

The answer became apparent on further study of the historic-district documents at the public library. I realized that the house's history of great schemes come to naught had begun with Mrs. Carr.

The Barn House, it turned out, hadn't been intended as a city house. The subdivision in which it had been built was originally part of a suburb called Lake View. The lots had been platted out and offered for sale in the 1880s. The promoters of the area were from a suburban community a little farther out called Ravenswood, and they called the new subdivision Southeast Ravenswood. They meant to distinguish the area from the city, the border of which was then a couple miles away. The lots were bigger—50 by 165 feet, compared to the standard 25-by-125-foot city lot—and the streets were wider. Mrs. Carr, I gathered, had bought one of the lots and built her house.

But the development had flopped. An 1894 fire-insurance map showed the buildings on each block; of twenty-one lots on our block at the time, there were buildings on only nine. (At the rear of the Barn House, I was interested to note, there had been a stable and what I guessed was an outhouse.) Several possible reasons for the slow progress suggested themselves, the most obvious being the financial panic that swept the country in 1893. But that explanation seemed inadequate. Other ventures launched in the same era—for example, the Chicago suburb of Oak Park, where my parents lived and Frank Lloyd Wright had built his early houses—had been mostly built up within a few years. Something else explained what had gone wrong in Southeast Ravenswood, and after some thought I decided I knew what it was: It had become urban.

That requires some explanation. However problematic urban life may seem at times now, 125 years ago it completely sucked. Cities as we know them today were sometimes exciting but more frequently terrifying novelties during the latter nineteenth century. In 1850, only three cities in the world had had populations greater than 1 million—London, Paris, and Peking. In 1900, after fifty years of chaotic but more or less continuous economic expansion throughout Europe and North America, the number of million-plus cities had risen to sixteen, one of which, Chicago, had been a sodden outpost of thirty thousand in 1850.

The shantytowns of the developing world today have nothing on the big cities of a century ago for squalor. In 1890, a year before construction of the Barn House, Jacob Riis had published *How the Other Half Lives,* a muckraking account of conditions in the tenements of New York. Riis reported, among other astonishing facts, that impoverished Jewish immigrants were packed into portions of the Lower East Side at a density of 330,000 per square mile, by far the highest rate of any city in the world; that a Bohemian cigar maker, living and working in a tenement owned by his employer, might expect to work seventeen hours a day, seven days a week during the busy summer season, at a piecework wage averaging six and a half cents per hour (less in the winter); that more than twelve thousand cast-off children, mostly employed as newsboys, bootblacks, and the like, lived in lodging houses operated by the Children's Aid Society; and that in one neighborhood during a cholera epidemic some years previously (presumably Riis refers to the outbreaks occurring in the years 1865–73), the poor had died at a rate of 195 per 1,000, which approached that of the medieval plague years.[5]

In 1894, William Stead, an English preacher and reformer, published *If Christ Came to Chicago!* It was somewhat derivative of Riis's book in terms of subject matter, describing as it did the only slightly less appalling state of the lower classes of Chicago, but Riis had nothing on Stead for style. Sample: "For the [police] station is the central cesspool whither drain the poisonous drippings of the city which has become the *cloaca maxima* of the world." Shorn of flourishes, however, Stead's message was much the same: The urban poor live in such wretchedness as you, gentle reader, can scarcely dream.

Some middle-class reformers were repelled as much by the foreignness of city dwellers as by their poverty. Riis, for one, had little good to say about Italians ("content to live in a pigsty"), Chinese ("a constant and terrible menace to society"), or the inhabitants of "Jewtown" ("money is their God"). Stead, notwithstanding his rhetorical excesses, was more tolerant, writing sympathetically about the enterprising rogues who served as precinct captains in the Chicago political machine, which he felt functioned as a sort of social services agency, at least for those who voted the right way. On the whole, however, the genteel view of urban life during this period can be characterized as: *Ooh, ick.*

The answer, in the nineteenth century as in the twentieth, was the suburbs. In 1886, the architect Daniel Burnham, the inde-

---

[5]Riis has a great deal more in this vein, which space doesn't permit my quoting, but here's one last statistic: Of the 1.4 million people discovered by the 1890 census to be domiciled in Manhattan, Riis noted, an estimated 1.25 million lived in tenements (that is, buildings housing three or more families). Not all of these were abjectly poor, but Riis was of the opinion that virtually all of the approximately 1 million persons living in tenements below 14th Street were, and thus his book shouldn't properly have been called an account of how the other half lived, but the other 71 percent.

fatigable urban booster whose landmark *Plan of Chicago* would be published in 1909, moved his family from the city's south side to the affluent suburb of Evanston, snootily asserting that he could "no longer bear to have my children run in the streets of Chicago." Evanston had been founded as an independent town (it had grown up around Northwestern University), but after the Civil War real estate developers, recognizing a market when they saw one, began building bedroom suburbs specifically aimed at businessmen commuting to downtown. One of the more influential was Riverside, Illinois, southwest of Chicago. Laid out between 1868 and 1871, Riverside had several things going for it: (a) It was designed by Frederick Law Olmsted and Calvert Vaux, who had earlier designed Central Park in Manhattan and in Riverside introduced the curving street pattern (in contrast to the standard nineteenth-century gridiron) that eighty years later became standard suburban practice; (b) it was built around a station on a commuter railroad that took workers to and from their jobs in the city; and (c) it was far enough out to be safe from the encroaching megalopolis.

Point (c) was where the developers of Southeast Ravenswood had screwed up. (They neglected point (a), too, but that was less crucial.) They had built their subdivision too close in, failing to take account of the likelihood of annexation.

Although the fact is little remembered today, all three U.S. cities that reached the 1 million mark by 1900—New York, Chicago, and Philadelphia—got that way largely through annexation. Philadelphia had been first, annexing the surrounding county in 1854 and increasing its land area by 2,000 percent. Chicago was next—in 1889, wanting to bulk up for the World's Columbian Exposition then four years away, the city annexed 120 square miles of hinterland and quadrupled its area. Last up was New York, then consisting solely of Manhattan, which merged with the independent city of Brooklyn and what became the boroughs of the Bronx, Queens, and Staten Island in

1898–99, giving the city a population of more than 3 million, after London the largest in the world.[6]

Annexation had obvious benefits for Chicago, but was perhaps less advantageous for Southeast Ravenswood. Once it had been a suburb, with all that that implies. After 1889, it was just another neighborhood in Chicago.

Real estate development in Southeast Ravenswood didn't flounder indefinitely. It was given a boost by the extension of the L to the community in 1907. But where before most of the development had been suburban in character—frame houses on large lots—now it was urban. Developers divided some lots and constructed Siamese two-flats—mirror-image pairs of brick apartment buildings having a common wall. Other lots were consolidated and large blocks of flats erected.

The result was a jumble, neither urban nor suburban in character. The magnificent nine-paned window on Mrs. Carr's entry stair had once overlooked a meadow; now it looked out on the brick wall of the neighboring two-flat eight feet away. The backyard and its stable stood in the shadow of a massive three-story apartment building that occupied a good portion of the frontage on the next street over.[7]

---

[6]Annexation continues apace today—witness Houston, which, thanks to Texas's permissive annexation law, grew from 73 square miles and 285,000 people in 1940 to 579 square miles and 1,954,000 people in 2000. The champ with regard to land acquisition, though, is Sitka, Alaska, which, owing to a quirk of local law and the scale of the state—the three largest U.S. cities in area are all in Alaska—has only 8,835 people but encompasses 2,874 square miles.

[7]This seems to have been a fairly general phenomenon, if you can trust playwrights. In Arthur Miller's *Death of a Salesman* (1949) we learn that when Willy Loman purchased his house in what presumably is an outer borough of New York it was surrounded by trees and flowers; now in his old age it's hemmed in by apartment buildings. This is generally taken as symbolizing the contraction of Willy's hopes. Symbol nothing—in those days it was a flat description of events.

You see the problem. Here was a house that had been conceived of, perhaps naively, as a country residence, with servants and lavish appointments. Thirty years later it was obsolete, built for a suburb that had never materialized in a world that was long gone. However many people may have had servants in 1891, it's a good bet no one in the Barn House's neighborhood, or for that matter most urban neighborhoods, had them in 1920. Mrs. Carr, one may reasonably conjecture, had ridden in a horse-drawn carriage; her neighbors thirty years later rode streetcars and L trains. Few now had sitting rooms and fireplaces; they lived in efficiency apartments with kitchenettes. Wealthy people still lived in big houses—in Chicago they gravitated to a string of lakeside suburbs called the North Shore, which started out rich and stayed that way. But not here.

Whoever owned the Barn House at this point—one presumes it was no longer Mrs. Carr—apparently decided to bow to the inevitable. In 1926, the building had been converted to a two-flat. (We deduced the date from old newspapers—the basement ceiling had been plastered to comply with a code requirement for fireproof barriers between floors of multiunit dwellings, and the newspaper had been stuffed behind the lath.) An additional kitchen had been installed on the second floor in the likely maid's room. Perhaps during the Depression and certainly by World War II, the building had been further (and illegally) divided into as many as seven apartments, most consisting of a single room with its own sink, dead bolt on the door, and possibly telephone and doorbell—the basement was a rats' nest of wires. We heard about crazy Walter who lived in the parlor, and a family that spent the war living in the front bedroom suite. Someone residing in the dining room had evidently owned a dog that was in the habit of begging to be let in; it had gouged deep scratches in Mrs. Carr's door.

Things had perked up briefly following World War II. A woman named Marge stopped by one day to tell us she had lived in the house as a child in the 1950s. Her family had shared the place with boarders at first, but by the time she left, around

1970, the house had reverted to single-family use. That suggests prosperity. The neighborhood as a whole saw a sizable influx of Hispanic immigrants, who moved into the big apartment buildings on the busy streets starting in the 1960s. But the older residents on the side streets for the most part stayed put.

Some may have had occasion to regret it. The neighbors told lurid tales, which possibly were exaggerated, but it seems safe to say that during the 1970s the community became, if not a slum, certainly a little raffish. Crime by all accounts got significantly worse. Late in the decade, we were told, a notorious Mexican drug family had established a sales operation in the "bad building" behind the Barn House; how long this remained in business we weren't able to ascertain, but drugs were available on a drive-up basis well into the 1980s. A drug kingpin, it was claimed, had lived in half of a four-flat across the street; the owner had sawn out much of the floor separating the upper and lower units, presumably in the interest of creating a dramatic architectural effect; one can easily imagine drugs having played a role in this process, if only as a source of inspiration, but whether the owner sold them can't be said to have been conclusively shown.

I was told gangs dominated the high school a block away, which was easy enough to believe, since as far as I knew gangs at the time dominated pretty much every city high school. Graffiti became noticeably more prevalent, as did vandalism, break-ins, robbery, shootings, and other common features of late-twentieth-century urban life. A woman was said to have set up shop as a hooker in an apartment building across the street; on inquiry I found that, neighborhood gossip notwithstanding, her occupation hadn't been definitely established, and some were of the opinion that she'd merely been friendly, taking home a succession of scuzzy male companions, one of the scuzzier of whom shot up the lobby on one occasion and the last of whom (I'm not sure if it was the same guy) had stabbed her seventeen times. In 1986, a few years after the murder at Mike's house, a teenage boy living across the street had been accosted a few blocks from home by gang members demanding his bicycle. When he refused to surrender it they shot him; he collapsed on some porch steps and died. That was the version Mike told in his newspaper account of the incident, anyhow. Another was that the boy had been selling drugs in a rival gang's territory and was killed in retaliation.

I make no claim that all this was dramatically worse than any other city neighborhood experienced at the time—far from it. In some neighborhoods on the south side, I knew from my brief stint as a wire service reporter, you could get an equivalent amount of action in a long weekend. But it was a lot for the north side— certainly enough to make one think: *You know, the suburbs don't sound so bad.* But the residents hadn't done what was arguably the smart thing and fled. Instead they'd organized a community patrol, which consisted of people driving around after dark with CB radios scouting for crime. Mike had refused to cooperate with what he considered vigilantes. That was putting matters a little strongly, I felt, but it had been a rough era. Mike told us about the previous owner of his house, whom he knew as Emil the Turk. Emil had been accustomed to beating his wife. On one such occasion the wife had called the police. The police arrived; Emil slipped them fifty dollars; they turned around and left. Emil picked up with his wife where he'd left off.

Our neighbor Ned told me the police had visited him one day after he'd mistakenly tripped the burglar alarm. The policemen admired the woodwork in his house and told him he was lucky so much of it was still there—in years past the local alderman had sent them around to strip the finery out of unoccupied old houses.[8] Ned himself had had to travel to Wisconsin to buy back a beveled-glass window that a previous owner of his house had carted off in 1947.

---

[8]Not, I feel obliged to say, the current occupant of that office, who is a nice man giving every appearance of honesty. Even if he didn't I'd still like to keep getting my garbage picked up.

The Barn House hadn't been plundered in this way, merely abused. Virtually every fine thing in it had been damaged or destroyed through carelessness or neglect. At some point, probably during the two-flat conversion of 1926, someone had gone around the basement bricking up the "joist ends"—the space between the top of the foundation wall and the flooring immediately above. The bricks were meant to be a fire-stop. But the bricklayer had used a type of mortar that expanded upon drying, pressing up on the floorboards above and causing the finished flooring around the perimeter of the rooms on the first floor to buckle. The dining room floor had been finished in oak veneer, with a parquet border of complex design. The buckling of the planking beneath had ruined it.

At every hand one saw signs of stopgap repairs and renovations done on the cheap. The worst example was the third floor. Originally, we guessed, the attic had been unfinished, but in the early 1930s a fire had burned through the roof, and whoever rebuilt it decided to convert the attic to living space. The original attic apparently hadn't had a lot of headroom, so the remodeler provided more by adding a long dormer along the front of the house, parallel to the street. Where the dormer intercepted the projecting bay, the remodeler had built the bay walls up higher, then topped them off with an awkward roof. To complete the job, the owner sawed off the eave running along the front of the house, which had been orphaned when the transept roof was raised.[9]

The result looked completely stupid. A three-year-old with a crayon could have produced a more attractive design. But the third floor was also one of the reasons we'd bought the house.[10] I

[9]If you're not following this, a drawing of the house as it stood when we bought it may be found on page 50.

[10]I don't mean to suggest it was the only reason. Whatever might be said for the immediate neighborhood, the house on the whole was well situated, being close to the lake, Wrigley Field, and the L, historically the armatures of redevelopment on the north side of Chicago.

worked at home; I needed an office. The bay windows in the attic offered beguiling views up and down the tree-lined street. A big maple stood in the front yard; though the leaves had long since fallen on the day we first saw it, the branches extended close to the windows. I guessed that having an office there would be like working in a tree house. But the job had been hopelessly botched—we'd have to reconstruct much of the front of the house, to say nothing of the rest of the building. Here was a home that had been built by naïfs and wrecked by knuckleheads. Restoring it wasn't a job we could just turn over to a contractor. We'd need an architect.

3

Many people agonize over the choice of architects. Not us. I knew a number of architects through my work; we spoke with three. Stuart designed jewel-box renovations, photographs of which appeared in national magazines; his work was exquisite, but a kitchen alone could cost $60,000.[1] Pete specialized in low-income housing; he did clever things with drywall and other inexpensive materials, but we were looking for something a little more pretentious. We settled on Howard. He was a big man; a mutual friend had described him as having "no physical fear," an assessment that was hard to argue with—I'd once braced myself in the back seat of Howard's car as he barreled at speed through a service station to dodge a traffic light. Such stunts commended Howard to me now. Manic bravery normally wasn't a quality one looked for in architects, but with the Barn House it couldn't hurt.

[1]The price in the early 1990s. It's a good deal more now.

Howard was a pretty fair architect, too, concentrating on projects in a traditional vein. His firm was housed in a stately old building downtown that I was surprised to learn had originally been an automobile showroom—auto showroom design has come down a jot since they built this palace. Now it was a fine arts building full of piano tuners and violin teachers, with high ceilings, grand staircases, and big windows. I found all this comforting, and presumably from Howard's standpoint that was the idea. If one's would-be clients discover their prospective architect's atelier is in a strip mall next to a Dunkin' Donuts, they start having second thoughts.

Howard spent a morning inspecting the Barn House with Mary and me, pointing out features of interest. One of the first he noticed as soon as we walked in the door. The floor in the front hall was finished in a fine-grained wood of a rich red color that we didn't recognize. Howard informed us it was heart pine, cut from the heartwood of virgin timber.

I'd never heard of heart pine before, and am not entirely certain I've got things straight now, but here's the story as best I can piece it together: Heart pine came from a tall, straight species called longleaf pine, which grew in a vast continuous band along the southeastern U.S. coast. Longleaf pine was slow-growing under the best of circumstances, but in the virgin forest longleaf saplings grew slower still due to competition for resources beneath the dense tree cover—I've heard of a tree three hundred years old that was less than a foot thick. As a result, annual tree rings and thus the grain were close-spaced and the wood was, for pine, unusually heavy—a board weighed as much as oak, and served equally well as flooring. By the early twentieth century the original stand of longleaf pine, some seventy million acres, had almost all been cut down. If you want heart pine now—it does make a handsome floor—you have to deal with a salvager, who ransacks old buildings destined for the wreckers or sends divers to the bottoms of rivers or lakes looking for logs sunk during nineteenth-century lumbering operations. Salvaged heart pine costs two to three times the price of new hardwood, which itself isn't cheap.[2]

I was fascinated to find such stuff in my house. It was like discovering the original owners had dined on buffalo tongue or hunted passenger pigeons. There was only one problem. Someone had sawn two large rectangular holes in the heart pine floor to install heating grates, which had long since been removed. One hole had been patched with maple, the other with construction pine. Neither came anywhere close to matching the original. There was surely a way to repair the holes less conspicuously; we just needed to figure out what it was.

Howard found another noteworthy item in the basement, where radiator pipes hung from the ceiling. They were wrapped in insulating material that in cross section looked like corrugated cardboard.

"Asbestos," he informed us. We'd need to hire a special contractor to haul it out, in all likelihood at exorbitant expense.

That was pretty much how the whole tour went—one happy discovery to two or three dismaying ones. Howard was more circumspect than others to whom we'd shown the house, many of whom had stared with their jaws slack. But the thought undoubtedly crossed his mind: *Thank God this isn't mine.*

Afterward we sat down for coffee on the red stools in the diner down the street. The day was cold and gray. Howard was uncharacteristically quiet. "The house has good bones," he said finally. He was referring to the method used to construct it, known as balloon framing. Balloon framing is commonly understood now to mean any kind of lightweight stick framing, but in fact it was a particular type of wood construction in which the exterior structural members rose the height of the building. When the joists and rafters were added you had a sort of cartoon outline of a house—a

---

[2]Some longleaf pine is grown on plantations now, but takes decades to produce an appreciable amount of heartwood. Even then the grain is likely to be coarser, since new-growth trees have greater access to sunlight.

balloon, I suppose—to which everything else was then appended. In the case of the Barn House, the exterior studs were two-by-sixes twenty-seven feet tall, while the floor joists were massive two-by-tens twenty-five feet long. The enormous boards were another product of the virgin forest, unobtainable now except through special order. The house was a relic of a departed era.

There was another long pause. "I bet we can save the light-bulbs," I said, thinking this funny.

A few days later Mary and I sat down with Howard in his office. He introduced one of his firm's associates, a young architect named Charlie, who was going to sit in.

Howard had taken some pictures of the Barn House and spread them on the table. We talked about what to do with the front of the house. I attempted to explain what I wanted.

"I'm seeing kind of a dormer thing on the left side here, and I think this bay over here wants to be a turret thing," I said. It wasn't my most eloquent moment. Howard and Charlie nodded. Charlie had said almost nothing the entire time. We shook hands and left.

A few days later Mary called me. "I just got a fax from the architects," she said. "Let me send it to you." The thin sheet emerged from the fax machine a few minutes later. It was a perspective drawing of the reconstructed Barn House, done in pen and ink. The original roofline (or what I could easily believe had been the original roofline) had been restored. A small dormer window overlooked the street on one side; on the other the projecting bay terminated in a graceful turret. It was precisely what I'd envisioned and what I'd ineptly tried to convey at our meeting with the architects. Charlie had designed it. He'd gotten it right on the first try.[3]

---

[3]Before and after drawings of the house may be found on pages 50 and 51. To give credit where it's due, I should clarify that the perspective rendering we saw initially was drawn by a talented illustrator named Bruce Bondy, who was working off Charlie's plans. The original fax is the frontispiece of this book.

Thus did we commence the process of design. It was surprisingly pleasant. Charlie, whom Howard had assigned to handle the brunt of the design work, was something of an anomaly—an architect without affectation or even much geekiness. Not all architects wear capes, porkpie hats, or bow ties, or sport glasses suggestive of nineteenth-century bookkeepers, or draw with broad-nibbed fountain pens of exotic manufacture using sepia ink, but you find these things among architects a good deal more than you do among the cashiers at Target. Charlie had none of them. He was one of those people who'd resolved to rise in his profession on the basis of genius alone. You may say I exaggerate his talents. It's true our project afforded few opportunities for the bravura displays by which architectural achievement nowadays is often judged—which is to say we didn't propose to heave up spectacular confections made of stainless steel, or whitewashed tubular monuments suggestive of ships stranded on mountaintops, or any other such heroic structure. The Barn House was an old frame house to start with, and assuming Charlie and Howard didn't radically exceed their instructions, that was what it was going to be when it got done. So I won't claim Charlie for the immortals.

But make no mistake—he had the gift. He had a wonderfully fluid drawing hand, with a hint of a tremor in it, somewhat reminiscent of the smoke in the voice of the better class of jazz singer. To see Charlie render a wiring schematic—and I know, because I was the author of the scribbled original—was to see a grocery list transformed into art, all done without apparent effort, like an early Michael Jordan layup.

I say without shame that I made Charlie's life miserable over the ensuing several months. I didn't do so intentionally, but luck had delivered an extraordinary instrument into my hands, and I meant to make the most of it. I wasn't the easiest client. I had friends who were unfamiliar with bearing walls and soil stacks and other essential structural notions, and who were chagrined when their ideas for remodeling were greeted with stifled laugh-

EXISTING BARN HOUSE

RECONSTRUCTED BARN HOUSE

ter. I didn't have that problem, but I had, shall we say, certain directions in which I wished to go. We advanced by a dialectical process. Charlie would submit a floor plan, which might for example show the master bedroom suite at the rear of the second floor. I would peremptorily decide that this approach was unsound and demand that the master suite be put at the front, where it had been in Mrs. Carr's day. I would redraw the plan in my amateurish way on onionskin tracing paper and send it to Charlie. Charlie would gamely do the whole thing over and send me new drawings. Studying the result, I would decide Charlie had been right the first time—there wasn't enough room in the front of the house for a master suite of the proper hauteur. It doesn't sound like the most productive system, and I doubt it would have worked with Frank Lloyd Wright. But Charlie and I got on well enough—partly, it must be said, because of Charlie's inexhaustible amiability, but also because he was a member of the Brotherhood of the Right Way.

The Brotherhood of the Right Way didn't hand out membership cards or hold meetings, but it was real just the same. Its adherents shared a simple belief: There was a right way to do everything, and one's task in life was merely to determine what the right way was, and then do it. That's not to say there necessarily was a single right way, although the more rigidly inclined members of the brotherhood might sometimes act as though they thought so. The truth was that the right way was a compromise between what you would do if you had unlimited time and money and what you could accomplish given that you didn't. Naturally this involved an element of judgment, and two exponents of the right way thus might differ from time to time on matters of detail. Nonetheless, all parties subscribed to the belief that there *was* a right way, or at any rate some finite number of right ways. In this they stood in contrast to the general run of humanity, which had no concept whatsoever.

Take the matter of home design. It seemed to me a basic rule of architecture that the inside of a house ought to bear some relation to the outside, but in my observation this principle was routinely flouted. The more common practice seemingly was to have the exterior and interior of the house drawn up by separate designers who never talked to each other and gave no indication of living on the same planet. Some joint House-Senate compromise committee would then take the two plans and attempt to cram one into the other—often, to my eye, with suboptimal results.

There's a woman I know well—it's fair to say she's like a sister to me.[4] She and her husband had added a two-story wing to their suburban home with a pair of handsome dormers facing the street. Inside was a master bedroom suite of sybaritic luxury, with an entertainment center, spotlit whirlpool bath, and so on. I was impressed, but while nosing about with that blithe disregard of privacy one can risk only with siblings, I realized that the bedroom gave no sign of the dormers. Opening some doors, I found an odd-shaped collection of tiny rooms concealed behind a wall—the dormers, pressed into service as closets. No offense to my sister, but this made no sense. The dormers had been built at considerable expense and equipped with windows. But the windows didn't provide natural illumination to the bedroom, where it might have served some purpose, but rather to the closets, where it didn't—if anything, the sunlight would fade the clothes. A small thing, you may say. But to me it was cheating.

Similarly, a home down the street from the Barn House had a fetching arrangement of overlapping gables and eyebrow windows and such that I felt certain must betoken an equally dramatic and ingenious interior. But when I had an opportunity to tour the house I found nothing of the kind. The volume enclosed by the overlapping gables was concealed by a ceiling—it was all dead space, though accessible by a door, revealing, as I recall, air-conditioning ducts. I was disappointed. One expected a certain

[4]Oh, let's not be coy. She's my sister.

amount of show in architecture, but to me this bordered on . . . eh, fraud is too strong a word. But it reminded me of the false fronts in old western boomtowns. In such matters Charlie and I were in entire agreement. We didn't hold rigid views about form following function, but we felt they both ought to be headed in the same general direction.

Our task was simplified by the fact that the Barn House had been well designed to start with. The front hall and the handsome staircase, for example—we'd merely have to restore them. How, I had no idea, but that was a detail for later. The parlor and dining room likewise were nicely proportioned, wanting only rebuilding. Even the inept effort to install a beam in the back of the house had simplified the problem of how to remodel a cramped Victorian kitchen in two useful respects: First, the beam builder had created a large space in which it was easy to imagine installing a modern kitchen; and second, he'd made hash out of everything that one might otherwise have felt obliged to save. Cabinets, some throw rugs, a couple I-beams—bingo, we'd be done.

Simultaneously with the process of design I prepared a written description of the project. I felt that if I carefully defined what I wanted done, and broke it down into manageable tasks in a methodical way, I would have, first of all, a basis on which to obtain well-thought-out bids from contractors (which in general proved to be the case, although there were surprises even so), and, second, the project would seem less formidable. I can't say the latter aim was successful. On the contrary, I scared the daylights out of myself. I'd gone through the house with a legal pad, noting the work that needed to be done in each room, then organized the work by trades, since that was how contractors priced jobs. The result was a "scope of work," with sections for concrete and foundation work, drywall, rough carpentry (subdivided by section of the house), flooring, tile, and so on—nineteen sections in all. The scope of work ran to eleven single-spaced pages with more than a hundred items, not counting options. You may ask: *Aren't we overdoing it a little here?* I don't deny there were eccentric aspects to the program. However, if your idea of planning is drawings on napkins, I'm happy to compare results.

Adherence to the right way was largely its own reward, but occasionally it paid off in practical ways. One was in connection with our application for a historic preservation tax break. Owing to the Barn House's location in a historic district, we were eligible for a state program that would freeze our property assessment for an impressive number of years if we restored the house to certain standards. What made matters tricky was that we were planning major alterations to the appearance of the house, and we were unsure whether the state preservation agency would approve. To assist in the process we hired a consultant named Vicki. She wasn't altogether reassuring, telling us of one application that had been rejected because the owner had proposed to install windows with muntins—thin wooden strips separating the panes—rather than the plain sashes originally employed. That didn't bode well for us. We were planning to tear off much of the front of the house, including the porch, the roof, the siding, and the windows, and rebuild them as Charlie had suggested, which certainly looked better and conceivably (in my opinion, probably) reproduced the original appearance of the house. But we had no proof, no old photos, no 1891 blueprints. I asked Vicki whether she thought our proposal would fly. *Worth a try,* she offered cheerfully. She suggested sending Charlie's scheme down to Springfield for an initial review.

A week or two later I got a call from Vicki. The state had granted preliminary approval of our project, based solely on the rendering of Charlie's plans. We would need to submit a detailed application in which I would have to justify the changes, but that was a formality. Perhaps the state's examiners, seeing the before and after (Vicki had taken care to include a photo of the house as it then stood), thought: *Anything will be an improvement.* But truthfully I don't think so. I'm convinced they took one look and said: *This is the right way.*

We'd passed a major hurdle, but there was still much to be

done. Charlie, Mary, and I spent weeks consulting and faxing drawings back and forth. In preparing my scope of work, I faced dozens of design decisions, some having largely aesthetic implications (wood siding versus vinyl?), others speaking to the basic habitability and convenience of the house. Many of these decisions were easy: Wood siding, absolutely—hang the expense. Five-eighths-inch drywall rather than half-inch. Hardwood flooring rather than tile or carpet.

Others were less so. It was all very well to profess a commitment to doing things right, but often I found myself having only a general idea what the right way was. This is a matter to which I'll return throughout this book, and in which I invested a great deal of time and thought. Even so I may as well confess that more than a few times we whiffed. I don't want to get too far ahead of my story, but perhaps the following observations won't ruin the suspense:

▪ You don't really need a bidet, unless you or someone in the family has issues I don't need to hear about. You also don't need a two-person whirlpool. (It may sound sexy, but it takes too long to fill.) On the other hand, you do need a separate room for the toilet.

▪ Ask yourself: Am I a bathtub person? Even if the answer is no, you still need *one*. Resale. Also kids.

▪ Maybe it's just me, but if the walls in your bathroom don't meet at ninety-degree angles, and the grout lines on the floor tile are noticeably out of parallel with at least one wall as a result, it's going to look pretty bush.

▪ Don't position the bathroom door in such a way that whenever you open it it smacks your wife in the butt.

▪ If you wind up with a shower stall having a conventional double-hung window in it (with translucent glazing, silly) because you have to have *some* natural light in the bathroom and glass brick and other such contrivances don't look period, you don't want to clad the windowsill in ceramic tile, because despite your best efforts water will infiltrate behind the grout and the tile will pry up. Instead, what you want is a sill made from a nice slab of marble, with a drip groove on the bottom and a silicone caulk seal all around. Take it from me, best fifty bucks you'll ever spend.

▪ Ceramic frogs, the kids' names, and so on may look cute in the bathroom tile now, but you'll be really sick of them in five years. We didn't do either of these things, and boy, am I glad. By the way, if you want some ceramic frogs, I can give you a whole box.

▪ Never use PVC pipe for your main soil stack, because plastic pipe transmits sound with excruciating fidelity, whereas cast iron, the alternative, muffles it. We didn't make this mistake—not for nothing did I pay all that money to Howard—but we heard of others who did. One was a rich lawyer who had hired an architect and a contractor and told them to spend whatever they needed to build the ultimate house, for which he compensated them with a percentage of the total cost of the job. "I *paid* these guys to spend my money," the lawyer moaned, but he was nonetheless obliged to listen to every appalling gurgle each time the toilet flushed.

▪ Yes, we spend a lot of time in the bathroom. You don't?

▪ You want to run a half-inch (at least) conduit to every principal room in the house with an electrical box at wall-outlet height near any place you're likely to have a desk or favorite chair. Internet connection. I did this for my attic office and the kitchen, and I'd have been smart to do it everywhere else. On the other hand, the fact that the kids can only access the Internet in the office (where I am) and the kitchen (where my wife is) isn't without its advantages in an era of chat-room deves.[5]

▪ Quartersawn oak. Remember these words.

▪ Epoxy paint on the basement floor. They use this stuff in nuclear power plants; chances are it'll survive your kids.

▪ You may not believe this, but if you let ordinary pine dry out long enough it takes stain beautifully. Unfortunately you have to look at it for ten years in an unfinished condition in the meantime. Fortunately the perfect excuse to give your wife when she bugs you about finishing the doors is that you're letting the wood age.

▪ If you install hardwood flooring, you need to put felt pads on the feet of all your furniture right away or after two weeks the place will look like it was overrun by rabid ferrets.

▪ Speaking of hardwood flooring, make sure the carpenters attach the plywood subflooring to the joists with screws—fewer squeaks. For that matter, if you've got an old house and the subflooring consists of six-inch-wide pine planks, never mind the plywood—just have the planks secured with screws, with the finished flooring nailed over that. Shrinkage due to winter

---

[5]Yeah, I know, everyone thinks Wi-Fi has rendered such concerns moot. Wait till your kid's MacBook elbows your PC laptop off the home wireless network. More generally, do you realize that, depending on which band of the radio spectrum your wireless network employs, you're sharing the line with cordless phones, vehicle location devices, industrial plastic preheaters, microwave motion detectors, TV wireless extensions, cordless earphones, wireless gumball cameras, remote controls, ham radio, and microwave ovens, plus who knows what technologies yet to be invented? That every thought you commit to the airwaves will be vulnerable to any hacker with a radio dish and a laptop? (Sure, trust encryption. The Germans thought the Enigma cipher machine was impregnable, too.) On the upside, contrary to what some may claim, you have nothing to fear from sunspots.

dryness will be spread over the whole floor rather than concentrated at the plywood joints and you won't have big gaps.

▪ If you've got the basement floor torn up, and the drainpipes beneath consist of hundred-year-old tile, replace them now or regret later that you didn't.

▪ The family room should adjoin the kitchen. Okay, everybody knows this. However, do they know to put a pass-through between the two rooms so that it opens over the kitchen sink, with windows in the far wall of the family room so whoever is at the sink can look out in the backyard and watch the kids play? They would if they talked to me.

▪ If you're putting in porch steps, and you live in a climate where water falls periodically from the sky, don't make the bottom step wood—it'll rot. Concrete is the thing. I speak from experience.

Notwithstanding these minor matters, planning the work on the house, from an architectural standpoint at least, presented no great difficulty. The real challenge was coming up with the money to pay for it.

4

Periodically in life one encounters things that are far more complicated than by rights they ought to be. Childbirth is one. I'm surely not the first person to think during the climactic moments of this supposedly joyous event: *This is the most idiotic way to reproduce a species I've ever heard of.* It is, after all, a basic biological process. It's had billions of years to evolve. You'd think by now we'd have worked up something involving ziplock bags, foam peanuts, and piped-in Mozart. But no. Instead we have buckets of blood, excruciating pain, and moronic medical residents, not to mention a non-negligible chance of deformity and death, all in an effort to squeeze an eight-pound sack through an aperture that can comfortably accommodate a jumbo frank.

I'm not claiming that financing the renovation of an old city house is in the same league with childbirth, agony-wise. But there are definite points of similarity. The pointless aggravation. (If you flunk the medical-resident admissions test, rest assured there's a place for you in the bank department in charge of dreaming up loan documentation requirements.) The endless waiting. The constant threat that all will end in disaster.

The thing was, at the time we acquired the Barn House, we were doing something normal people didn't do—we were taking a decrepit house in a declining city and fixing it up, in contrast to the usual American practice of moving to the edge of settlement and starting from scratch. Confronted with such an eccentric act, those in the business of lending money were taking no chances. Don't misunderstand; it's not that no one had ever requested a loan to rehabilitate an old city house. Indeed, so many had gone before us that at financial institutions specializing in home improvement loans for city houses a well-defined process had evolved. Up to a point it made sense.

Here's how it worked. One started with the house. It perhaps was in need of repairs, but it was more or less intact; a price had been struck for it, and a mortgage loan obtained. Very well; that was the bedrock upon which all else relied. One then needed to obtain a construction loan to pay for the renovation, and upon completion of the work, a final mortgage that paid off both the original mortgage and the construction loan and provided long-term financing for the finished house. It seemed simple, and in outline it was; but it entailed a hundred intricate steps as rigidly prescribed as a Japanese Noh drama. Certain acts had to be accomplished in a certain order. To deviate from the script in the smallest detail was to invite catastrophe. We knew one couple who attempted to obtain a construction loan after interior demolition was under way—a fatal error. They'd failed to confirm their home's baseline value; their loan application was rejected.

The house's value was the key thing, you see. At the outset this figure could be confidently stated—that is, the price you just paid. One then proposed to take the house, a sagging but patently saleable commodity, and demolish large parts of it. To a degree this was true of any home improvement project, but city houses were often in such an advanced state of dilapidation that they had to be gutted, with all or most of the interior finishing removed, the utilities yanked out, and the walls taken down to the studs.

Gutting a house reduces its value to an appalling degree. The value of the property at its nadir may be the price of the land on which the house sits minus the cost of razing what's left. The home owner doesn't see it in such stark terms, of course; he's destroying the house in order to save it. The lender can afford no such confidence; he must plan for the worst. (I'm trying to put myself in the lender's shoes here, not without effort.) Except in rare cases the home owner has no prior experience; he may well be a fool, and even if he isn't, he may be launching a project he lacks the resources to complete.

One encountered such people from time to time. When I was just out of college I came home about an hour past dawn one morning to overhear an argument under way in an old house across the street from my apartment. The house was occupied by a young couple with a small child. Over a period of several months the husband had disassembled most of his front porch, presumably with the idea of rebuilding it. At the time of the argument the porch consisted of the wooden deck plus the roof above, the latter propped up precariously by two-by-fours at the corners. There were no pillars, railings, or steps—I remember one day the small child and a little friend having a peeing contest off the side. The only access from the sidewalk to the front door was a stepladder propped against the deck where the stairs had been. The fellow had gotten the project to that point perhaps a month or two previously. There'd been no progress since.

That was the subject of the argument. "You take the whole front porch apart and then you just leave it like that! I can't get into my own house!" the woman shrieked. "I can't *live* like this!" (Many a rehabber has heard these words.) The woman may have thought she had problems, but the party who arguably had worse ones was the holder of her mortgage, the value of whose collateral had just gone down the pipe.

Thus the Noh ritual. The lender will want, first of all, abundant documentation establishing that the loan applicant is a person of means; he'll want an appraisal, to confirm the starting value of the house; he'll want plans indicating in detail the work to be done; he'll want a contract with a qualified builder to perform the work for a fixed price, plus an oversight process to ensure that the work is done competently and in a timely manner; he'll want tax returns and plats of survey and credit checks and builder's references and a building permit and insurance policies and four or five million other things that at the time I imagined had been dreamed up by a bunch of former fraternity rush chairmen cackling: *Let's see if we can get the dumb son of a bitch to do* this. However—again, I'm trying to be evenhanded about this—it may well have been the case that they were the product of some bean counter waking up in the middle of the night in a cold sweat and thinking: *We're sinking $200,000 into* what? Finally—this is the tricky part—he'll want assurance that the finished house will be worth what it cost to restore it, or more precisely, worth the value of the outstanding loans.

For us this was no sure thing. We'd purchased the house with a $200,000 mortgage. The architects estimated that renovation would cost $250,000 if nothing went wrong. Comparable houses in the neighborhood (Ned's, for example) typically sold at the time for far less than $450,000. Luckily, one gut rehab in the vicinity had been completed and sold prior to our arrival— another Queen Anne a block away. Initially, we were told, the owner had put it on the market for $650,000. One hopes this didn't represent the actual amount of money invested in the property, because there had been no takers. The owner had been obliged to reduce the price sharply, eventually striking a deal at $456,000. Allowances having been made for differences in size and finishes, that figure established the upper limit of the financing we could obtain for the Barn House.

This is a point worth enlarging on. In fixing up an old city house, the chief lending constraint wasn't so much what you could afford personally (although naturally that entered into it), but rather what the neighborhood would support. Trouble was, a city house commonly was such a shuddering wreck that the obtainable funds undershot what was needed by a hilarious margin. The Barn House required reconstruction of the most fundamental sort—I-beams! Roof! Walls! We had of course included the more conspicuous repairs in our cost estimates, but—I blush to confess it—we'd left other items out. For example, I'd have been hard put to come up with a persuasive riposte had some keen-eyed loan officer sat down with me and asked: *So, this house—were you thinking of having doors?* The numb fact was that the money we expected to have at our disposal wouldn't suffice to complete the job, and we were gambling that more would magically materialize at timely intervals en route. Anyone who embarked on a large-scale city rehab in those days can no doubt tell a comparable tale. The bank, one suspects, wasn't entirely oblivious to the implacable fiscal facts and, notwithstanding its appetite for documents, simply took a great deal on faith. I know we did (or anyway I did—I hadn't explained to Mary in detail about the loose ends in the budget). One had the sensation throughout the project—and bear in mind, this was above and beyond the usual concerns about tradesmanly competence and schedule slippage and so on—of careening down a mountain road in a car without brakes, having no definite notion of what lay ahead and no certainty of success, knowing only that, the frantic descent having commenced, there was no alternative but to continue—and this in a race that went on for years.

We encountered one unexpected obstacle early on—the matter of insurance. The bank wanted to see a copy of a valid hazard insurance policy with a liability limit of at least $1 million. What heart-stopping disaster would run to that kind of money I didn't care to contemplate, but the amount wasn't the issue. Rather, it was this: Our regular carrier refused to insure a house that was unoccupied. We explained that we couldn't occupy the house; we were renovating it. This concept proved difficult for the agent to grasp. His was a suburban company; his idea of home renovation was recarpeting the guest room. A house so far gone that you couldn't live in it while working on it was beyond his comprehension. We had several exasperating conversations; it was like explaining quantum mechanics to a sheep. We hunted around and found another carrier. The carrier sent out an inspector. More problems. The company would only insure the house if we replaced the main electrical panel. The old one was a fire hazard.

I couldn't argue. I'd seen more impressive-looking apparatus in a tackle box. But I couldn't legally replace the panel myself; the job had to be done by a licensed electrician. I asked around. Friends who were also renovating a house suggested a man named Lee. He'd done some work for them; they were satisfied with the quality; the price had been reasonable. The only drawback was that Lee was hard to reach. However, it was my lucky day—I got him on the first try. He agreed to stop by the following morning to replace the panel. I said I'd leave the rear basement door unlocked so he could get started. This was perhaps an unorthodox procedure for someone I hadn't yet met, but I felt the lack of insurance acutely—I was certain the house was going to burn down at any moment. (Indeed, for months every time I turned the last corner en route to the Barn House I felt genuinely relieved to find it was still standing.) I felt I had no time to lose.

I was late getting to the house the next day. The basement door was open; I could hear noise inside. Walking into the room where the fuse box was, I found a tall, gaunt black man with a salt-and-pepper goatee fussing with a piece of pipe. I guessed he was in his sixties. He wore horn-rimmed glasses, what I recall as a tan army-issue sleeveless T-shirt, and baggy khaki fatigue pants. On his head was a baseball cap with a black, red, and green flag insignia above which was the word AFRICA. He was smoking a long, thin cigarillo. He looked like a cross between Fidel Castro and Malcolm X.

He looked up as I entered. "How do," he said in a drawling baritone, extending his hand. "You must be Ed. I'm Lee."

I had one of those watershed moments one encounters from

time to time. You'll appreciate that the total package Lee presented at that moment was, even by city standards, pretty out there. Then again, I knew if I wanted somebody in a blue workshirt with *Vern* embroidered on the pocket I should have moved to the suburbs. I stuck out my hand and we shook.

Lee had a courtly manner and a dry sense of humor; he was one of those people it was impossible to dislike. He showed me what he'd done. He'd installed a temporary new service panel next to the old one and switched over the cabling. Then, his sense of aesthetics offended by the derelict basement wiring, he'd ripped out the worst of it, replaced it with conduit, and installed a couple of ceiling lights. The result was a great improvement—we'd easily pass insurance inspection. I asked him how much.

"Seventy-five dollars," he said.

The city guy learns at an early age never to appear surprised by anything, and that skill came in handy now. The typical quote for a new main panel at the time was on the order of $1,000. Granted, what Lee had done was only a quick fix. The temporary panel was essentially a long-term equipment loan. Still, $75 was startlingly cheap. I'd need someone to install the permanent service and possibly help with other work; I could see already that there would be little slack in the budget. Lee offered the prospect that I'd be able to conclude the project without having to knock off gas stations in the late stages.

My friends proved to be right—it was never easy to reach Lee. If he wasn't home when you called, you could leave a number with whomever answered, presumably one of his kids; but the chances of the message getting through weren't high. Later a friend told me that Lee was often unavailable for long stretches because his wife had thrown him out of the house. "He's quite the charmer," she said by way of explanation, with what seemed to me a silly grin. But I was willing to put up with that. Lee, too, belonged to the Brotherhood of the Right Way.

My earlier excursion on this subject may have given the impression that the right way was the exclusive province of the professional crowd. Not at all. I had learned about the right way from my father, who was as working-class as they got.

Long experience with my father had taught me two things about the right way: (1) Doing things properly would produce a beautiful result in which one could take great satisfaction when the job was finished; and (2) there was such a thing as taking it over a cliff. In the latter department, for example, we had the matter of haircuts. When I was small my father had been the household barber; his idea of a proper haircut was to make you look like you had just been inducted into the Marines and to take a full hour doing it. In matters more worthy of his attention, however, my father did magnificent work. My parents had the only hundred-year-old house in northern Illinois in which every wall was straight and every corner square, testimony to what could be accomplished with infinite patience and a truckload of cedar shims.

My father's general approach, for better or worse, had rubbed off on me. As the significant others in our respective lives will surely agree, it was a mixed blessing. My parents once had an argument about the proper method of sanding the floor in their bedroom. My mother reasoned that all they needed to do was sand around the perimeter, because there would always be a rug in the middle. My father bridled at this suggestion, because it wasn't right, and I have to say my sympathies were with the old man. On the other hand, I also have to admit I don't know whether they ever sanded the middle of the floor or not, because it has been covered by a rug for nigh on forty years.

An adherent of the right way reconciled himself early in life to certain intransigent facts. The first was that the right way was only sporadically the easy way, and as such was rarely going to be on sale at The Home Depot. Another, which is perhaps the first restated, can be expressed in the form of a lament: *If I abandoned my principles,* the righteous person might say, *life would be devoid of meaning. On the other hand, I could probably make a lot more money.* One knew certain persons who when rehabbing a house would re-side only the front, because that was the part you saw from the street. This offended the sensibilities of any right-thinking person, but was boatloads cheaper. In fact, one observed with chagrin, this sort of blatant chiseling had become routine in American home building, where people (my sister, for one) thought nothing of buying a house with brick in front and vinyl siding everywhere else.

I understood cost-benefit analysis, the laws of supply and demand, the greatest good for the greatest number, and that sort of thing. That didn't mean I had to like the result. I didn't live in the city because it was economical; I didn't propose to live in an old house because it was cheap. The world could do as it liked; I—you can imagine what a trip I was to live with—was going to do it right.

My goal in getting people to work on the house, therefore, was to hire disciples of the right way whenever possible. There were several reasons for this. The first, naturally, was that the job would get done properly without my having to hover constantly over the proceedings like a fretful mother. Second, and I may as well be frank about this, people who liked to do things right had a tendency to undercharge. Finally, an adherent of the right way was a party with whom one could profitably consult. We'll return to this matter in a moment.

A month before we were scheduled to close on the Barn House we got a call from the appraiser asking if we knew there was a hole in the roof, the sequela to the aforementioned deck. We admitted that we did. We'd become accustomed to being thought of as crazy people. My family in particular thought fixing up the Barn House was an act of the profoundest folly. My brother John, who was on his second house, and for whom I'd wired two kitchens, four bathrooms, a bedroom, a garage, an attic playroom, and sundry other portions of miscellaneous premises, offered the opinion that the Barn House was a bigger project than his and the old man's houses put together. That was an exaggeration in one sense, true in another. We'd gutted probably half of my parents' home, and my brother had done the same with maybe 40 percent of his, but not all at once, and the breadth of the work in both houses was nowhere near as extensive as in ours. Truth was, we'd signed up for a much larger project than we were initially willing to admit.

We needed to replace all the pipes and wires throughout the house and out to the street. (We omitted the sewer tile, but shouldn't have, to our subsequent regret.) We had to replace all the plaster. There was a point early in the project where I thought I might save the odd wall here and there, and walked around marking Xs on sections I wanted to preserve; reality eventually set in, but quite late in the project there was still one chunk of original plaster and lath approximately eight square feet in area that I planned to save, partly because it was intact and partly because it was a token of an era long past; however, the fit was upon the lads that day (I wasn't present) and it all wound up in the Dumpster. The heating system needed to be completely redone. We needed to install an air-conditioning system, intercoms, an alarm system, telephone and cable TV wiring. Sixty percent of the flooring needed to be replaced and the rest refinished. All of the existing windows save two were destined for landfill. The front porch—junk. Likewise the repulsive turret roof, a fair number of the doors (the rest would have to be refinished), much of the woodwork, the fireplaces, plus much more that's painful to recall and that we'll get to soon enough anyway. Suffice it to say we had a full plate.

Two weeks before closing the current owner phoned. There had been a drenching rainstorm the previous night; in the middle of it, the electricity on the second floor of the house had failed. He'd been unable to restore it, and had the idea this might queer the deal. Perhaps it should have; probably at least I should have taken advantage of the opportunity to strike a harder bargain. But

I didn't. The truth was I didn't care. I expected to replace all the wiring anyway; it was immaterial whether it worked beforehand or not.

I planned to do some of the work myself, but given the scale of the project I knew I wouldn't be able to accomplish more than a fraction of what was required. I began soliciting recommendations for general contractors. Finding a good contractor was a challenge under the best of circumstances, and living in the city made it more difficult still. I'd heard many bizarre tales.[1] But I wasn't too worried. I'd heard about Eddie, whom I had reason to believe was well acquainted with the right way.

Eddie was a Polish immigrant—Chicago at one time had had the largest concentration of Poles of any city except Warsaw.[2]

[1] The following was sent to me by Lisa, who worked at my newspaper. I thought to paraphrase it but find I can do no better than the original:

"When my boyfriend and I bought a small three-bedroom house [in the city] about ten years ago the first order of business was to gut the dungeon of a kitchen we had inherited. Somehow or another the boyfriend met and hired a couple of beatniks that he met in a bar in Wicker Park to do the kitchen job. He was particularly drawn to them because they were self-proclaimed communists that guaranteed the job at a very reasonable price. The drinking probably helped too. Of course the remodeling took twice as much time as promised—about three months of washing dishes in the bathtub and eating only what we could barbecue in the backyard. Our commies would show up to work for a couple of days then disappear to parts unknown for weeks. Typical contractor behavior, but we couldn't figure out what they were doing in the meantime seeing how we were their only clients. Turns out our socially conscious, tree-hugging communists spent their off hours organizing protests against every organization that looked at them cross-eyed and spent a lot of time in jail as a result. We found this out when I turned on the six o'clock news just in time to see the cops arresting our contractors for disturbing the peace during the Promise Keepers Convention at Soldier Field. Seems this was their life's mission. Not as part of a group or anything. Just the two of them and maybe a girlfriend once in a while. Remodeling was just a side job for earning bail money. They did a great job on the kitchen though."

[2] Not anymore. The second largest city in Poland, Lodz, has now grown to 789,000 people, which according to the *Tribune* exceeds the number of Poles in Chicago by a small margin.

He'd arrived on a tourist visa in 1978, but the political troubles that eventually sparked the Solidarity movement made it seem unwise to go back. He'd been a grade school teacher in Poland, but lacking accreditation in the United States and having long been fascinated by construction anyway had gone into the remodeling business. Our friends Beth and Zet had been his clients; they described him in rapturous terms.

"We were remodeling our kitchen, and on one side there was a staircase coming down and a boot room with walls separating everything," Zet said. "We were thinking about removing the walls and opening up the space but weren't sure if we could. Eddie said the walls weren't structural and suggested we take them out and put in a railing on the stairs instead. He said, 'If I were a child, I would want to sit at the top of the stairs so I could look out at the trees in the yard.' I thought: *I want this guy.*"

We invited Eddie over. He was a compactly built man with a neatly trimmed beard and a precise manner of speaking. We sat at the dining room table in our town house and discussed the work. One question regarding which we had come to no firm conclusions was the method of heating the house. The Barn House when we bought it was heated by hot-water radiators. They had been installed some years following the house's original construction, and the pipes were exposed. The radiators themselves were bulky. We assumed without having given the matter much thought that we would remove the pipes and radiators and install ductwork for gas forced-air, by far the most common type of home heating in the United States. In addition to being relatively cheap, forced air had the great advantage that you could use the ducts to air-condition the house in the summer.

Eddie was unenthusiastic about forced air. The rooms in the house were large, he pointed out; it wasn't as though we couldn't spare the space for radiators. Concealing ductwork, on the other hand, would require us to install false ceilings or soffits, either of which from the standpoint of appearances was something of a kludge. More to the point, radiators provided the best heat. He thought we should just conceal the pipes, easy enough to do while we had the walls open.

As he spoke I realized with budding certainty that he was right. The house I had grown up in had been heated by radiators; it had been comfortable even on the coldest days. When I came inside after jumping in the snow, I could sit on a radiator and warm up. In contrast, the places I had lived in that were heated by forced air always seemed to have cold spots. In our newly constructed town house, for example, the furnace was located on the second floor. To heat the first-floor kitchen, the blower had to force the naturally buoyant warm air down ten feet, then twenty feet laterally beneath the floor, then up through the registers. The system didn't work very well; you were fighting basic physics. We froze in that kitchen on cold days.

I considered. We were going to rearrange some rooms; we would need to install additional heat in a few locations. As far as I knew old-fashioned radiators were no longer available. I had seen baseboard heaters that I knew used hot water. I asked Eddie whether I could use them.

Eddie shook his head. A radiator contained a large reservoir of water. A baseboard heater, on the other hand, consisted of a straight piece of pipe with perpendicular fins at intervals to radiate away the heat. The two didn't have the same . . . at this point Eddie stumbled. He had reached the frontiers of his English. But I saw what he was driving at.

"Thermal mass?" I said.

"Thermal mass," he said. A baseboard heater didn't contain much water; it would cool off quickly, and with it the room. An old-fashioned radiator contained a great deal of water and would stay warm for a much longer time. You couldn't operate radiators and baseboard heaters off the same furnace, or at any rate off the same pump; they had different cycling requirements. No matter, Eddie assured me—I could get all the radiators I needed secondhand.

Thermal mass was a basic engineering concept, but not every contractor understood it, particularly in an age when hot-water heat was no longer widely used. Here was a fellow, I decided, who knew the right way to do things, and would go to some trouble to do them. I needed to talk to other contractors and get other bids, but this was my guy.

5

We'd first viewed the house in January and taken possession in May. It was now early June. We still had a great deal of planning to do and hadn't hired a contractor, but we were far enough along to know there were sizable portions of the house we'd need to demolish. We hadn't yet arrived at the conclusion, immediately obvious to nearly everyone else, that the house would need to be completely gutted, but even so there were truckloads of material that needed to be pulled down and removed. This wasn't a task that required advanced skills, and we wanted to economize. I got on the phone.

One thing any guy working on an old house discovers is how easy it is to recruit other males to assist with demolition. Ask for help painting, or hanging wallpaper, or any other mundane chore and you're sure to hear some feeble excuse. But give a guy a chance to spend a couple hours reducing parts of a century-old building to rubble and he's there. Over a period of several weeks I asked perhaps thirty male friends and relations if they'd be willing to spend a few hours ripping down walls. Close to two dozen agreed. Clearly I was tapping into some atavistic male impulse. If I'd promised they'd also get to fire automatic weapons I'd probably have gotten the whole squad.

You may suppose my friends were drooling jamokes. Not at all. I had a surgeon in there, a dentist, an architect (Charlie, who wasn't reluctant to get his fingers dirty), a judge, several writers, a former contributing editor for a national magazine, a computer programmer, a newspaper production manager, a video producer, a college dean, an auto service manager, a lawyer, an accountant, and miscellaneous other intellectuals, professionals, and men of the world. If the house had fallen in on the bunch of them, the average intelligence of the central United States would have noticeably declined. As it was they attacked the house with the elan of the Mongols sacking Kiev. The house echoed with the sound of blows, the squeal of rending lumber, and the crash of falling debris.

The surgeon and the editor went downstairs to pull down the basement ceiling. About forty-five minutes later they came back up. They were completely covered with fine black dust, which had poured out from behind the lath and plaster. The only parts of them that weren't completely grimy were the whites of their eyes. They looked like Welsh miners. "I think we've established that your house was heated by coal," said the surgeon, making a facial expression I took to be a grin. A few hours later he was back at the hospital rummaging through someone's internal organs, presumably having washed his hands first. Demolition wasn't something most guys wanted to make a career out of, but it lent life a certain tang.[1]

---

[1] It's worth pointing out that the male love of destruction has nothing to do with testosterone per se. On one of my early trips to the Barn House I took along my eldest, Ryan, then three years old. Thinking to keep him occupied while I worked elsewhere, I gave him a little hammer and pointed him at a

There was no end to the surprises one might encounter in an old house. I'd heard of people who found that the previous owner had stuffed bags of cocaine into cracks in the walls (whence, one supposes, the term "crack cocaine"); who on their first walk-through were obliged to step over a body in the living room (sleeping rather than dead, one presumes, although I imagine the matter wasn't subject to close investigation); who, while removing the wall tile in the upstairs bathroom, fell through the bottom of the tub and the floor beneath (there had been an undiscovered leak), their legs dangling in the downstairs hall. Nothing quite that dramatic happened to us, but we did find quite a few curiosities, the following among them:

1. A Victorian-era high-button woman's shoe.[2]

2. A one-pint glass milk bottle from the T. H. Bates company, 410 Otto St.—PURITY GUARANTEED, patented Sept. 17, 1889.

3. An 1891 Liberty dime, perhaps lost by one of the workers who built the foundation wall near which it was found by Ryan, and subsequently lost a second time by us.

4. An 1897 train schedule wrapped around a radiator pipe, indicating the date at which the owner of the Barn House had given up on the original heating system and installed one that actually worked, a matter to which I'll return.

---

disposable stretch of wall, then proceeded to get tied up in a phone conversation. When I went to check on Ryan thirty minutes later, I was startled to discover that he'd laid waste to a good fifteen square feet of plaster and in the process had given himself a blister. I had to buy him work gloves.

[2]Howard the architect, who went on to become chief curator of the National Building Museum in Washington, D.C., told me many years later that numerous women's shoes turned up in walls during construction projects at that institution, which was housed in a building erected in 1886. This led him to think either women in D.C. had some mighty odd habits or else carpenters thought shoes were a token of good luck.

5. The skeleton of what was probably a pigeon (there had been a hole in the eaves where they roosted), but having an appearance of such antiquity that one couldn't rule out the possibility that it was an archaeopteryx.

6. A portion of the June 14, 1923, edition of the *Miles City* (Montana) *American*. Miles City, I happened to know, had been a crew change point on the Chicago, Milwaukee, St. Paul & Pacific Railroad, better known as the Milwaukee Road. Perhaps someone in the house had been a trainman.

7. A 1921 visitor's guide called *This Week in Chicago*, modestly reporting that Chicago, the "World's Fourth City" (in population; today it's twenty-seventh), had "a record of development in population, wealth, education, and civic achievement of which the world can furnish no parallel in rapid and permanent growth."

8. A walled-up set of built-in shelves containing nothing, which I nonetheless found gave me the creeps, having read at a too-tender age Edgar Allan Poe's *The Cask of Amontillado*.

9. Several hundred feet of gas pipe used for lighting—disconnected, we established, although with gas pipe you never knew. A friend removing some old pipe in his house one day smelled gas and thought at first it was a trace of earlier days but soon realized, mercifully before the house exploded, that the pipe was still connected to the main.

10. The original house wiring. Houses in the 1890s commonly were equipped for both gas and electricity, lest the latter prove a fad. Old wiring is commonly called knob-and-tube wiring, referring to the insulators from and through which the wire is strung. The Barn House electrical distribution system used basically this type of wiring except that it dispensed with the knobs and tubes, consisting merely of wires pulled through holes drilled in the framing and soldered together. Most of the

old rubber and cloth insulation had rotted away, exposing the bare copper, fortunately no longer carrying current.

11. A 1972 issue of *Gallery* magazine proving that Brady Bunch–style haircuts didn't look any less ridiculous when you took your clothes off. [3]

12. A box of .38-caliber bullets with five missing, wrapped in a newspaper dated 1972 and stuck above a header in the attic. Clearly 1972 at the Barn House had been quite a year.

The work that first few weekends was partly exploratory—we needed to establish what was salvageable and what would have to be replaced. One task was to see what the exterior of the house looked like under the ugly brown shakes. To my satisfaction we found close-spaced cedar clapboard, grimy but in better shape than one might have expected. Though the shake installer had done his best to conceal it, the Barn House had been a handsome structure at one time, and the thought that it might be again now seemed less far-fetched.

The back of the house I wasn't so sure of. A room had been added to the rear of the kitchen in the 1930s—probably, if one judged from the quality of the work, by the same palookas responsible for the roof in front. The room was poorly proportioned, the doorway was too narrow, and the ceiling had partly fallen in—this was the room with the hole in the roof where the deck had been nailed on. On the other hand, it was already there, an advantage if the basic construction was sound. That was doubtful, but one wanted to be methodical. One Saturday I sent my brother Bob out back with a pick and shovel to plumb the depths of the addition's concrete footings. The building code in Chicago required that footings extend at least forty-two inches below

---

[3] I'm informed Brady Bunch haircuts have made a comeback in some quarters. So?

grade, beneath the frost line. If the footings hadn't been done properly, the addition would have to be demolished.

Bob strolled out to the front of the house forty minutes later. He was of the view that the Barn House had not been one of my shrewder investments. I detected the glimmer of a smirk.[4]

"Ed," he said, "do you know your house is built on sand?"

I went back to look. He'd dug down about three feet. Sure enough, I saw about eight inches of topsoil, and beneath that what to all appearances was beach sand. The entire neighborhood, I now recalled, had been built on an old sandbar, a vestige of the days when a glacial lake had covered the region. I remembered a house we'd looked at some time previously, in a neighborhood a little to the north, a charming place except for the fact that it leaned about six inches out of the vertical, like a picture knocked askew. The Barn House wasn't that bad, although it's true the floors in the rooms in the front of the house were two to three inches lower at one end than the other, due in all likelihood to settlement of the central chimney, which defect one seldom noticed except on the third floor, where one had the impression of walking up a hill. I'd long since deferred that problem for later, and decided not to worry about the sand either, since there wasn't much I could do about it at that point. Instead I concentrated on the footings for the addition, which as feared went down only thirty inches and had been poured without benefit of forms, the concrete having simply been dumped in a trench. I'd seen more care used making mud pies. That settled that. The addition would have to go.

---

[4]I had it coming. Once, on the first day of a fishing trip, I caught a fish and Bob didn't. The next morning at breakfast I announced to our group that Bob and I had always had a friendly rivalry, but that midway through high school, by which time Bob was an inch taller than me and twenty-five pounds heavier, I had come to the realization that violence was immature. "From then on," I declared a bit too grandly, "I resolved to outdo Bob based on intellect alone."

By now I was firmly persuaded that no competent thing had been done to the house since the last of the original carpenters had packed up his tools and walked out the door. Everything accomplished subsequently bespoke expedience and cheesiness. One afternoon I walked around the attic and noticed slabs of cheap pressboard that had been nailed up in a vain effort to lend some finish to the space, and was so offended to have such rubbish in my house that I began ripping off pieces and hurling them out the window. Recognizing that this process lacked system, the following weekend I built a chute, which extended from an upper-story window to the Dumpster (actually, a succession of Dumpsters) we had by now more or less permanently parked in the driveway. I was proud of that chute, a sturdy piece of apparatus made of two-by-twos and salvaged Masonite held together with drywall screws.[5] I'd constructed it in the rain. It wanted elegance, I concede. Indeed, from the standpoint of slovenliness, the property lacked only a car up on blocks. No matter; the current state of affairs was temporary. We'd arrive at elegance in due course.

The chute proved particularly useful in disposing of cellulose. Cellulose is a dirty gray material having the appearance of loose cotton. It had been used to insulate the attic joists at the time of initial construction—there was no insulation in the walls, the builders of the era having been of the view (rightly enough) that you lost more heat through the roof of a house than out the sides. I'd been told the cellulose was made from ground-up scrap paper, the best they could do in the days before fiberglass. It was foul beyond description.[6] To get at it you had to pull down the attic

[5]Gus in the movie *My Big Fat Greek Wedding* thinks the answer to all of life's little problems is Windex, and many have a touching faith in superglue and duct tape, but for lasting resolution of vexatious situations, in my opinion, you can't beat drywall screws and a Makita cordless driver-drill.
[6]A certain school of thought holds that cellulose is just as good as fiberglass and a lot cheaper. I'm willing to concede this may be true of new cellulose.

ceiling, whereupon it fell on you in a clump, covering you with filth and filling the air with dust that left you coughing and wheezing and wiping your eyes. Most of the guys were good for about two hours of this before they decided they had better things to do. I, on the other hand, had to spend days at it.

Late one morning I began shoveling cellulose down the chute. There was a brisk wind out of the south. As the cellulose slid into the Dumpster, clouds of dust billowed off and drifted down the block. I guessed this wouldn't endear me to the neighbors. Sure enough, after about twenty minutes someone emerged from a two-flat a couple doors up and stormed toward the Barn House. It was an older man whose name I later learned was Joe. Joe was in a rage. "What are you doing there?" he demanded. "That stuff is *poison.* It causes *cancer.*" He planted himself near the Dumpster, his fists on his hips, and glared up at me. "It's asbestos, isn't it?"

I was in no mood for palaver—I'd been hawking up cellulose all morning. The thought crossed my mind to reply that I was increasing the value of Joe's property merely by hauling this despicable crud out of the neighborhood and I didn't want to hear any beefs about his house getting dusty. But I repressed the impulse. One wanted to be neighborly. "No," I hollered down. "It's cellulose. It's not going to hurt anything. I'll be done soon. Please be patient."

Joe glared awhile longer, then stalked off. *Fabulous,* I thought glumly. *Maybe the wind will blow out of the north tomorrow and I can tick off the other half of the neighborhood.* Truth was, Joe had nothing to worry about—the real asbestos was already gone. I'd called up asbestos abatement firms based on the size of their ads in the phone book and had gotten quotes of up to $5,000. One of the callees turned out to be an old pigeon-racing buddy of my father's. (Long story. Don't ask.) He volunteered to do the

---

Hundred-year-old cellulose, however, isn't something I want leaking particulates into *my* breathing space.

work at cost—$1,100. The process had been completely invisible to me. I arrived at the Barn House one day to find the stuff gone—pipe insulation, floor tile. It was one of many breaks we got that for a long time we considered just luck.

I got on the wrong side of a lot of people that summer. Across the street from the Barn House was a meeting hall of the Jehovah's Witnesses. One Sunday morning while I was out shoveling debris into the Dumpster, two women strolled by with armloads of Witness literature.

"Shall we give him one?" one said in a voice just loud enough for me to hear.

"He's working on Sunday," said her companion. "He's an animal—he doesn't even *have* a soul."

Others were friendlier—my soon-to-be-neighbor Gabe, for one. Gabe was a city guy of the old school. He was a five-foot-six Vietnam vet who called himself a Puerto Rican hillbilly—he'd been born in Kentucky to Puerto Rican parents while his father was in the military. Though he'd moved to Chicago when he was nine, he still spoke with a thick Hispanic accent. Now a foreman at an injection-molding plant, he lived with his extended family in the two-flat next door to the Barn House.

Gabe stopped by to chat occasionally while I was en route to the Dumpster, filling me in on the neighborhood. He warned of the "bad building" behind us—although drugs were no longer openly sold there, he'd had a few run-ins with some of the residents, whom he described as Mexican riffraff. During one confrontation, his antagonists (kids, presumably) asked why he, a fellow Hispanic, was on their case. For Gabe this wasn't a question that required a lot of soul-searching. "I'm a home owner!" he replied. A short time before, he told me, a departing tenant had set a fire in a garbage cart shoved up against his garage, scorching the paint. The fellow had then rammed his truck into Gabe's garage door, knocking it off the track, and had stolen some jacks and tools.

On the whole, however, things were calmer than they had been, I was given to understand. Apart from the occasional irruption of graffiti, overt signs of gang activity had largely ended. That's not to say crime had disappeared. The police report in the local newspaper chronicled a steady drone of burglaries, robberies, assaults, vandalism, and the occasional drive-by shooting within a mile or two of the Barn House; every time I talked to Mike he seemed to know about some new murder or shooting that had occurred nearby. But that was true pretty much anywhere in the city. The main thing, I gathered, was that crime wasn't in your face to the extent that it had been a few years previously. You didn't have, as my friends in Bucktown did, a car bombing on your block, or surly youths loitering on the street corners; the residents no longer felt obliged to patrol after dark. On warm evenings, it's true, you could often find a sizable aggregation of young men hanging out in the parking lot at the muffler shop drinking beer, but mostly they were working on cars, and while I can't say that the sight did much to dress up the street, as far as I knew they never did any harm. I had a friend who lived in a neighborhood called Rogers Park on the far north side of the city; he was active at his kids' school, and one of his jobs was to stand at a certain location on a certain street during afternoon dismissal and keep an eye on a drug lookout stationed across the way. That sort of thing hadn't been necessary for some years in the Barn House's neighborhood. Nonetheless, you had occasional vivid reminders that you were living in the city, a matter to which I'll return.

The work in the Barn House that summer was filthy and tedious, but I remember those days with great fondness. Despite the occasionally hostile reception, I liked the neighborhood. Now that it was full summer, the mature trees lining the parkways had formed a canopy over the street. By city standards it was quiet and spacious. True, we were on a flight path for O'Hare airport; we were a short distance from two busy commercial streets; the L line and a commuter train line were about two blocks away; at rush hour many motorists trying to avoid the backup at the intersection (the city had dug up the sewers) took a shortcut down our street. Still, it was quiet compared to, say, a foundry.

Most of the time there was parking, too, except when the Jehovah's Witnesses had services, which is to say, pretty much constantly (services at the time were conducted in multiple languages and were held in shifts), and my impression was that we got a lot of overflow cars owned by teachers and students at the nearby high school. You also had the problem, which didn't become apparent till later, of people who would come home drunk and park in front of your driveway like mopes (we had the only driveway on the block, and one of few in the neighborhood, but look, you nitwits, our car was parked in it), although I will say the cops were pretty good about ticketing. Things could also be tight when the Cubs were in town, because we were just outside the restricted-parking district around Wrigley Field (not that anybody paid much attention to *that*), and people took advantage to park near us and walk to the game. But most of the time you could find parking without much difficulty, often right in front of the house.

Part of the charm of the place in those early days was that it was completely overgrown. No outside maintenance had been done in years. The front yard was full of violets; the backyard was like a forest glade. Weed trees—box elders and trees of heaven, mostly—had grown up at the rear of the lot, blocking the view of the apartment buildings behind us. Three enormous elms along one side fence filled most of the sky with their branches. There was a big cottonwood; a huge maple plus several smaller ones; three blue spruces planted front and rear in a not entirely successful stab at home improvement; a mulberry; a pear tree, of all things. Now that the leaves had grown in, what with the spruce in the front yard, low-hanging branches from the maple and a honey locust on the parkway, and a row of bushes along the front sidewalk that were a good six feet tall, you could barely see the house—arguably an advantage under the circumstances. Matters couldn't stay like that, I knew, but I was reluctant to cut the stuff down. I have a picture of my older two children in the backyard when they were small, surrounded by an Eden of trees, shrubs, and wildflowers; it recalls W. Eugene Smith's famous photograph *The Walk to Paradise Garden.* One had the sense of a landscape reclaimed by the wild.

My male relations, who continued to assemble periodically to assist with demolition, took a more practical view of things. Where romantics might gush about nature, they thought: *What this needs is some Agent Orange.* Late one afternoon as we relaxed on the derelict front porch after a day of wrecking walls, I noticed an exchange of glances. My brother-in-law Tom, who had a luxurious mustache that gave him a somewhat piratical appearance, stood up and stretched.

"Ready?" he said to the others.

"What's up?" I asked. One always wanted to keep the members of my family separated, lest there be unrest.

"Relax, Ed," said Tom with a sidelong look. "This will only take a minute." Producing hedge trimmers and other implements previously concealed on the premises, the boys proceeded to assault the bushes and whatever other vegetation was in reach in front of the house.

"You *guys!*" I protested. I confess I did so without much conviction, and they paid no attention anyway. In ten minutes they were done. The bushes had been shorn to a more conventional size.

To be sure, there was plenty of vegetation left. Late in the afternoon a few days later I sat out on the landing off the rear of the third floor drinking a Mountain Dew. There was a jerry-built stairway there, presumably constructed as a fire exit when the house had been converted to apartments. From the top step I looked out into what to all appearances was a forest. Neighboring buildings were visible through gaps in the leaves. A few houses down I could see the big catalpa tree in Mike's backyard. It was almost July now and the tree was full of enormous white blossoms. In the trees closer at hand birds flitted from branch to branch. We lived on a flyway; migrating birds followed the Lake Michigan shoreline and roosted in the nearby cemetery. We saw more birds than I'd ever seen in my life—blue jays, robins, cardinals. We'd planned to tear off the raggedy steps and replace the back door with a window; now I started to think better of it. The scene was so pretty. Maybe someday we could build a deck up here. The project had barely begun, but I was content. I was fixing up my old house.

After a time I was roused from my reverie by a voice in the distance—an angry voice, I soon realized. Every so often it paused, then resumed. I was overhearing one side of a quarrel. I went downstairs and out into the backyard to investigate. The angry voice was coming from an open window in the bad building across the alley. The speaker was male; the words consisted chiefly of profanity: "You fuckin' *bitch*." From time to time when the voice paused I could hear a barely audible response.

The man seemed to be growing more and more irate. At any moment I expected to hear blows and screams. I went inside the house and dialed 911.

When I came out again a short time later I noticed Betsy standing in her yard two doors down. She had heard the argument, too.

"I called the police," she said.

"So did I," I replied.

By now all was quiet—either the argument had subsided or he was cutting up the body. I listened for a few moments; nothing. It seemed to me my presence was no longer urgent, and I was overdue for supper. I consulted with Betsy. She said she would wait until the police arrived. I turned to go.

"Welcome to the neighborhood," Betsy called after me.

———

I wasn't present when the kids began calling the place the Barn House, and no one now remembers who invented the name, but I suspect it was my daughter Ani,[7] the more verbal of our (then) two. The term wasn't affectionately meant. Mary had taken the kids to inspect progress on the house, and they were unimpressed. Demolition by late summer was well advanced, and much of the framing was exposed. We'd swept up periodically, but bits of plaster and other debris lay in neglected corners, fragments of wood lath hung from the studs, and grime covered every surface. I seem to recall Ani on her return commenting disdainfully, "It's a *barn* house, Daddy," and wrinkling her nose. In any case the name stuck; we called the place the Barn House for the next five years.

[7]Her spelling, not ours, which she adopted in eighth grade. She was Annie during most of the events in this book, but if I use that spelling now I'll never hear the end of it.

6

Other than the possums, which we'll get to by and by, I can't honestly say that anything about the Barn House surprised us. While we weren't without our illusions, for the most part we expected the house to be a project from hell, and it was. Still, I'd be lying if I said we never wondered whether we were crazy to take on the job. It wasn't so much that investing in the house alarmed us. We were uneasier about the city.

I don't mean to exaggerate the risk. At the time we bought the Barn House, Chicago, like most cities of any size, had its share of reviving neighborhoods. But cities as a whole, and Chicago in particular, were still on a downward slide. Sure, in some parts of town you could get a pretty fair flourless chocolate cake. The fact remained that, as of the early 1990s, Chicago had been losing population steadily for more than forty years—to be precise, 837,000 people, at the time the most of any city in the modern world not purposely destroyed or emptied out.[1]

---

[1]This figure has now been exceeded by Detroit, which as of 2005 had lost 963,000 residents since its 1950 peak. War-ravaged cities have had greater

Adjustments having been made for scale, the story was largely the same in most older cities. At the time we bought the Barn House, it could be argued in all seriousness that residing in one of the great central cities of the United States, or at any rate of its eastern half, was a vanishing way of life. Between 1950 and 1990 Boston lost 30 percent of its population, Philadelphia 31 percent, Baltimore 32 percent, Cincinnati 33 percent, Minneapolis 33 percent, Washington 35 percent, Buffalo 43 percent, Detroit 44 percent, Cleveland 48 percent, Pittsburgh 51 percent, St. Louis 54 percent. New York lost 824,000 people in just ten years, from 1970 to 1980.

In some parts of Chicago almost nothing remained. In 1981, the *Chicago Tribune*, to illustrate a series about the city's economic prospects called "City on the Brink," had published a striking photograph of what apparently had been a residential neighborhood not far from the Loop, the city's central business district. The picture had been taken from some elevated point. In the distance was the downtown skyline surmounted by the Sears Tower, with a cluster of low-rise buildings in the middle distance. The landscape in the foreground was almost completely empty. The streets and sidewalks were still there, and the utility poles and streetlights; one could see street signs, some parked vehicles, and here and there a house or other structure. The rest was prairie.[2]

---

losses; Berlin's population as of 1946 had fallen 1.3 million from the prewar level. Undoubtedly the most dramatic example of urban decline is ancient Rome, whose population is thought to have fallen from roughly one million during imperial times to about 50,000 in the Middle Ages.

[2]My friend Philip Bess, an architect and baseball fan, published an equally arresting illustration of urban decline in a booklet entitled *City Baseball Magic: Plain Talk and Uncommon Sense about Cities and Baseball Parks* (1989). The booklet contained two fascinating maps. One depicted the environs of Tiger Stadium in Detroit in 1921, nine years after the park was built. The second showed the same neighborhood in 1986. The maps showed not just the streets around the stadium but the buildings, represented as black shapes. At first glance it was scarcely possible to believe the maps depicted the same district. In 1921, Tiger Stadium had been part of a densely built-up com-

I'd seen a neighborhood disintegrate firsthand. When I was young my family had lived in a community on the far west side of Chicago called Austin.[3] As city neighborhoods go, Austin was reasonably well equipped with the amenities. The housing had been solidly constructed—brick two-flats and apartment buildings, frame single-family homes.[4] The parochial schools were good, the public ones fair. There was a magnificent regional park, Columbus Park, with woods, a golf course, and a lagoon, the masterpiece of a wonderful man named Jens Jensen, one of the giants of American landscape design. There was a fine old town hall and a library on a village green of sorts, vestiges of the day when Austin had been part of an independent town. The com-

---

munity, with buildings occupying virtually every lot. In 1986, easily three-quarters of the buildings were gone. Some close to the stadium had been torn down for parking; others had made way for an expressway cut through the heart of the area. Still others had been replaced by larger structures. But most had simply disappeared, presumably having been abandoned or burned out and demolished during Detroit's long decline.

[3]Austin had an unusual past. In the nineteenth century it had been part of Cicero, a thinly settled township that it shared with Oak Park and what would become the town of Cicero, future headquarters of Al Capone. In the late 1890s there had been a row over the extension of the Lake Street L into the township—the go-getter Austinites had been in favor, whereas the rustics of Oak Park had been opposed. After the usual machinations surrounding transit in those days (an ailing town trustee had been dragged from his bed at one a.m. to vote in favor of the extension, breaking a tie, after opponents had gone home), Austin prevailed. Out of spite, the residents of Oak Park and the rest of Cicero engineered a complex annexation election in 1899 in which, over the opposition of Austinites, they voted Austin into Chicago while retaining independence for themselves. This made Austin the only neighborhood I ever heard of that wound up in the city because it had been kicked out of the suburbs.

[4]There were a few remnants of Austin's early days as well. At the end of our block a large white frame building stood at the rear of a lot, where it served as a garage. One day when I was six or seven—this was in the 1950s—I looked up at the double doors in the upper story of the building and realized with a shock: *That's a hayloft. This is a barn.* I felt I had discovered some priceless artifact of early human habitation, like the cave paintings at Lascaux.

munity was well served by transit and the expressway system. Shopping was convenient. The tree-lined streets were pretty.

Yet when presented with a modest challenge—namely, an influx of black people in the 1960s—the incumbent residents of Austin had bolted for the exits. The core of the community changed from virtually all white to 90 percent black between one census and the next. In a few city neighborhoods racial turnover had no visible impact other than a change in the predominant skin color of the residents, but in others, including Austin, it was accompanied by rapid physical decline. In the years following my family's departure in 1966 our old block had deteriorated to a shocking degree. Washington Boulevard, just down the street from our house, had once been lined with handsome courtyard apartment buildings; within a decade or two half the ones on our block had been torn down. Many of the buildings on the main commercial artery, Madison Street, were boarded up or razed. Similar scenes played out all over the city's west and south sides, and in other cities throughout the United States.

A familiar story, I know. Still, it seemed to me, looking back at what had happened, that the deterioration of places like Austin hadn't been at root a consequence of racial change. Race merely brought the matter into higher relief. The real problem was that most of the people who lived in cities didn't particularly want to be there. The city was just a way station en route to some distant dream. When I was a child there were Chicago neighborhoods that were even then on their third or fourth waves of immigration. People moved in, built a community, and then, having attained a degree of middle-class respectability, cleaned out their closets and left. The city was a convenience, like an old car or a starter house, and if everyone bailed when the going got tough, well, what else would you expect?

In those days, from what I could see, only a few people lived in the city because they genuinely wanted to: (1) the rich, who could afford the choicest real estate and insulate themselves from urban inconveniences;[5] (2) the bohemian element, which had been sizable in Chicago at one time, although its numbers had dwindled by the time I began to notice such things, which is to say, the early 1970s; (3) gays, who constituted a highly visible community by the same period; (4) kids just out of college; and (5) Italians. Okay, maybe the Chinese, too, but I spent more time in Italian neighborhoods, several of which had persisted since the late nineteenth century, which for Chicago was unusual. Why Italians lingered while others fled warrants further investigation, but we'll leave that for another book.

There was one additional group that I was only dimly aware of as a child and didn't become fully acquainted with till after college: people who fixed up old houses. As a kid I attached no special significance to this sort of thing. My family fixed up old houses and I thought everyone did. Only gradually did I realize this wasn't so, and that the practice was mainly limited to a few neighborhoods, most prominently Lincoln Park on the north side, much of which consisted of picturesque (or at least potentially picturesque) brick town houses built not long after the fire. Having discovered the phenomenon, I knew at once that I'd

[5]Even the rich couldn't always manage it. In Chicago after the fire, the wealthiest section of town was Prairie Avenue, a street of mansions south of the Loop. But the soot, noise, and congestion due to rail lines in the vicinity soon made living conditions intolerable. In 1882, Bertha Palmer, the wife of a wealthy hotelman and the queen of the local social scene, moved her family to a mansion on the north lakefront, then mostly undeveloped. Chicago's other moguls soon followed, and by the turn of the century Prairie Avenue had emptied out. Many mansions were torn down or fell into disrepair and the district became mostly industrial. Mrs. Palmer didn't have to move twice, however. Her north lakefront neighborhood, which became known locally as the Gold Coast, remained one of the wealthiest urbanized areas in the United States more than a century later. I cite this last point because it's fashionable in some quarters to portray the rich as predators who take over a neighborhood for a time, then abandon it for the next urban bauble. On the contrary, observation suggests that, whatever predatory qualities the rich may have, once they settle into a place, they stay quite a while.

found my life's work, or anyway an important part of it, and that someday I'd find such a neighborhood and fix up an old house myself.

I should acknowledge here that considerable controversy has attended the process of fixing up old city houses, as evidenced by the terms used to describe it. The expression "urban pioneering" first surfaced in the 1950s, enjoyed a vogue in the 1960s, and turned up in magazine articles well into the 1970s. The term suggested plucky frontiersmen establishing civilization in the wilderness and was objected to for that reason, inasmuch as it cast the previous residents in the role of the savages.[6] By the 1980s the expression had largely been supplanted by "gentrification," with its odor of class struggle. The word had been coined in 1964 by the British sociologist Ruth Glass to describe the influx of professionals into the working-class districts of London. Glass saw this primarily as a matter of the moneyed set displacing the proletariat, a phenomenon of which she did not approve. Her attitude has largely carried the day in academia. You'll spend a long afternoon at the library before you find a sociologist with a positive word to say about gentrification.[7]

Criticisms of gentrification often ran to extremes, but there was an element of truth to them. While it would be an exaggeration to describe gentrifiers as callous exploiters, they tended to be a bit, shall we say, self-indulgent. When I leafed through old-house magazines in the years before we bought the Barn House, I was struck by how often those who restored antique homes seemed to be childless (at least children didn't figure in the accounts) and had jobs that gave them the time and discretionary income to pursue what was essentially a hobby. I read about peo-

[6]I recognize that Native Americans weren't crazy about having been cast as savages either.

[7]That there's a smallish (if vocal) pro-gentrification camp in the academy I freely allow, but we'll return to such matters later.

ple who planed their own wood, rebuilt houses using antique nails, replicated high Victorian parlors with ornate wallpaper and tasseled curtain tiebacks.

That wasn't for me. At an early stage I'd formed a different idea. I wanted to fix up an old house, sure. But my real ambition was more modest, or so I thought: I wanted to live an ordinary middle-class life in the city.

At the time we bought the Barn House it was an open question whether such a life was going to be possible. Again, don't get me wrong. It's not that the city was on the verge of collapse; as I say, some parts of it had unquestionably turned around. In the course of preparing a magazine story I'd obtained a computer disk from a local planning agency with the fine-detail returns from the 1990 census, known as census tract data. Then I persuaded a fellow with a computer mapmaking business—I tell you, I went to town on this piece—to use the data to generate a color-coded map of Chicago showing the up-and-coming areas of the city, as indicated by rapidly rising property values. By far the largest district was a roughly rectangular area comprising the Loop and environs plus the north-side lakefront. In all it took in about twenty square miles, a not inconsiderable portion of the city, and one that closely corresponded with my windshield impression of the improving parts of town.

I didn't need computer maps to tell me that the city was considerably livelier than it had been when I was a child. I lived in several gentrified communities in Chicago before I got married; one of them was a district on the north lakefront then called New Town. It was a bustling, noisy neighborhood, popular with gays and kids who had just gotten their first jobs in the big city. The streets were crowded with yuppies in running shoes, hookers, men in leather vests and nipple rings, and little old ladies pushing wire shopping carts.

Nonetheless, it seemed to me that something was missing. One day in the mid-1980s I interviewed the proprietor of a local independent supermarket and his wife. He was a pillar of the business community and spoke with satisfaction of improvements in the neighborhood. At the end of the interview I asked him about something that had been on my mind—whether he could see raising a family there. He looked thoughtful for a moment. "Not really," he said finally, then turned to his wife, a woman of considerable chic, if I may say so. Her answer was brisk: "No."

You see where I'm headed with this. By the early 1990s fixing up an old house wasn't unusual. Fixing up an old house in the city wasn't exactly unheard of either, although it put you in more rarefied company. Fixing up an old house in the city with an eye to raising a family there, however—I don't claim nobody did it, but you were definitely out on the fringe.

Mary and I wondered what we were getting ourselves into. Life in the city was all very well when you were young and single with nothing at risk but your own hide and a security deposit. Putting your family and a considerable fraction of your lifetime income on the line was a different matter. We had no illusions about making a fat, or for that matter any, profit on the Barn House, but we weren't so wealthy that we could afford to squander our money. Schools, crime, recreational opportunities for the kids— we had only the vaguest idea about such things. Our own urban childhoods offered no guide. The city had changed enormously during our lifetimes. When I was growing up, an elaborate social infrastructure built around Catholic parishes had greatly simplified the job of raising a family; how much of this remained we didn't know, but we suspected much of it was gone. Who knew what burdens we were foolishly about to assume?

If we were on the cutting edge of anything, we had no sense of it. On the contrary, I was struck by how little interest there seemed to be in ordinary urban life, as distinct from the bright-lights-big-city version, even among those who might be expected to harbor some fondness for the less traveled road. As a writer interested in seeing what other writers had to say, during the time we worked on the Barn House I read or at least browsed through a dozen book-length narratives about building or renovating some habitable place—the sort of topic that naturally inclines the literary imagination to ponder the makings of the good life and the putting down of roots. All the books were written by American authors over the past twenty-five years. Not one was about a house in the city.[8] Curiously, most of the books weren't about houses in the suburbs, either. Typically the house was in a small town—preferably a small college town, with a good library, a coffee shop, and witty neighbors—or else out in the country. In that respect the books largely coincided with the view of most Americans, who according to surveys preferred rural or small-town life, or at least thought they would. Few fantasized about the city, whether writers or not.

As for TV, that mirror of the times—well, if you were a city guy whose lifestyle coincided in some way with that depicted on *Seinfeld*, in its fourth season when we bought the Barn House, or *Cheers*, then in its last, TV had you pretty well covered. In the matter of fixing up old city houses, however, different story. I won't say home improvement shows never featured houses in the city; more commonly, though, and you'll forgive me if I generalize here, they featured residences in suburbs or small towns, with city houses dragged in whenever the producers felt the need for something exotic and couldn't come up with a house built of termite droppings. *This Old House*, if memory serves, once featured a house in London that required a system of pumps and reservoirs to compensate for the nonexistent street pressure—apparently the municipal water supply consisted of hollowed-out Elizabethan

[8]The closest I've found is *This Damn House!* by Margo Kaufman (1996), which describes a home with apartment buildings on either side of it and street people napping on the lawn, which makes it pretty urban in my book; but the locale is Venice, California, a beach town about twenty-five miles from downtown Los Angeles.

logs. Interesting, sure, but the unspoken and perhaps inadvertent message was that the city was not a place where ordinary folk lived. In 1990, Bob Vila had spent a season of his *Home Again* program renovating a two-flat in the Wicker Park neighborhood of Chicago, presumably because his sponsor at the time was Chicago-based Sears; the opening show had him driving around the neighborhood with a local real estate agent, who pointed out various properties that had sold for what were then substantial sums. Peering through the windshield at the unprepossessing street scene, Bob struggled to remain noncommittal, but his expression plainly said: *You've got to be kidding.*

To a large extent it was a matter of appearances. Assuming you weren't after the urban noir look, cities, or at any rate Chicago, weren't very telegenic. Suppose we wanted to video the drive to the Barn House. Things would begin well enough. We would cruise up Lake Shore Drive, which wound through a park with Lake Michigan on one side and a wall of high-rise apartment buildings on the other—as gorgeous an urban panorama as one could hope to find. The impression of elegance would persist for several blocks once we got off at the Barn House exit and headed inland past more high-rises and patrician old apartment buildings. Then we would reach a commercial street called Broadway.[9]

---

[9]Broadway, as one might suppose, is one of numerous city streets throughout the United States named after the famous thoroughfare in Manhattan. Originally it had been called Evanston Avenue, after the Chicago suburb toward which the street leads. Evanston was named for John Evans (1814–1897), a doctor who helped establish the first insane asylum and school for the deaf in Indiana; Mercy Hospital in Chicago; the Illinois Medical Society; the Illinois Republican party; and Northwestern University. Having been appointed the second territorial governor of Colorado, Evans was instrumental in the development of that state and helped found what is now the University of Denver. A fellow like that is worth naming things after. One concedes that Evans was instructed to resign as governor of Colorado after a massacre of Native Americans on his watch. However, that wasn't why Evanston Avenue was changed to Broadway. In 1913, in one of those spasms of Second Cityism that peri-

Here urban fantasy gave way to urban reality. A partial list of sights en route to the Barn House at the time we bought it included:

▪ A restaurant whose sign proclaimed ARNOLD'S FOOD. Arnold typified the let's-call-a-spade-a-spade approach to Chicago restaurant management, which held that you ought to strive for unambiguity in your communications, lest the public be confused. Elsewhere in the city, it must be said, restaurateurs in the Arnoldian mold were giving way to your more typical yuppie froufrou types, who gave their establishments exotic names in romance languages that one suspected meant "toilet fixture" when translated back into English,[10] and who were already making appearances in Arnold's backyard (see the seventh bullet point below). But for the most part shopkeepers on the road to the Barn House still clung to the old ways.

▪ A sign advertising ESP PSYCHIC ASTROLOGY—ESPIRITISTA Y CURANDERA—TAROT CARD READING. One-stop shopping for all your supernatural needs.

▪ A currency exchange[11] with a bus stop in front patronized by unsteady middle-aged women who, if you intruded a millimeter or two too far into their personal space while making a left turn, would shout obscenities and give you the finger.

---

odically grips Chicago, a north-side business association succeeded in getting the name changed during a reorganization of city street nomenclature, apparently with the aim of lending the avenue an aura of glamour and excitement. I won't say this hope was entirely ill-founded, but results were a long time coming.

[10]I'm thinking of "trattoria." You have to admit it makes sense.

[11]A currency exchange in Chicago is a street-corner establishment that cashes checks and provides other routine financial services. Such businesses are apparently unique to Chicago and stem from the days when Illinois law prohibited branch banking.

■ A gas station seemingly much too large for the available business, which I visited only once in those years, on which occasion the other persons on the premises consisted of one other customer, the night manager, a hooker, and a male screamer.

■ A defunct Thai restaurant, the right side of which appeared to have been sat down on and squashed.

■ A local institution known as Byron's Hot Dogs, consisting of a tiny one-story building surrounded by a parking lot. Byron's was one of hot dogdom's holy places, an establishment where a hot dog with everything meant everything but ketchup, ketchup being to a hot dog what black velvet was to art.

■ An upscale Italian restaurant with a sidewalk café and a name in a romance language.[12]

■ A hospital whose administrators, like hospital administrators everywhere, felt the best way to improve the neighborhood was to tear down all the buildings in it and put up parking lots.

■ A residential loft over a vacant storefront, which for years appeared to be undergoing an extremely deliberate process of construction. Apparently at some point the owner tired of the project and decided it was done, because flowerpots and other signs of domesticity appeared; but even now, unless what is being conveyed is some outré design statement, the building seems to be missing a few bricks.

■ A Mexican meat market.

■ An L line.

■ Two cemeteries that stretched along either side of the street for close to half a mile. The land rose slightly through this stretch, and what with the trees, timeworn monuments, and

---

[12]The restaurant did, in fact, call itself a trattoria.

rolling terrain made for a charming scene, at least on the left, where a rusty chain-link fence enabled you to actually see some of it. Unfortunately, on the right, the view was blocked by a high barbed-wire-topped brick barrier having the charm of the Berlin Wall. Too bad. The wall concealed Graceland Cemetery, the final resting place of numerous local luminaries, among them Ludwig Mies van der Rohe and George Pullman, the founder of the Pullman sleeping car company, a man so loathed by his employees that tons of concrete and steel rail were laid atop his coffin lest the working class sneak in and desecrate his grave.

▪ A Burger King.

▪ A Filipino-American community center.

▪ A small strip mall with a self-service laundry, pizzeria, and so on. Actually, I don't think the pizzeria was there when we bought the Barn House, but at the time I wasn't taking copious notes.

▪ An apartment building with what appeared to be an astronomical observatory on the roof—that is, a round structure topped by a hemispherical copper dome (empty, I later learned).

▪ A post office in a style I thought of as Depression moderne, notable chiefly for having a large mural of the social realist school painted over the service windows depicting the march of progress in Chicago, as evidenced by steel mills, railroads, stockyards, and noble workers, which I particularly admired because even the intellectual scientist-type guy, with whom I naturally identified (in fact, it's a self-portrait of the artist, Henry Sternberg), was portrayed as having massive sinewy arms.

▪ A bar whose logo was a black cat, which I had been told was patronized by Hispanic transvestites. When I first heard this I misunderstood and thought the club was patronized by Hispanic trans*sexuals*, leading me to think: *Boy, I bet they haven't got a joint like* that *in Cedar Rapids.* Eventually I got straightened out on this detail, and have since ascertained that the club saw its share of "queens, butches, nerds, bears, flames, [and] closet cases,"[13] lest I give the impression that the client base was excessively narrow.

▪ A leftist bookstore.

▪ A storefront church.

▪ A Mexican fast-food restaurant named El Grande Burrito with worn linoleum and leaky steam radiators.

▪ A muffler shop that usually had a couple dozen vehicles parked in front of it in various stages of disassembly.

▪ A tavern called the Blue Bird Lounge that sold beer by the quart.

▪ A public high school having the appearance of a Norman castle that was notable for: (a) having been featured in the movie *My Bodyguard* (1980), about a kid who needs protection to keep from getting beat up, for which purpose the school seemed an apt choice; and (b) being the alma mater of the ventriloquist and comedian Edgar Bergen, the creator of Charlie McCarthy and cocreator of actress Candice Bergen.[14]

▪ The diner where we had huddled with Howard, owned as it happened by the same fellow who ran Arnold's, which offered

---

[13] I found this out on the Internet. You can find out anything on the Internet.

[14] I mention this in recognition of the fact that Edgar Bergen's heyday is long past. Fame in the United States being a fleeting thing, it's perhaps also advisable to state that Candace Bergen's most recent claim thereto was having starred in the title role of the TV sitcom *Murphy Brown* from 1988 to 1998.

a breakfast of scrambled eggs, hash browns, sausage, toast, and coffee for three dollars and change, and in my observation never closed except for the time the city shut it down for a week for paying off on the electronic poker machine.

▪ A dilapidated wooden church.

▪ A submarine sandwich shop run by a succession of immigrants, including one from Jordan, with whom I once got into a discussion of Queen Noor.

▪ A restaurant in the old-Chicago mold whose logo was a bee, which was decorated with tiny Christmas lights and NFL paraphernalia, served pretty fair ribs, and didn't have smoking and nonsmoking sections so much as smoky and really smoky.

▪ A self-storage warehouse that had once been the factory that produced the iconic 1960s appliance properly known as the Lava Lite.

▪ Another L line. From this point on things get a little repetitive, so we'll bring the tour to a close.

You're thinking: *Arnold's Food. A psychic astrologer. A transvestite bar. I could make a miniseries out of material like that.* No doubt. My point is that taken in the aggregate it didn't amount to much. The street had an unfinished quality, as did the city as a whole—you felt it had started on the long road to urbanity but never quite arrived. Getting it the rest of the way was what city folk hoped to accomplish. But how soon they might do so no one then could say.

One summer evening after a day's work at the Barn House I returned home to find the family in a tumult, with the kids crying and Mary grim. Shortly before my arrival Ryan and Ani had been jumping on the bed; Ryan had fallen and hit his teeth on the bedpost. Now his two upper middle incisors protruded at a gruesome angle. Mary drove to the hospital while I sat in the backseat with my arms around the small boy in my lap. Except for the occasional whimper he was quiet, which wasn't reassuring. Ryan had the characteristic, common among males in my family, of complaining in inverse proportion to the severity of his problems, the extreme example in this regard being his great-grandfather, who'd walked into the hospital with advanced pancreatic cancer, of which he'd given no sign, and died five days later. Admittedly that wasn't a likely outcome of the present crisis; disfigurement, on the other hand . . . eh, better to dwell on the positive. My brave little guy.

At the hospital the X-ray technician asked Mary if she were pregnant. "I don't know," she said. "I might be." Not wishing to chance it, I held Ryan while the technician made the exposures. When the prints were ready the doctor pointed out the adult teeth already growing in Ryan's upper jaw. They were intact. Although Ryan would have to endure a prolonged period of toothlessness, eventually the adult teeth would replace the damaged ones, which the doctor had now removed.

We were immensely relieved, but another issue had presented itself: Mary was in fact pregnant, as we confirmed not long after. In itself this was no surprise. We'd bought the Barn House in anticipation of a third child and promptly set about producing one, recognizing that home renovation and gestation were lengthy processes we didn't have time to pursue sequentially and so would have to endure together. We weren't unmindful of the fact that if a domestic emergency arose I'd likely be elsewhere, but Ryan's encounter with the bedpost had made the practical implications more apparent—and Mary would bear all the burden. What's more, we now had a deadline. Assuming we didn't want the simultaneous stress of fixing up a house and tending a newborn, we needed to be done by April of the following year, 1994.

7

By late summer the architectural drawings for the Barn House were approaching completion and some seventy cubic yards of former interior finishing reposed in a landfill, but we were still nowhere near the commencement of construction. I was growing impatient. Part of the problem was the unorthodox nature of the project. In addition to the general contractor, who would handle most of the heavy construction, I had to hire subcontractors for everything else, mainly the mechanical systems. In August I went to Charlie's office to use a drafting table to prepare drawings of the air-conditioning ducts. I did this out of exasperation with the HVAC guys, HVAC standing for heating, ventilating, and air-conditioning.

I never did figure out what the problem was with HVAC guys. Perhaps it was excessive exposure to chlorofluorocarbons. Collectively they were the most argumentative bunch of people I'd ever met. I had three prospective HVAC contractors plus George, my father's sheet-metal worker buddy, come in to look over my project; each one told me to do the opposite of what the previous fellow had said. One advocated having the registers high and the returns low (conditioned air comes out of the registers; stale air returns, as one might suppose, via the returns); the next said to have the returns high and the registers low. One wanted to have the registers diagonally opposite from the returns; another wanted to have them all on the same side of the room. Normally one gets a bead on the right way by interviewing knowledgeable parties and arriving at a consensus, but here that strategy had gone inexplicably awry. The experience was disconcerting. It was like asking directions to the interstate and having one person gesture across the street, a second over yonder, and a third at the North Star.[1]

The one point on which all the contractors agreed was that I was out of my mind. Maybe I was, but I was the owner of the house and it was my money. I figured the least they could do was humor me. We had a number of conversations along the following lines:

CONTRACTOR: You want to have separate systems for heating and air-conditioning?

ME: Yeah.

CONTRACTOR: Nobody does that. They run heating and air-conditioning in the same ducts.

ME: I know. I don't want to do that. I want to use radiators, with ducts for the air-conditioning.

CONTRACTOR: It'll be expensive.

---

[1] I hadn't then been introduced to the mystical HVAC concept known as "flow," the practical import of which is that it doesn't matter where the registers and returns are located, as long as flow—that is, air movement—is thereby obtained.

ME: How expensive?

CONTRACTOR: Real expensive.

ME: Give me a ballpark idea.

CONTRACTOR: How much do you want to spend?

ME: How much do I *need* to spend?

CONTRACTOR: A lot.

CONTRACTOR'S ASSISTANT: Why would you want to use radiators instead of forced air?

CONTRACTOR: Oh, it's the best heat.

ME: Exactly. It's the best heat. That's why I want to do it. I'm trying to get a *price*.

CONTRACTOR (gesturing skyward, as if pulling a number out of the air): $25,000.

Thus my dour mood. It was wearing to be constantly thought of as a lunatic, and now I could see it was going to be expensive, too. I had hauled up on an inescapable fact of life: For any object having to do with human shelter, be it repainting the birdbath or heating the house, the building trades offered a certain path—to be fair, in late-twentieth-century America, a pretty wide path—and as long as you kept within it you had only to pick up the phone, collect estimates, hire a vendor, look in on the workers periodically, and in the end write a check. Despite all the kvetching you heard, and I say this sincerely, the fundamental competence of the American home-building industry with respect to any well-defined task in what was after all a complex and perilous business—consider the fell consequences if the plumber overlooks a gas leak—was one of the wonders of the world.

Strike out into the bush, however—try to get your project

done in a way that tradesmen weren't accustomed to doing—and God help you, you were on your own. It's not that you couldn't find anyone willing to take on the job; I'd found Eddie, after all, who after an hour's inspection had a far more detailed idea of what needed to be done to my house than I did. But he was an exception. Most contractors lacked his grasp, and if you didn't feel like paying extravagant sums, I'd come to realize, you needed to break the assignment down into what from their perspective would seem manageable tasks.

I made two decisions. First, I would repipe the radiators myself. I'd never done this before and had no idea what was involved, but how hard could it be? Second, I'd prepare my own engineering drawings for the air-conditioning ducts. The attic framing was complicated; routing the ducts would require somebody to, you know, think, and in the course thereof one might make a mistake and underbid a job that required an expensive solution. If I could eliminate some of the uncertainty, my theory was, perhaps I would get a more reasonable bid. I did, although in retrospect it must be said that HVAC was one of those businesses exhibiting the Law of Conservation of Price—namely, all bids for a job are the same, the only difference being how much comes out of your pocket and how much comes out of your hide.

At any rate, it was pleasant that August day to stand languidly in the drafting room of Charlie's high-ceilinged office and look down on the great avenue and feel a kinship with Dankmar Adler and Louis Sullivan, two of the most eminent names in Chicago architecture, who had done the same thing in an office in the building next door about a hundred years before. Then I told myself it was time to quit daydreaming and buckle down to work. I started with what was known as a sepia print, a reproduction of Charlie's original floor plan having, as the name suggests, a brownish cast to it. Using ink eradicator I obliterated unnecessary details—they vanished at a stroke—and drew in the lines indicating the ducts, registers, and returns. Adler and Sullivan, and pretty much every other architect in America, had done their drawings in much the same way for the previous 115 years, since the introduction of blueprinting to the United States from the UK, where it had been invented. The whole enterprise, what with the rolls of brown-toned drawings, the simple tools—you kept your compass point sharp using a pad of sandpaper—and for that matter the antique airy room, in the middle of which was a narrow spiral staircase leading up to a gallery crammed with books and ledgers, had a distinctly nineteenth-century feel to it.

Well it might. Although I didn't know it at the time, I was working in the twilight of an era then passing into history: the time when architects designed with pencil and paper. The Barn House was the last project in which Charlie was able to display his fluid hand in routine drafting. Shortly after he finished our job, his firm took out most of the drawing tables and installed computers, and he worked almost exclusively with mouse and keyboard from then on. He still did (and does) renderings for presentation purposes by hand, but nobody after that got an ordinary blueprint from Charlie that he wanted to take home and frame.

Whatever might be said for my drawings from an artistic standpoint, which wasn't much, making them was a useful process—it obliged me to think the project through. I saw now why the HVAC guys had been reluctant to bid realistically for the job. On the third floor, for example, I'd blithely proposed running ducts through a labyrinth of existing wooden framing behind one of the chimneys. On applying the higher cortical faculties to the problem I realized it couldn't be done. I decided I'd have to drop the ceiling in the front bedroom and run the ducts through the space thus created, which would simplify the routing to a considerable extent, and while I wouldn't say the result was elegant, at least the thing was physically possible.

When I'd finished my drawings, Charlie sent them out to the repro house; the copies were delivered to my home a day or two later. I mailed sets to several potential bidders, including a young journeyman named Pete, who'd been recommended by George. We had a somewhat tense negotiation—I had a price in mind, and was determined to get it—but eventually we came to an agreement: $9,000 to install all the ductwork, coolant lines, and control wiring; hook up the air handlers and condensers; and get the whole thing to work. That took care of the VAC. For the H, I was on my own.

Meanwhile I was still in the process of hiring a general contractor. I wanted Eddie if I could afford him, but prudence suggested learning how his prices compared. I'd spoken to two other contractors besides Eddie—we'll call them Matt and József. In July I'd sent all three the scope of work, a bid sheet, and a set of preliminary plans. One by one they'd shown up to walk through the house and take notes.

One morning I was carting debris out of the house into the Dumpster. Matt was sitting on the front steps jotting notes on a pad. He was a young fellow, wearing shorts and looking jaunty. "So," I said, "what are you going to charge me? Three hundred thousand dollars?"

Facetiousness with contractors is always a risky business. "Probably more than that," said Matt, continuing to write.

"Right."

Matt looked up. "I'm serious," he said.

The day seemed suddenly cooler. The limit of what we could afford was $250,000.

I spent several nervous days awaiting the arrival of the bids. Once they were in hand I spread them on the desk and compared the bottom lines:

JÓZSEF $219,000

EDDIE $235,000

MATT $317,000

Well now. A spread of nearly $100,000 on a $250,000 job represented a significant difference of opinion. However, closer examination partly allayed my concern. I suspected I was merely seeing the ignorance surcharge—the padding a contractor added to his bid as insurance against what he didn't know.

The usefulness of an uncertain grasp of the facts is often underappreciated in commercial dealings. Ideally you wanted to discover which of the parties chasing your business knew more, but sometimes it was enough to find out which of them knew less. The three bids were instructive in this regard. Two were fairly close while one was an outlier. Either Matt knew something the others didn't or he didn't know something they did. The early returns favored the latter, but one wanted to be sure. I got Matt on the phone. Among other things he had priced exterior demolition at close to $15,000, compared with $6,000 for József and a little over $4,000 for Eddie. When I asked about this, he said he felt it would take four men two weeks to finish removing the cedar shakes. Two of my brothers had ripped off a sizable portion of the siding in an afternoon. No way would four guys need two weeks to dispose of the rest.

Then there was the quality of Matt's work, as evidenced by his previous jobs, which I'd gone round to visit. It was competent by the standards of the day but to my eye betrayed only an intermittent acquaintance with the right way. One project had involved adding a bathroom. To avoid having to rejoist the floors to accommodate the drain pipes, Matt had placed the pipes on top of the existing floor, then put a false floor on top of that. To get into the bathroom you had to step up six inches—an inexpensive but clumsy solution. Charlie's architectural drawings would prevent the worst such improvisations, but no drawing could anticipate every design decision that might arise, and I didn't want to have to watch the carpenters' every move.

Matt having been eliminated from consideration, I turned to József. Like Eddie, he was what the architects had termed an ethnic contractor. Unlike Eddie, he'd been incurious about many aspects of the job, and in general hadn't been very communicative. It was hard to imagine working with him. I'd seen a few of his jobs; the work was tolerably done, but there were small things that bugged me—gaps between trim boards and so on. I'd have to keep a close eye on József's workers, too.

Eddie's bid was higher than József's, but not unreasonably so. The quality of Eddie's work, from what I had seen of it, was impeccable. For $16,000, the difference between his bid and József's, I'd get a guy who would do the job right—in my opinion money well spent.

Just a couple problems. The first was that the bottom line wasn't really the bottom line. I'd structured the bid to make rehabilitation of the house's siding optional. It was optional in the sense that there were two ways to handle the work—repair or replace—and I'd asked for bids on each. It wasn't optional in the sense that I could omit the work altogether. After some consultation with Eddie, we decided we could wash and paint a third of the siding, salvage another third from the doomed addition and reuse it elsewhere, and replace the last third. That would cost $30,000. So the true cost of the job wasn't $235,000, but $265,000.

At this point the disadvantage of doing things the right way became apparent—it was usually more expensive. For example, I'd asked Eddie to bid on modular replacement windows designed to fit into the existing frames. Trouble was, as Eddie pointed out, the existing frames had the structural integrity of wet cardboard. Much of the wood was rotted and out of true; to install new sashes in such junk was foolish. It was better to replace everything, including the frames. Hard to argue with, but it would cost another thirteen grand.

Then there were the gutters. I'd requested bids on galvanized steel, but Eddie urged copper instead. Copper was attractive and durable and required minimal maintenance; if not abused it would last the life of the house. It cost more, though. After some discussion we decided to use copper at the rear of the house—a quirky choice, I suppose, but it made sense to me. The roof of the rear addition was flat and would be sealed with a rubber membrane poured in place. The gutter supports would be embedded in the rubber; to replace the gutters you'd have to replace the roof. Galvanized gutters eventually would rust, and while they might outlast the roof, they might not—and I didn't want to have to replace the roof just because I'd cheaped out on the gutters. Thus copper. Add $1,200.

So it went. A little more for concrete work. A lot more for carpentry—a new iteration of the drawings indicated much more framing than originally envisioned. A little more for roofing; I can't remember why. Eddie shaved his contractor's markup. It helped a little, but not enough. By the time we were done, the price of the job had ballooned to more than $284,000.

The obvious and for practical purposes only solution was for me to do a lot of the work myself. I'd always planned on doing some work, because I enjoyed it; now I'd do so because I had to. The electrical and heating systems—they were my problem now. Other work I decided to subcontract myself, to save the contractor's markup—plumbing, air-conditioning. Some work we omitted altogether. Woodwork refinishing, for example—some other time.

We got the price down to $213,000—not an extravagant sum, given the breadth of the work required, but it was a little deceptive. To cite one obvious difficulty, while I was a fair electrician, I didn't know jack about heating. Worse—this was the part I hadn't explained in detail to the bank—even after all the money in the budget was spent, the house still wouldn't be done. Woodwork refinishing was a case in point. An unwary loan officer might consider this task a dispensable luxury—who cares if the woodwork was a little scuffed up? But the truth was, the old woodwork we'd piled in the basement was more than scuffed up; it was probably wrecked—in the fever of demolition the boys had shown a little too much zeal. While I hadn't ruled out the possibility of reusing some of what we'd salvaged, chances were we'd need to install new. Remilling woodwork to match the opulent original would be an expensive project—more than 5,000 feet of oak and poplar stock worked into four different shapes using custom-made knives. We could use cheap stock moldings, of course (though I cringed at the thought), but even that would cost thousands of dollars I didn't have and had no immediate prospect of getting. Some work had never been on the bid sheet—painting and decorating, chimney relining. Rebuilding the fireplaces. Repairing the dining room floor. Finishing the third floor, where my office was to go. All required. All unbudgeted.

But it was too late now. Interior demolition was now well advanced. Decrepit as the house had been when we bought it, it was now completely uninhabitable. The project was fairly launched; we wouldn't come up for air for another three years.

8

I was by now fairly desperate to get the work under way, but one obstacle remained. We still faced the delicate matter of getting a building permit.

Some controversy attends the question of when a building permit is required. To hear some tell it, you're supposed to get a permit every time you change a lightbulb. That wasn't the attitude in Chicago, where the common view was that you should never get a permit if you could possibly avoid it. I'd known people who had built major additions entirely on the sly. Partly that simply reflected the instinctive distrust of authority in a working-man's town—obtaining a permit wasn't going to materially advance your project; it merely gave someone the opportunity to tell you to stop, or that you were doing it all wrong. Chicago being Chicago, it also gave someone an opportunity to put his hand in your pocket.

There was also the matter of the building code. Chicago—I imagine this is true of many older large cities—didn't use the uniform national building code that smaller municipalities typi-cally adopt. Rather, it enforced a code of its own devising, the peculiarities of which were legend. For example, for years the city had demanded that the water supply in every building be con-nected to the feed from the street main using something known as a wiped lead joint. It's unnecessary to explain what such a joint was other than to say it required copious amounts of the heavy metal lead. Lead in drinking water causes mental retardation. Many who've had dealings in Chicago will find a lot explained right there. Eventually the lead-joint requirement had been re-scinded, but a great many other oddities remained, with some new ones added.

There was the matter of purple primer, for instance. The city had decided to permit the use of drainpipe made of polyvinyl-chloride, commonly known as PVC. The joints in PVC pipes were secured with glue. Before daubing on the glue it was neces-sary to apply primer, which cleaned and softened the parts to be joined. So far so good. The twist in Chicago was that the primer had to have purple dye in it.[1] This enabled building inspectors to determine that you had in fact used primer, as opposed to spit or taco sauce or (I suppose this was the real fear) nothing, thereby producing a substandard joint and subjecting posterity to the em-barrassing possibility that the waste line on the upstairs toilet would give out immediately following the arrival of someone's prom date. I appreciated the thought, but there were manifestly so many thousands of other things that a creative plumber could screw up that I wondered why anyone would single out primer. One far greater risk, for example, was that the plumber would saw through all the floor joists to accommodate horizontal pipe runs, something that happened constantly and which in terms of po-tential seriousness was comparable to removing the home owner's

[1] I don't mean to suggest, incidentally, that purple primer is unique to Chi-cago, but it's far from universally required.

spinal column. I speak from experience; someone had done it in my house, causing Bob the engineer to come as close as I ever saw him to betraying agitation.[2]

The code had a great many other problematic clauses, of which I can give only a sample. All house-current wiring had to be placed in ductile metal conduit. I'd spent thirty years learning to bend pipe and had no personal objection to it—on the contrary, I thought it was a worthwhile investment. There had been multiple safety-related changes in wire manufacture in my lifetime— cloth-and-rubber insulation had given way to the more durable plastic TW; TW to the more heat-resistant THHN or THWN; copper wire to aluminum and back to copper when aluminum proved more prone to fires. In a house without conduit you had to chop holes in the walls to replace the wiring, or more likely just live with the danger; with conduit you merely pulled the old wire out of the conduit and ran new. All that having been said, virtually every other habitable place on earth permitted armored or plastic-sheathed cable in residential service, which was much cheaper to install.

The drain line for a dishwasher had to have a one-inch "air gap," to preclude what in my opinion was a somewhat unlikely scenario involving the siphoning of contaminated water. The dishwasher also had to have a cutoff switch located nearby, in case the home owner wished to repair the wiring but couldn't find the fuse box.

Oh, and grease traps. Grease traps in most of the world had gone out with chrome dinette sets, but the code in Chicago still required them, even though if used with a garbage disposal they'd rapidly fill with odious slop. Professional home builders in Chicago had adopted the tactic of installing a grease trap until the plumbing inspector had signed off on the job, whereupon the

[2]His actual words, and I'm quoting as closely as I can remember, were, "Oh, my. We'll have to do something about *that*."

trap was removed and saved until needed again. I got the impression from plumbers that there were only a couple dozen extant grease traps in Chicago, which had been making the rounds from job site to job site since 1958.

In light of all this, obtaining a building permit struck some as foolish. But I intended to get one anyway, for two reasons, one obvious and the other possibly not. The obvious reason was that we had a Dumpster in the driveway and were about to tear off the front porch, the back of the house, the siding, and a good portion of the roof. For a period of several months the building would have gaping holes in it covered with big blue tarps. If an inspector happened by, we were hardly in a position to claim we were just cleaning out the basement. The less obvious reason was that building permits were a bulwark of civilization, and however stupid or seemingly pointless the process, to get one was to step back from the abyss.

You may think I exaggerate, and of course I do, but less than might be supposed. Here's an episode that illustrates the matter in all its complexity. A few minutes after midnight on June 30, 2003, a tier of wooden porches at the rear of a renovated three-flat in the Lincoln Park neighborhood of Chicago collapsed without warning, the floors pancaking on top of one another as the floors of the World Trade Center had done on September 11. Thirteen people were killed, all twentysomething professionals with (till then) bright prospects. Another fifty-four were injured.

In the ensuing media coverage, the following emerged:

1. At least 114 people had been standing on the porches or associated stairs at the time of the collapse, all attendees at a party that was just then breaking up.

2. In hindsight this was really, really stupid.

3. Chicago was one of the few if not only cities in the country in which it had become routine practice in certain neighbor-

hoods to build oversized wooden porches or decks behind walk-up apartment buildings for the purpose of having blow-out parties.

4. Prior to the fatal accident, overloaded porches had been collapsing in Chicago for years, although usually without serious injury to the occupants.

5. Notwithstanding (3) and (4), no public or private regulations governed the number of people permissible on a Chicago porch.

6. The aforementioned parties often involved charcoal or gas grills; the porches on which the grills stood were almost invariably made of wood; wood was combustible. Furthermore, the original purpose of back porches was to provide not a venue for socializing but rather emergency egress, which, as one chagrined young partygoer pointed out, put Chicago in the possibly unique position of permitting wooden fire escapes.

7. In view of (1) through (6) above, Chicago had barely scraped the surface of potential porch catastrophes.

8. The individual who had renovated the building and constructed the porches a few years previously had obtained a building permit, but hadn't indicated new porches on the plans submitted for approval. Getting a building permit for a non-controversial subset of the work actually contemplated was a time-honored dodge in Chicago, the idea being to obtain a building-permit placard to stick in your window while avoiding, or at least delaying, official scrutiny. The persons responsible for the 1930s defacement of the Barn House, for example, had gotten a permit to "move two windows" and then had proceeded to rebuild much of the third floor. True, the premises would eventually be visited by city inspectors, who presumably would notice that the work failed to correspond to the

plans, but the typical Chicago property owner figured he could cross that bridge when he came to it, if you catch my drift.

9. Getting back to our subject, the porch-collapse building had been in fact visited by inspectors, but—I make no accusations—even though the porches were new and unpermitted, said inspectors hadn't brought this to anyone's attention.

10. The porch floor joists were two-by-eights but, according to city officials, were required by code to be two-by-tens.

11. The building code didn't actually *say* two-by-tens, but merely referred to an industry standard set by the American Forest and Paper Association, which city officials contended was a well-known document but which none of the local builders interviewed by reporters admitted to having heard of.

With these facts in mind, few in Chicago would dispute the following: (1) Getting a building permit was an important civic duty; (2) it was still a pain in the butt.

I'd heard the process was arduous. Charlie told me his firm's clients sometimes hired expediters whose job was to stand in line waiting to get the paperwork approved. I didn't intend to go that far; I didn't figure I had to. The people who needed to fear the process, I felt, were either small-time chiselers who were trying to sneak a mother-in-law apartment into the basement, or else Republicans.[3] I, on the other hand, was getting professional advice. I had a formidable collection of drawings, with impressive-looking title blocks and symbols and inscrutable instructions such as 16" ɸ TYP. and SHT MTL CRICKETS AS REQD, and embossed stamps say-

---

[3] It's not just people in Chicago who think this way. Once while walking in the mountains near Tucson, Arizona, I stepped on a rusty nail. The doctor at the emergency room asked if I'd been given a tetanus booster recently. I couldn't remember. Learning that I was from Chicago, the doctor asked, "Are you a Democrat?"

ing STATE OF ILLINOIS * LICENSED ARCHITECT. In addition, I had the perhaps silly idea that getting a permit would be fun. I did my own taxes, too. For excitement I don't claim either ranked with bungee jumping, but they were challenge enough for me.

City Hall in Chicago—properly known as the City-County Building—is a large cubical edifice occupying a full city block in the Loop. It's split down the middle. The eastern half contains the administrative offices for Cook County, of which Chicago constitutes the larger part; the western half houses those for the city. The city half is where most of the excitement is. The ground-floor lobby is a study in marble and terrazzo, impressive in a 1930s B-movie kind of way, full of cops, clerks, and scurrying citizens, with quiet eddies here and there where well-fed parties in expensive suits conferred with leaner individuals—lawyers, likely—regarding matters of dizzy import, such as the Bears game.[4]

One applied for construction permits at the building department, which was on the eighth floor of the city side. One saw fewer people in expensive suits, and more nervous-looking nebbishes such as myself. Inquiring at the counter, I was told to fill out a form stating the particulars of the project. One of the blanks to be filled in was the value of the work. I completed the form and

---

[4]I had lived in Chicago too long to be overawed by City Hall. In the late 1980s the city and the state of Illinois agreed to build a pedestrian tunnel under the sidewalk connecting City Hall to the state office building across the street. The city began digging on its end and the state began digging on the other. When the workers met in the middle they found that the floor heights of the two halves of the tunnel differed by nine inches—not bad if you were boring through Mont Blanc, but this was a tunnel of maybe seventy-five feet. It turned out that the engineers designing the tunnel had consulted old blueprints, which commonly express floor heights in terms of a standard downtown reference point known as the "city datum." At least that's what the drafter of the plans for the state office building had done. The dope who had prepared the plans for City Hall, however, had expressed the floor heights with reference to the bottom of the building. The tunnel workers fudged the difference with a ramp.

handed it to the sad-eyed man behind the counter. He studied the form for a moment. "You sure it's going to cost this much?" he asked.

Clearly I wasn't supposed to be. "More or less," I said.

The sad-eyed man looked at me and sighed. I'd gotten a similar look from an old cabbie when, as an eighteen-year-old summer fill-in driver, I stood at a counter in the cab barn and filled out a federal tax form with the amount of tip money I actually made.

"The form is used by the county when they reassess your property after the work is done," the sad-eyed man said.

"Oh," I said. I took back the form and scratched off a zero.

The next stop was the zoning man, a youngish fellow in a polo shirt. The zoning man glanced through the drawings, then pushed them back. "You need to get a driveway permit," he said.

"No," I said. "It's an *existing* driveway."

"Doesn't matter," he said. "You still need to get a permit." He gestured toward a counter on the far side of the room.

This was unexpected. I could understand permits for new construction, but who ever heard of getting permits for things built twenty years before? The notion seemed to open the door to all manner of bureaucratic meddling: *We're sorry, sir, but we shouldn't have given out that driveway permit to start with. And while you're at it, tear down that eyesore of a house, too.* I also knew from Mike Royko books that the sale of driveway permits had once been a lucrative sideline for unscrupulous Chicago aldermen. While I was reasonably sure those days were gone, I wasn't eager to put the matter to the test. Plus, there were sure to be more delays and fees.

No use complaining, though. I went to the indicated counter and explained my problem to the woman sitting behind it, one of those stout bottle blondes who, in Chicago as in probably every other city, accomplish all the useful work of government. She handed me a form.

"Fill this out and bring in a photo of the driveway," she said.

"A photo?" I said stupidly. I didn't see the point, but at least they weren't asking for an environmental impact study. I rolled up my blueprints and went home to get the camera.

A couple days later I returned with an envelope full of driveway pictures. I handed one to the woman behind the counter. She studied it, then handed it back.

"Your driveway is cracked," she said. "You'll have to get it repoured."

"Repoured?" I looked at the picture. The driveway had some cracks across one corner. The affected area amounted to about a square foot. Repouring seemed absurd. More important, it would take days, maybe weeks depending on whether they expected me to replace a corner or the entire driveway. It was already the end of September. How much longer it would take to get a building permit once I got the driveway permit I didn't know. I was planning major structural work that would leave much of the house open to the elements. If I lost a month we would be working outdoors in the depths of a Chicago winter. I thought of Napoleon on the banks of the Dnieper.

I looked down at the remaining driveway photos and had an idea. Shuffling through the stack, I placed a different one on the counter. "You know," I said, "I've got another photo here."

The picture showed the driveway from a different angle. The cracked corner wasn't visible.

The woman looked at the photo, then at me. All of us encounter these little face-offs with destiny at some point in our lives. In some the fate of nations hangs in the balance. Others are about driveways. "Let me ask the boss," the woman said. She picked up the photo and walked into a nearby office. A few moments later she returned and shoved the photo back across the counter.

"Okay," she said.

"Thank you," I said. One down.

Back to the zoning man. He looked through the drawings for a second time. I hoped he would find nothing to object to, but no. "Can't do this," he said, pointing.

I leaned over. On the drawing for the third floor Charlie had labeled one room OFFICE and another FUTURE BATH.

This problem I understood. Months earlier Charlie had faxed me a page from the city's building code about the "minimum number of exits." It was written in typically opaque building-code style, but after some study I gathered that, if you had a two-story house, the city would let you get by with one set of stairs between floors, but if you had a *three*-story house, you needed two sets of stairs, both serving all three floors. The idea was to provide an alternative fire exit in case the first was blocked.

In the Barn House, the first and second floors were served by two stairways, but the third floor as originally built could be reached by only one. An exterior fire staircase had been added at the rear of the building, presumably when the house was divided into apartments, but the wood was rotting and we were going to demolish it. Charlie had made several stabs at designing a replacement stairway, but none had been satisfactory—too big, too ugly, blocked the windows on the lower floors, and so on. There was no way to fit another interior stairway into the floor plan. In the end we deferred the question. We left a door at the back of the attic, but with no stairs attached; the door opened into the void. (Well, not the void exactly; the doorway deposited you on the roof of the second floor, which jutted out below. But there was no deck or railing.) Charlie had drawn in rooms on the third floor but added notations indicating that the finishing work would be done at some future time.

That wasn't good enough for the zoning guy. He wanted me to scratch out FUTURE BATH and OFFICE and write in STORAGE.

I considered. Though a small thing, this was a more emphatic declaration than I cared to make. Charlie and I had discussed an exterior spiral staircase, which would be less obtrusive than a bulky wooden one. We'd arrived at no decision, but a spiral staircase now seemed like a better solution than going on record as saying the third floor would be devoted to storage forevermore. I asked the zoning guy if I could amend the drawings. *Sure,* he said. I would find a place to do so out in the hall.

I gathered my drawings and went out in the hall. I found several rows of tall tables. Various parties were scattered about with drawings strewn in front of them, furiously scribbling. I found an unoccupied spot and prepared to do the same. I didn't know exactly where the spiral staircase should go, but figured as long as I got it somewhere at the back of the house we could work out the details when the time came. I marked up one set of drawings. The staircase looked as if it had been drawn by an alert preschooler. Well, Charlie could make art out of it later. I marked up the other copies.

Back inside. Next stop was the plumbing man. There was little on the drawings having to do with plumbing, and what there was I had mainly done myself. This consisted of a 3-D schematic of the pipes showing the various risers, drains, and vents, the original for which I had laboriously sketched out in pencil. Charlie had taken my diagram and rendered it into an intricate arrangement of parallel lines punctuated by curlicues and doodads.

The plumbing guy flipped through the drawings and found the diagram. "You forgot to put in the diameter of the pipes," he said.

This was true. Nobody had said anything about pipe diameters.

"You also need a grease trap." Damn, the grease trap. I'd forgotten.

Back to the tables in the hallway. I wrote in some plausible pipe diameters and a little box labeled "grease trap." I copied these notations to the other copies of the drawings. Back inside.

Flip, flip, flip. Pause. The plumbing man reached for a rubber stamp, smacked the drawing with it, wrote in his initials, handed back the drawings. Now we were getting somewhere.

Next the electrical man. I'd done the original diagram for the electrical drawings, too. In contrast to plumbing, however, with the electrical work I knew what I was talking about. The electrical man took the drawings. Flip, flip, flip. Pause. Smack. Scribble. Three down.

Last stop. I approached the architectural examiner and handed over the drawings. Flip, flip, and so on. Another pause. The pause lingered. Trouble.

"There's a problem with these stairs," the examiner said, pointing to the spiral staircase I had drawn.

"What's wrong?" I asked.

"For fire stairs you need a thirty-six-inch-wide tread. You've only got thirty inches here."

Crap. I'd made the spiral staircase five feet in diameter so it would be less conspicuous. I didn't want a piece of apparatus six feet in diameter bolted to the back of my house; the place would look like an oil refinery.

"I don't get it," I said. "You see houses all the time that only have one set of stairs up to the third floor."

"That's an existing condition," said the examiner.

Huh, I thought. An existing condition. That put matters in a new light. Evidently it was illegal to *create* a building code violation, but not illegal merely to have one. Low thoughts crowded my mind. I wanted to be law-abiding, you understand. However, on a short-term basis, I was . . . well, let's say I was willing to walk through the valley of the shadow of death. I gathered my drawings, went out to the tables in the hall, scratched out the spiral staircase, and wrote in STORAGE.

By now it was near the end of the day. The architectural examiner I had talked to initially was no longer on hand. Instead I spoke to a professorial-looking fellow in glasses. He inspected my drawings, then reached for his rubber stamp.

I cleared my throat. "At what point does the city usually come by to inspect?" I asked. The examiner had undoubtedly heard this before, and had seen the scribbles on the drawings. He gave me a stern look. "The inspectors can come by at any time, without notice," he said. He paused, then continued in a milder tone: "But on average they come by sixty days after the permit is pulled."

I thanked him, picked up my drawings, paid the fee to the cashier, and received a cardboard placard reading BUILDING PERMIT in bold type. Nine months after first laying eyes on the Barn House, we were ready to begin the serious work at last.

A couple days later I got a call from Eddie. He was experiencing severe stomach pain. He had been in to see the doctor; he feared the worst. He was sorry, but he had to withdraw from the project. I wasn't to worry, however. He was turning the project over to his cousin Tony, in whom he had great confidence.

It was now early October. Already the days were growing noticeably cooler. The work hadn't yet begun, and my project was in the hands of a man I'd never met.

9

Tony was unlike anyone else I knew in the building trades. The thing was, and I marvel at it to this day, he returned phone calls—and what's more, he returned them promptly. This trait is exceedingly rare among contractors and tradespeople, as anyone who has dealt with them knows, which in turn is exceedingly mystifying, since it seems to defy ordinary expectations of rational behavior. It wasn't like you were trying to collect money from these guys or serve them with a summons. On the contrary, typically you were proposing to pay them—in many cases pay them a lot—to pursue the calling in which they were nominally employed. Yet it might take a week and three or four attempts to get one to call you back. It was the damnedest thing. They couldn't spend *all* their time hunting, or sleeping it off, or whatever it was they did. Even people in the business didn't understand it. "Don't these guys have *families?*" my plumbing contractor, Kevin, once plaintively inquired, speaking of the journeymen he had to coax into accepting a paycheck. Of course, then I spent a week trying to get Kevin to call me back, so he was hardly one to talk.

Tony was different. No doubt I'm being unfair in saying this, but I can't help thinking it was because he wasn't native born, and so was unfamiliar with the way business in America was done. At the time he began work on the Barn House, he'd been in the United States for not quite twenty years, having emigrated from Poland in the early 1970s. By training Tony wasn't a contractor but a civil engineer, one of what, to those left behind, must have seemed like a frightening number of professional people draining out of Poland in those days—our cleaning lady had been an attorney. Leaving Poland wasn't easily accomplished, but Tony contrived to obtain a passport and a tourist visa—how, I didn't inquire. Having arrived in the United States, he got the visa extended. Time passed; Tony didn't return to Poland. Deportation papers arrived. Tony married an American woman of Polish descent—a lovely lady, I hasten to say, to whom he remains married to this day. The point was, he stayed.

Immigrant communities in the United States often specialize in certain trades. In Chicago, Koreans run dry-cleaning shops, Thais and Vietnamese open restaurants, and Mexicans work as landscapers. Poles in Chicago commonly get started cleaning houses and office buildings—Tony in fact had run a cleaning crew for a time. The other trade open to Poles was construction. Why this should be so isn't entirely clear, although the cost of entry is low and Poland's vocational schools are said to turn out excellent tradesmen. Tony had never been to vocational school, but he'd grown tired of emptying wastebaskets and swabbing toilets. He acquired two partners, both Polish immigrants, one a writer and the other a stuntman. (A movie stuntman. I had to ask that this be repeated, too.) One may ask what there was for a Polish stuntman to do in Chicago. Apparently not much—the fellow was amenable to Tony's suggestion that they go into the siding business. Tony knew nothing about siding, but—you can see why I liked the guy—figured he could learn. Here his professional background was helpful, since as a former engineer he was acquainted with such concepts as plumb, level, and true, which gave him a leg up right there. Plus, he was honest, industrious, and shrewd.

The siding business lasted only a season; the writer and the stuntman went back to Poland. With winter coming on, Tony decided he would expand into general remodeling. A few sessions of eating dirt were enough to convince him he wasn't cut out for manual labor. He decided to become an entrepreneur.

In Chicago in those days—I don't claim things are drastically different now—there were a number of remodeling firms of somewhat shady reputation that ostensibly were general contractors but in reality were mainly sales organizations, making their money on brochures and smooth talk. A job having been sold and a contract procured, an expediter would then set about finding someone to do the work. The screening process wasn't rigorous. If you had a truck and tools and could stand upright unassisted— tovarich, you got the job.

In bidding on such work, Tony developed a two-part strategy. First he'd visit the job site, partly to look over the project but mainly to schmooze the home owner. Over a cup of coffee he'd review the items to be accomplished, taking care to omit some essential task. The alarmed home owner would pull out her copy of the contract to show Tony the agreed-upon scope of work. Tony would smile, concede she was right, and note the contract's bottom line. Thus prepared, he'd submit his bid—on a $7,000 job, say, he might calculate that he could do his portion for $3,000, bid $4,000 (which would cause the general contractor to squawk, but not throw Tony out of the office), and settle for $3,800, putting him $800 to the good.

That showed a certain cunning, but the devious part was this—Tony would then do a competent job. The happy customer would sign the completion form and pay the general contractor, who in turn would pay Tony. Meanwhile, the subcontractors hired to work on other houses would bungle their assignments, tick off the home owners, and get fired without being paid, whereupon the general contractor would ask Tony to salvage the jobs. Tony would visit the home owners, ask to see the contracts (he needed to see what had been done and what hadn't, didn't he?), then bid as if starting afresh. The general contractor, anxious to avoid having the jobs botched twice and aware that his outlay up to that point had been basically zip, was disposed to accept any reasonable offer. If some of the fired subcontractors' work could be salvaged, so much the better for Tony.

After a few years of subcontracting to other companies, Tony was sufficiently well established to strike out on his own. Eventually he was joined by his brother Jerry, his junior by fifteen years. Jerry worked for Tony for a while, then started his own company. He and Tony had agreed to pool their resources for the purposes of our job.

As the preceding makes evident, Tony was well suited to work on the Barn House, but I didn't know that when we first met. All I knew was that Eddie had recommended him and that Tony, on the basis of the half hour's acquaintance we had prior to signing the contract, seemed like a nice guy. I don't claim it was a shining example of due diligence. Looking back on it now, in fact, I'd say most people do a better job checking out strangers they pick up in bars. But it was now early October, with not a nail driven. I signed.

Almost everyone who worked for Tony and Jerry was of Polish or at least Eastern European extraction, except for those in trades that had become the province of other ethnic groups, the example coming most quickly to mind being Mexicans, who, in addition to landscaping, had cornered the market on drywall. Alex, my real estate guy, who did some rehab on the side and thus had occasion to hire, was of the view that Polish drywallers were, relative to the Mexicans who had supplanted them, older, slower, more expensive, and possessed of a greater proclivity to drink. I have no personal knowledge of any Polish worker with the last failing, although now that I consider the matter it might explain the unfortunate fellow who kept falling off the ladder and suffering grievous bodily harm. For the most part, though, the Polish workers were skilled and hardworking, and I grew fond of all of them, particularly the noble Chester, the head of the framing crew. Tony employed them, or at least a large subset of them, through an arcane system of labor subcontractors, the details of which were elusive but which had the effect, as I understood it, of shielding him from adverse financial consequences when business slowed down. Tony was perhaps unschooled in some fine points of American business practice, but he was no dope.

At an early stage of the program I developed great confidence in Tony, which was perhaps surprising in view of the somewhat rocky start. The back of the house had to be demolished, to aid in which process Tony and Jerry had hired a Polish fellow with a backhoe. I wasn't present when the work began, but judging from the results the backhoe man had gotten a little carried away. I'd instructed that the rear of the kitchen was to be knocked down, but that the floor joisting—the century-old, twenty-five-foot-long two-by-tens—was to remain. The backhoe man had consigned the floor joists to history, and while he was at it had knocked off a corner of the limestone foundation, destroyed the cellar door, and for all I know would have flattened the rest of the house, except that at the climactic moment the goddess of home improvement had decided, *enough of this malarkey*, whereupon the backhoe popped a hose, spraying hydraulic fluid over the ruins and bringing progress, if one could call it that, to an abrupt halt.

When I arrived at the Barn House the next day I stood in the basement and surveyed the scene. The back of the house had the appearance of a bombed-out cellar on the western front. Above me yawned the heavenly vault, occluded to some extent by the upper reaches of the neighboring elm trees, then showing the first tinge of autumn. The splintered lumber formerly constituting the kitchen, the rear addition, the second-floor porch, the rear deck, and appurtenant structures lay in an untidy heap behind the foundation wall. At the edge of the wreckage stood the crippled backhoe, the ruptured hose hanging limp. I knew nothing about backhoes, but I bet you twenty dollars that with a length of garden hose, a couple clamps, and a quart of brake fluid I could have gotten it operating well enough to move it. It wasn't my backhoe, however, and frankly—my serenity on this point now strikes me as remarkable—it wasn't my problem. Tony would fix it. (Actually, through some division of responsibilities not clear to me at the time, it was Jerry's job to fix it, a matter in which Tony seemed to take a grim satisfaction; I could only assume Jerry had hired the backhoe guy.) The backhoe man showed up later that day and spent a good hour ineffectually maneuvering the shovel, presumably in an effort to retract it to the point that he could extricate his machine and drive it to the repair shop; but eventually he abandoned the effort, and apparently the backhoe as well. All I know is it wound up parked on the street a half block away, where it remained for a month or so until purchased by the Irish water-service installers Kevin had hired, who had wonderful brogues and the wit to deduce that here was a pigeon ripe for the plucking. Demolition was completed by a crew of Mexicans, too freshly arrived to have learned the art of drywall, who removed the shattered remnants by hand.

I observed these proceedings with detachment. I had decided, on the basis of some ineffable vibe that I can't persuasively explain but that till then had seldom steered me wrong, that the project was in good hands. Besides, I had other fish to fry. I had to figure out what to do about the radiators.

I t's customary in old-house books to rhapsodize about the carpentry, the smell of fresh-cut pine and manly sweat, the scream of the circular saws, and other signs of a construction project in progress, but if you don't mind we're going to go easy on that part. I don't mean to minimize the importance of the Barn House's carpentry, or to deprecate in any way the quality of the work, which was a wonder to behold. Indeed, particularly with respect to the framing of the multi-angled turret roof, I regretted more than once that we were going to have to cover it up, and gave some thought to leaving it exposed, either by giving the room a rustic treatment or somehow putting the framing under glass. The latter idea was facetious, of course, and Charlie talked me out of the former. Still, when it came time to put up the dry-wall, I felt as though I were draping a muumuu over Catherine Deneuve.

Anyway, while carpentry will get its due in this book, I'm not going to dwell on it. I was more interested in other aspects of the house—namely, the electrical and mechanical systems. It was the Remco Thinking Boys' Toys talking. Carpentry had its points, I conceded that. You got to pound intractable objects with a hammer, grip mouthfuls of nails, and operate power tools shaped like an assault rifle. It tickled the Y chromosome to do such things from time to time. But one didn't want to get carried away. My brother John, for example, was one of those guys who thought nobody could call himself a man who hadn't framed a hipped roof, the kind that slopes down to the eaves on all four sides. Please. It was a useful skill. Knowing how to light a fire with two paper matches in the rain was a useful skill. But the breed of individual who had taken apart clocks as a child and cars as an adolescent knew there was more to life than lumber. Way more. I'm speaking of pipes, ducts, and wires.

Houses nowadays have a lot of pipes, ducts, and wires. Indeed, in any restored home one principal difference between the updated version and the original is the vastly greater amount of stuff hidden in the walls. If you'll excuse my once again getting ahead of my story, we tallied up the reels for the different types of wire and cable we installed at the Barn House, not only for the 120-volt AC supply but also for the intercom, the telephones, cable

TV, and so on; the total ran to fourteen thousand feet—and we hadn't installed the extensive data wiring common today, nor an infrared-controlled sound system. We did install an alarm system, but I didn't do it myself, and so don't know exactly how much wire it required, but looking around the premises afterward I guessed it had to be another one thousand feet, meaning we used close to three miles of wire and cable all told.

When we were well into our project I visited a new house constructed for a friend, who had made provision for every electronic gadget then known; his basement utility room looked like a telephone exchange. "Cool," I said when I saw it, and I spoke sincerely. I loved this stuff. I won't claim I understood it in detail. My alarm guy, one of those carefree electronics geniuses to whom the word guru could be unsarcastically attached, used to explain how the various systems worked, larding his conversation with such terms as "zero crossing" and "trickle current" and the like, as if I knew what he was talking about. Up to a point I did—I'd subscribed to *Popular Electronics* for a year at age fourteen—but inside of fifteen minutes he'd always left me in the dust. No matter. I was in my element and happy.

It would be a while before we got to the wiring, though. First came the pipes.

When the likely expense of renovating the Barn House first became apparent, I considered doing all the pipe fitting required, including that for the plumbing in addition to the heating. But the more I thought about it the more I realized this course was impractical. It was partly a question of time and partly one of skill. I had seen enough plumbing work done to know that it involved considerable craft. Among other things we would have to run some gas lines, which required threaded pipe. I knew, as all red-blooded lads should, how to thread pipe, having found it useful as a means of dodging plaster duty on days when the electrical business was slow. It required jigs and dies and cutters and vises; copious amounts of thread-cutting oil, the scent of which to this day takes me back to the blossom of my youth; and a thing called a reamer, about which I'll say only that if you thought *Marathon Man* was a movie to chill the blood, wait till you see the remake done with a reamer. But I hadn't had primary responsibility for hooking the pipes together, and with my father's example vividly in mind, I decided that if leaks were an inevitable part of the learning process, it was best not to start out piping gas.

The water-supply piping was less problematic than gas from the standpoint of leaks, and for a time I considered doing that. I had a pretty thorough general knowledge of plumbing arcana. I could speak with confidence of P-traps, street elbows, and unions (the steel kind, not the labor organization); I had gone to the plumbing supply store as a boy, looked the counterman in the eye, and ordered couplings, hermaphrodite fittings, and two-inch nipples—plumbing terminology isn't for the easily embarrassed. But that was just the start. Plumbing, I knew all too well, was an esoteric art. There was the mysterious matter of the "wet vent," which I understood in a general way, but not so I could pass the journeyman's test. I had caulked the joints of a four-inch cast-iron soil pipe with the exotic fibrous vegetable known as oakum, a vinelike commodity that I imagined had been harvested from the mighty baobab by pygmies in the rain forest, as a prelude to having my father and George seal the joint by pouring in molten lead heated to 700 degrees Celsius in a miniature furnace. But I had never poured the lead myself, and given that we needed to install a good deal of cast-iron soil pipe in addition to the gas pipe, I felt that now wasn't the time to learn. I'd have time to acquire one new trade but not two, and the one had better involve work I couldn't otherwise get done, or only at exorbitant expense. I've earlier alluded to my difficulties with heating contractors. I resolved to do the heating myself.

I knew little about heating systems, but the topic held a primitive fascination for me. The Barn House was a veritable museum of heating technology. Originally it had been heated with a gravity warm-air system, by far the simplest type of central heating, which operated by convection. Comparable systems had been used in ancient times. One needed a heat source at the base of the house and a system of flues. The heated air became buoyant, rose through the flues, and warmed the rooms. When the air cooled, it sank and returned to the heat source via a central return duct. One enjoyed a steadily circulating air flow for as long as the heat source kept operating, without the need for fans or other expedients. In consequence, according to one gushing account I read, the system was "wonderfully silent."

It's fair to say the version in the Barn House was also wonderfully ineffectual. The flues had to run through the center of the house rather than the exterior walls, lest the rising air cool off too quickly. No heat was provided near the windows, where heat loss in winter months was most severe. So far as we could tell, in the Barn House there had been only one duct to the second floor, to the sitting room that adjoined the master bedroom. The master bedroom itself had been heated by a fireplace. The rear bedroom, from what I could tell, had had no heat source at all.

A heating system like that might suffice for some balmy Sunbelt town, where the locals spoke of the coming ice age when the temperature dipped below 50 degrees Fahrenheit, but this was Chicago. Mrs. Carr had shivered through the winters for only six years. In 1897, she had replaced the original heating plant with a gravity hot-water system—we knew the date, you'll recall, because a train schedule from that year had been stuffed around one of the radiator pipes. Radiators had been installed and holes for the pipes drilled through the floors. The pipes themselves were exposed to view. Few traces of the gravity warm-air system remained by the time we bought the house other than patches in the flooring where the registers had been.

A gravity hot-water system also worked by convection, electric pumps not having become practical when the technology was first devised. A boiler in the basement heated water, which became buoyant and rose through supply pipes into radiators in the rooms above. Having shed its heat, the cooled and now denser water returned to the boiler via a separate set of return pipes. The system worked solely because of the difference in density between hot and cold water; it had no moving parts.

A gravity hot-water system had the considerable advantage that it worked. Its disadvantage, if one judges from the literature available today, was that it required an extensive practical knowledge of fluid dynamics. In order to ensure balanced delivery of heat to radiators on different floors, one might tap off the side or the top of the supply pipe to take advantages of minute differences in the heating gradient of the water in the pipes (or so I read today— there was no evidence that whoever installed the Barn House's heating system had been aware of such niceties). None of this was of importance now; an electric pump had been installed long previously, and the water now flowed through the system because the pump forced it to. But I didn't know that yet. I didn't know anything. My ignorance of what lay ahead was complete.

The one other type of central heating system then in common use was steam. It was never used in the Barn House, although my neighbor Ned's house had it; I mention it solely because it was cool. The ingenuity of steam heat appealed to me. It depended on the fact that water when boiled expands to sixteen hundred times its liquid volume. (Or maybe seventeen hundred times; every time my brother-in-law the Ph.D. figures this out he gets a different answer.) The steam penetrated to the farthest reaches of the system without pumps. You could heat the largest house, or for that matter an apartment building—most apartment buildings constructed in Chicago before World War II are heated with steam to this day. Another advantage of steam was that it required no special skills on the part of the pipe fitter. It was merely necessary that the single pipe connecting each radiator to the furnace (or rather, judging from Ned's house, to the basement supply loop) ascend continuously en route, so that when the steam gave up its heat in the radiator and condensed, it would flow back down to the boiler as water. The steam, meanwhile, would continue to flow in the opposite direction—all of this occurring, mind you, within the confines of *the same pipe.* As I say, it was ingenious. Supposedly it was also more dangerous than a hot-water system, since the steam operated at higher temperatures and pressures than a hot-water system and presented a greater likelihood of a boiler explosion.[1] While this may have been so, a likelier mishap in my observation was that all the water would boil off, with unhappy consequences. I knew a guy rehabbing a steam-heated house—a Victorian town house of baronial splendor, it made the Barn House look like a chicken coop—who went on vacation one winter and left the place in the care of a buddy. Unfortunately he had neither installed a system to replenish the boiler water automatically (Ned had one of these), nor conveyed to his friend the resultant necessity of refilling the water by hand. The boiler ran dry, the heat stopped, and the water supply pipes froze and burst. I wasn't present to view the result, but I gather it wasn't pretty.

Radiators, whether heated by water or steam, presented some problems. They were big and clunky. They took up floor space and were difficult to move. They collected dust. They were in the way when you wanted to paint the room or install carpet or flooring. The valves sometimes leaked. Trapped air had to be bled out of hot-water radiators periodically; the steam ones hissed when the heat came up. They were a bitch to paint.

Their only real advantage was that they provided the best heat. In a well-designed system, the force of the water flow didn't di-

[1] I learned this from studying the works of Dan Holohan, who has published books about maintaining old heating systems and operates a Web site, heatinghelp.com. Dan was kind enough to answer a few questions for this book and I have no reason to doubt anything he says. However, had I read his books before embarking on the installation of the heating system in the Barn House, I would never have had the nerve to start.

minish appreciably over a long pipe run. (In part this was a matter of decreasing the pipe diameter with distance, taking advantage of the Venturi effect to increase the water's velocity.) Rooms in the far corners of the house stayed as warm as those near the furnace. The system was quiet—at night all you could hear was the faint whirring of the pump. It didn't blow dust around the house. The room temperature didn't fluctuate markedly as the furnace cycled on and off—the hot water in the radiators kept the room warm even after the pump stopped. If you came in some night chilled to the bone you could sit on a radiator to warm up. Plus we already had the furnace and most of the radiators.

We also wanted central air-conditioning, and that meant ducts. But since the ducts would only be used for cooling, and since the exterior/interior temperature difference in the summer was 25 degrees at most, versus 70 degrees or more in the depths of a continental winter, one could be a lot more casual about locating the registers.

I was, in my way, quite systematic. I wanted to have the heating system properly engineered, to avoid hot and cold spots. Charlie recommended an engineer named Kent, who had done work for his firm. Kent, a taciturn young fellow with a mustache, had come out to the house and spent a day measuring radiators, inspecting the furnace, and making notes on a legal pad. I gave him a copy of the blueprints, and later sent him detailed information about each room in the house on a form he had given me: dimensions, size and orientation of windows and exterior doors, type of insulation, and similar matters. I gathered that he entered all of this into a computer program that calculated heating requirements.

In the fullness of time a cylinder arrived in the mail containing several large sheets of rolled-up onionskin—a schematic of the house marked up in Kent's brisk hand, showing the locations of the radiators and the routing and diameter of the pipes. I spread them out on the table, studied them, and—Charlie had likely warned Kent about this—proceeded to redo them. Kent had estimated the heating capacity of the individual radiators and assigned them to different locations based on the needs of the rooms. But he hadn't taken into account the *shape* of the radiators. He had tall ones standing next to low windows, wide ones in places only narrow ones would fit. He had, moreover, drawn the main supply pipes in the basement on the assumption that the furnace would be in the front of the house, whereas I had now decided I wanted it to be in the middle. I also had various ideas about minimizing the visual clutter of the pipes, and leaving enough room to mount the air-conditioning ducts, and other technical minutiae concerning which there is no need to bore the reader. The upshot was that I got out my own roll of paper and, as I had done so often before, redrew the plan.

Meanwhile I set about purchasing more radiators. This entailed going to the secondhand radiator yard out on Milwaukee Avenue and dealing with Peter, an enormous monosyllabic Ukrainian in his twenties who was perhaps not Fulbright scholar material but compensated by having impressively oversized muscles of the sort formerly seen in *Li'l Abner* cartoons, which were undoubtedly handy in his line of work. Here again I had the sense of having been transported to another age. Cities had been built by the likes of Peter, mighty men who accomplished monumental tasks—you try taking a radiator apart—using appropriately scaled tools, in Peter's case the biggest pipe wrench I had ever seen. Peter presided over a forest of used radiators of all descriptions, removed from buildings that were being wrecked or renovated. Some of the radiators were small—these were still being manufactured. But mostly I was interested in the big ones, which to my knowledge hadn't been made since the 1960s. The largest specimens, dating from the era before wall insulation, contained more steel than you found nowadays in some cars. One took a selfish pleasure in purchasing these mammoth fixtures; it was like owning the Brooklyn Bridge. I strode happily around the radiator yard selecting a half dozen radiators of the proper size, arranging with Peter in a couple of cases to add or subtract fins.

The requisite number of radiators having been assembled, the next job was to move them to the desired locations in the house. Initially I had hoped to get the carpenters to do this. They were built like trucks, and had already helped me move the furnace from the front chimney to the rear one, a formidable project. But Tony and Jerry begged off. Some of the radiators were crushingly heavy and had to be moved to different floors. They felt trying to manhandle them up and down the narrow steps was foolish. "Somebody could get killed," said Jerry. *Some people have no sense of adventure,* I thought. But there was no arguing with them. I wondered aloud: "What am I supposed to do?"

"Rent a crane," Tony suggested.

A crane? They let civilians rent cranes? I figured I'd have as much luck leasing an aircraft carrier. However, on looking in the phone book later—the phone company in those days published a separate volume of the Yellow Pages for commercial users, a copy of which I providentially happened to have—I found that there was in fact a category of listings entitled "Cranes—Rental." Before I could begin phoning, though, Tony called up with a reference of his own. Inside of half an hour I was talking to Cleo, who was—who knew such people existed?—a freelance crane owner-operator. The rate was $85 an hour, four-hour minimum. He could come out in a few days.

If ever there were a good time to bring in a crane, this was it. The rear of the house had now been demolished and the debris hauled away, but construction hadn't yet begun. The house's backside was open to the weather, covered only with a tarp at the end of the day; it would be easy to swing radiators in and out. The only problem was getting the crane onto the property. The driveway at the side of the house was too narrow. Tony suggested taking down the rear fence and having the crane enter the backyard from the alley. It sounded like a sensible idea to me.

We were scheduled to move the radiators on a crisp day in early November. Tony had earlier detailed a couple of carpenters to dismantle the back fence. I'd been down the street on an errand when Cleo arrived with his crane; he had maneuvered it into the backyard on his own. As I walked up the driveway, I could hear a hissing sound from the rear of the house. Coming round to the backyard, I saw the crane. It was close to the house, with its boom raised and its jacks lowered. It had four immense wheels, each the size of a ten-year-old child. In the cab was a stocky man whom I took to be Cleo. He didn't look anywhere near as cheerful as a man who owned his own crane might reasonably be expected to be. A glance showed why. The hissing sound, now quite loud, was coming from the crane's front tires. They were both punctured.

I found out what had happened. With the rear fence removed, Cleo had driven over the concrete slab at the back of the lot. The slab, you'll remember, had been intended for an unbuilt garage. Now it was covered with matted debris. The debris concealed embedded bolts intended to secure the garage walls. Those at the front of the slab had been bent flat long ago. But those at the rear, near the fence, still pointed up. What was the harm? Nobody ever went there.

Cleo had driven over the bolts. He'd already called the repair service. He wasn't sure if the tires could be repaired. New ones would cost $400, more than he'd make on the job.

Cleo seemed strangely calm in the face of this disaster. Resigned is probably a better description. One puncture, now—that would have suggested an accident, in theory preventable, and he might have felt entitled to be angry. But *two*, precisely spaced— think about it, what were the chances?—that was fate. Cleo, an honest suburban boy sucked into a developing urban quagmire, surely sensed that he'd been doomed the moment he'd taken my call. There was no sense in complaining. He'd gotten his crane into position and was ready to work.

So we did. The project proceeded with what in my book was

military precision—in fact, given what one hears about such things, it probably exceeded military precision by a considerable margin. On a clipboard I'd listed the current and final location of each radiator, with the moves scientifically ordered to minimize extra work; each radiator was tagged with a number and its destination room. I'd arranged for a squad of stout Polish carpenters to be on hand, along with the requisite dollies and hand trucks. The first radiator was an impressive twenty-one-finned monster so massive it bent passing starlight. We (well, the Polish carpenters; I supplied high-level guidance) muscled the radiator onto the dolly, then pushed it to the rear of the house, wrapped cables around it, attached Cleo's hook, and gave the signal to hoist away. Then we scrambled to the appropriate floor, hauled in the dangling behemoth, set it on a dolly, disengaged the hook, trundled it to the designated location, and tipped it off the dolly. We repeated the process thirteen times. I had allowed four hours for the job; we were done in maybe two. Even Cleo was impressed. "This was a real nice job," he allowed ruefully, surveying the scene. I wrote him a check. He didn't ask compensation for the tires and I didn't volunteer any, which was perhaps ungenerous on my part, but I was a desperate man. I left a few minutes after what was surely the world's largest tow truck arrived.

The radiators having been properly situated, my task now was to connect them. The time was growing short. It was already November. So far we'd been fortunate; the weather had been mild. But the bitter Chicago winter would soon arrive. Though we'd removed much of the plumbing, we still had running water, a toilet and a sink, and I wanted to keep them operating if possible. To do that, though, I needed heat in the house.

10

A natural corollary of the fact that there are a limited number of ways to do things right is that there are a more or less infinite number of ways to do them wrong, or, if one wants to leave human agency out of it, a very large number of things that can *go* wrong, wrong being broadly defined in the context of home renovation to include everything from getting stuck with a really yucky basement-floor paint color to having the house collapse. We pretty much ran the gamut during the time we labored on the Barn House, and this despite the fact that we had the pride of Polish manhood (I intend no snarkiness) working on the job. Quite a few more things would have gone wrong had I not opportunely intervened. Mistakes and near-disasters are a feature of any construction project, of course; the only specifically urban aspect of the bungling that occurred in city houses was that, since there was generally more to do, there was more to get screwed up.

One day a couple weeks after construction began I arrived to find that the bricklayers were about to begin laying the masonry foundation for the reconstructed addition. By this time trenches had been excavated to the requisite depth (I didn't personally measure that it was forty-two inches, but the formwork had been done in a manner sufficiently authoritative that I felt certain someone had), and the concrete footings poured to a few inches above the level of the surrounding earth. The foundation wall was next. It was to be constructed using what Charlie called a split-faced CMU, short for concrete masonry unit, which was a sort of upscale concrete block. It looked like every other concrete block on all sides except one, which had a bumpy surface that made for a loose approximation of what architects called rusticated masonry, which is to say, stone tooled to look as if it had been wrested from the earth by a caveman with an ax. Whatever may be said for rusticated masonry, split-faced CMUs in large quantities were excruciatingly ugly—tart it up how you will, a concrete block is still a concrete block—but in sparing amounts (we needed only four courses) they made for an economical alternative to the limestone used in the Barn House's original foundation, which we were so certain was prohibitively expensive that we hadn't bothered to get a price.[1]

The bricklayers had laid out the first course of blocks but hadn't yet mortared them in place. I noticed a problem right away—all the blocks had only one rusticated face. That was fine for a straight run of wall, but the outside corner blocks needed to be rusticated on two sides, as anyone having experience at Legos, or for that matter an IQ above one, will immediately grasp. Lacking the requisite materials, the bricklayers were evidently planning on using ordinary blocks at the corners, the flat ends of which promised to

---

[1] It's doubtful we could have gotten some at any price. Judging from its slightly yellowish cast, we guessed that the original foundation blocks were Joliet limestone, which derived its color from its high iron content and the quarries for which had long since closed.

give the wall the appearance of having divots in it. I pointed this out to the person supervising the bricklayers, a natty young fellow with a leather jacket and a cell phone, the trappings of command in the trades. The fellow said that corner blocks of the sort I had in mind were unavailable. I replied that I knew for a fact that they were. I knew no such thing, but it stood to reason—not always an infallible guide in the construction business, but give me a break. The head bricklayer wasn't buying it. After a minute or two of fruitless disputation I told him to call Jerry. Jerry told him that of course you could get corner blocks, kolachkybrain. (The conversation was in Polish, and I could hear only one side of it; I deduced the above from a certain stiffening of expression.) The bricklayers weren't happy, since the job was delayed, but the corner blocks were obtained in due time.[2]

Then there was the matter of the chimneys. I realized I was going to have to hire someone to work on them at an early stage of the project. The house had two, each a formidable construction of brick. One rose through the center of the house; the other, near the front of the building, rose along an outside wall. The front chimney had three flues and the central one four, for a total of seven. Why this extravagant number I don't know. Only one flue was in use when we bought the house, for the gas furnace; two others served inoperative fireplaces. That left four unused, one in the front chimney and three in the central. A flue seemed an unlikely thing to need a spare of. I could only suppose that the

[2]An oddity of bricklaying, or at any rate of Polish bricklaying, is that one commences by placing a layer of tar paper on top of the concrete footing, and then putting the first course of bricks on top of that. The purpose of the tar paper, I suppose, is to prevent ground dampness from seeping into the bricks (concrete blocks are notoriously prone to moisture problems, and require not only tar paper but an application of sealant after the wall is erected). However, the result is that the bricks are not, strictly speaking, attached to the foundation, but rather are sitting on top of it. I noticed this after the bricklayers had finished their work and pointed it out to Jerry, who hadn't previously

central chimney had been mainly intended to do what central chimneys had always done—namely, hold up the rest of the house, in our case the heavy wooden beams supporting the floor joists. This practice is frowned on today, and caused Bob the engineer great distress, but the chimney seemed well suited to it. It measured seven feet by a foot and a half at the base, which, granted, was smaller than the colonial chimneys you saw preserved here and there on the East Coast, which were the size of small hotels, but still impressive compared to the glorified stovepipes installed in new construction today.

We wanted to restore the inoperative fireplaces to working order, which in the case of the living room fireplace wouldn't be easy. Its flue had been diverted to serve the furnace and its firebox had been closed up with a cast-iron plate. The hearth tile was gone, although the shallow recess in the floor where it had been remained; someone had futilely attempted to conceal the depression with squares of thin vinyl tile. If there had ever been a mantelpiece there was no sign of it now.

None of the flues, we established, had ever been lined. Although the masonry looked solid from the outside we had been given to understand that if we burned wood in a hundred-year-old unlined chimney we were taking our lives in our hands. The chimney tops were crumbling, and the one on the outside wall had to be made taller—city code required that it be two feet higher than anything else within a ten-foot radius, and the peak of the rebuilt turret would be only eight feet away.

I knew two ways of lining chimneys. The more common

---

given the matter much thought. We pondered the newly constructed wall for some moments without coming to any conclusions. Later I realized the whole house was built the same way—the floor joists, and thus the building (both the old part and new), weren't bolted to the foundation wall; they just perched on top of it, held in place solely by friction and gravity. Granted, it wasn't like somebody was going to tip the foundation up on one end and let the house slide off. On the other hand . . . well, one remembered *The Wizard of Oz*.

method was to insert a stainless steel tube. The ballpark price we heard was a thousand dollars per three-story flue. Notwithstanding its stainlessness, the steel tube was subject to corrosion and would eventually require replacement. The other method, which we heard about from a friend, involved the creation of a "solid flue." A cylindrical rubber bladder—basically a giant condom— was shoved down the flue and inflated. The bladder was then agitated while a watery grout was poured into the space between it and the surrounding brick. After the grout solidified, the bladder was deflated and removed. The result, theoretically, was a cylindrical flue with a solid masonry liner bonded to the brick. The liner wasn't subject to corrosion, and arguably added to the chimney's strength. It was also cheaper than stainless steel.

Our friend was enthusiastic about solid flue and to me it made perfect sense. I called the contractor whose number he gave me, Paul. It was only later that I discovered our friend had never actually gotten around to having solid flues installed himself.

Paul seemed like a nice enough guy when he came out to the house. We agreed that he would line the three flues in the outside chimney. He would also add to the chimney top and re-route the furnace exhaust so it used a different flue. At some point I would have the living room firebox rebuilt so I could use the fireplace again, and later still I would see about getting a hearth and a mantel.

One evening shortly after work on the chimney began—I hadn't visited the job site in a couple days—I got a call from Paul.

"We ran into a little problem," he said.

There are three people in this world from whom you don't want to hear that you have a little problem. One is your heart surgeon, another your tax accountant, and the third is your chimney guy. I asked Paul what was up.

Paul explained that he'd inserted the bladders into the flues in the outside chimney and begun pouring the grout. Unbeknownst to him, the wall of the house concealed an old crack that extended most of the height of the chimney. When the flues were half filled the lateral pressure of the grout had caused the chimney wall to buckle outward half an inch. Paul had immediately stopped pouring and the buckling had progressed no further; nonetheless, the chimney was in peril of collapse.

I grant you there's nothing specifically urban about calamities of this kind. Anyone who renovates a hundred-year-old structure, and it may as well be in an alfalfa field as in a city, puts himself in the position of having people he barely knows tell him the side of his house is about to fall off. Still, I was . . . well, I was nettled, I'll say that. I asked Paul what he proposed to do. He said that the chimney's buckled outer wall would have to be taken down and rebuilt.

I suppose I sighed. I asked Paul what all this was going to cost me. Well, he allowed, the lateral pressure of the liquid grout was an inherent risk of the solid-flue process. (Later I heard about a house where the grout had burst a weak spot on an inside wall and filled up the bathroom.) He would take down the bricks and re-lay them at no charge. I assuredly sighed at this point, with relief. The only problem would be finding replacements for the bricks that had cracked.

That didn't look to be easy. The bricks were a deep red, quite handsome really, of a uniform color. Though common enough in old buildings, I had never seen anything like them in new construction. A previous owner of the Barn House had replaced a few chimney bricks with others of an almost-but-not-quite shade; they were conspicuous at fifty yards. The corner of the chimney where the replacement bricks had to go was the one closest to the street; I fretted that if the job was a hodgepodge it would be the first thing anyone approaching the house would see. But Paul had an idea. He was replacing a chimney in the western suburbs; he thought the bricks were similar to mine. He would get some samples.

I got a call from Paul a few days later and went out to the house. He showed me some of the salvaged bricks. When I got home I called Charlie.

"They're a dead match," I said.

"Naw," said Charlie. Charlie had a capacity for appreciating small wonders that was comforting at such times.

"I'm serious. Only problem is they're an eighth of an inch too short."

"That's nothing. You can finesse that with mortar."

It was even so. Paul dyed the mortar black to match the color of the original. (The contrast of the black mortar with the red brick was striking; one wonders why such things aren't done more often. No doubt the answer is that no one thinks to ask.) When he finished a few days later, the repair job was undetectable except at close range. As it happened we weren't done with the chimneys, but for now another bullet dodged.

Installation of the heating system now commenced in earnest. Now that the radiators had been conveyed to the right rooms, I had to hook them up. It may be difficult for the reader having no knowledge of these things to appreciate the magnitude of this task. Imagine yourself trying to install radiators, a task you know nothing about and have never seen done—in fact, all you know about radiators is what you can pick up from looking at one, which I assure you isn't much. No doubt, you suggest, it's simply a matter of getting the pipes from point A (the radiator) to point B (the furnace). Well, sure. One can say the same of putting a man on the moon. It's the details that are a ballbreaker. We start with the matter of bushings.

A bushing is a sort of metal collar used to make a big hole into a little one. You screw the bushings into big holes in the base of the radiators. The bushings have little holes that you hook the radiator valves into. One may ask why the radiator manufacturers hadn't furnished their products with little holes to start with, rather than yawning two-inch orifices such as might be needed to connect the radiator to the cooling pipes for a nuclear power plant. I can't say. Perhaps someone was on the take from the bushing cartel. No matter—I had to take out the old bushings and replace them with new ones. The radiators having been rearranged and the thermal characteristics of the house having changed (we were going to insulate the walls, of course), the pipes were all different sizes.

The existing bushings had been rusting in place for ninety-seven years—for all I knew they had fused inextricably with the radiators' molecular structure and were held in place by the strong nuclear force. The only tool I had with even a gossamer promise of removing them was an eighteen-inch-long pipe wrench. It was a stout little instrument manufactured by the Ridgid Tool Company, best known for its calendars depicting busty maidens wielding oversized Ridgid tools with come-hither looks and God knows what salacious intent. Still, eighteen inches, whatever the busty maidens might think of it, wasn't going to do me a lot of good with a radiator bushing. I wrestled the wrench onto bushing A on radiator #1 on the third floor (one always pipes radiators from the top down), and gave a tentative tug. Nothing. I ratcheted up the joules and applied—well, I won't say hernia-inducing torque, but certainly enough to pop the bolts on, say, an automobile wheel. Still no go.

I was discouraged, but only momentarily. I knew what I needed, and browsed around the house in search of it. Those who have been down this road before will know what I was after: a cheater pipe. I found one in the basement. I had laboriously unscrewed several hunks of the old threaded radiator feeder line and hadn't gotten around to discarding them, or more accurately, the neighborhood metal scavengers (more on them later) hadn't yet spirited them away. I found a five-foot length of pipe an inch and a half in diameter. If I slipped it over the handle of the wrench I would be able, through the principle of leverage, to apply substantial additional force, which would either budge the bushing or snap the wrench, a sight worth seeing either way.

I strode purposefully back up to the third floor, grappled the wrench onto the bushing again, slipped the cheater pipe over the wrench handle, then looked for a suitably Archimedean place to stand. The preliminaries having thus been efficiently addressed, I applied prodigious force. Nothing happened initially, but one felt—one *sensed*—internal seismic shifts, as ancient and implacable forces conceded the jig was up. I gave it a little more gas.

The sucker turned.

Oh, yes. It wasn't *happy* about the situation, and I needed to reseat the wrench and cheater pipe multiple times in order to coax the bushing through the better part of a revolution before I could finish the job with the wrench alone. But it turned.

One recognizes that in the context of pivotal world events—the battle of Midway, for example, or the invention of movable type—the loosening of a radiator bushing doesn't loom very large. But it was (so to speak) a turning point for me. I had established, first of all, that the stupid bushings *would* turn, a matter of which till then I'd had no personal experience. More to the point, they would turn on my say-so. It's all very well to know, in an abstract way, that humankind can harness the forces of the universe. One still wants firsthand assurance that they'll toe the line for you.

For a time thereafter things proceeded with reasonable dispatch. After I had removed the old bushings, I screwed in new ones of appropriate size, having first daubed the threads with a white Teflon crayon. I did this because plumbers always did it, or else used a sort of gray ectoplasm called pipe dope (Teflon was more high-tech), having in my mind the idea that the stuff would prevent leaks, although Kevin the plumbing guy later informed me that the true purpose was to reduce friction and enable me to screw in the new bushings to pinnacles of tightness previously undreamt of, thereby ensuring (I guess) that the next guy who had to remove them would likewise bust a gut. This done, I noodged the radiator into its final position using a crowbar. (Well, not final final; I had to move it around numerous times for the drywallers and floor sanders and such, but you know what I mean.) I screwed the valve and return elbow (the part that hooked to the pipe on the other side of the radiator) into place, marked the floor immediately below, and drilled holes for the pipes that would drop through the floor. Then I walked downstairs, looked up at the holes in the floorboards above, and considered the matter of pipes.

Although this won't mean much to you unless you're the type who spends your lunch hour prowling the plumbing aisle at the True Value, pipe fitting these days is an order of magnitude simpler than it was when my father renovated houses, largely as a result of the substitution of lightweight, easily worked, and (no surprise) cheaper materials such as copper and plastic for cast iron and steel. The introduction of new products—vinyl siding is the obvious example—has arguably led to an erosion of quality in many construction trades. Plumbing isn't one of them. Some will dispute the merits of plastic pipe—when used for drains, as I've already pointed out, it can be embarrassingly noisy; the fumes from the glue used to assemble it can be toxic; and there is some lingering concern about whether noxious chemicals can leach from plastic pipe into drinking water. (The current research consensus: Don't worry about it.)

Copper pipe, however, is superior in almost all respects to the material it replaced, threaded steel. It's vastly easier to install, for one thing. Cutting and threading steel pipe involved numerous steps using tools that would fill a small machine shop. You clamped the pipe in a vise; cut it to length using a cutting-wheel tool that you clamped against the pipe and then rotated, screwing the wheel progressively tighter until you had sliced through the pipe; reamed out the burr; applied a thread-cutting die set into a multiarmed die holder having the appearance of an airplane propeller; squirted on oil to reduce friction; muscled the die through an arc of ninety degrees or so; applied more oil; rotated the die another ninety degrees; and so on till the thread had been cut to the necessary depth. Then you removed the pipe from the vise, flipped it around, clamped it in the vise again, and threaded the other end. On a good day cutting and threading a single length of steel pipe took two adolescents twenty minutes (I suppose if we had really busted our humps we might have done it in ten), without even getting into the business of fitting all the pipes together and stopping the innumerable leaks.

Soldering copper pipe, on the other hand, required one merely to cut the pipe using a tube cutter, which was similar to a steel-pipe cutter but maybe one-fifth the size; burnish the ends to a shiny finish with sandpaper to ensure proper bonding of the solder; daub on a jelly-like substance known as flux, which melted when heated and distributed the solder uniformly around the joint; assemble the pipes and fittings; and then solder the whole mess together using a portable torch. The work required some skill, and carried with it the not insignificant risk of setting the house afire, but in terms of physical exertion it was a frolic in the daffodils compared to fitting steel pipe. Plus it was twice as fast and, since the pipes were light, could be done without a helper.

Soldered pipe had one other large advantage as well. Threaded pipe had a tendency to leak at the joints—sometimes copiously, as my father had discovered to his sorrow and my amusement, but more often in minute amounts that no amount of tightening could entirely eliminate. Even in the best of circumstances a few joints would weep, which rankled the old man's perfectionist soul, but there was little he could do about it except wait a few weeks till rust plugged the gaps. A properly soldered joint, in contrast, was watertight from the start.[3]

[3]Another advantage of copper pipe, in my limited observation, is that it doesn't plug up with lime scale to the extent that galvanized steel does.

The upshot of all this was that while piping a house full of radiators using threaded steel pipe wasn't a practical possibility for one man with limited time, few tools, and no experience, it wasn't out of the question using copper. That's not to say it would be easy. I'd sweated pipe, as plumbers say, exactly twice before, both times small jobs at my mother-in-law's. Unfortunately, by the time I began working on the Barn House I'd forgotten how I'd done it, as I discovered one morning when I spent an hour trying to hook up a temporary water line for a toilet and wound up burning a hole in the pipe with the torch.

Now I was faced with repiping the entire house—perhaps a thousand feet of pipe and hundreds of solder joints—and I had to get it finished before the arrival of sustained subfreezing temperatures, perhaps six weeks. Or at least get it finished enough to start the furnace. Here I had done one smart thing. In designing the piping I had divided it into two loops, one supplying the radiators in the front of the house, the other those in the back. Each loop was to be isolated from the other and from the furnace by valves. My plan was to finish one loop and stub out the other as far as the valves—a matter of a few inches of pipe. Then I could shut the valves on the unfinished (indeed, unstarted) loop, open the valves on the finished one, fill the system with water, start the furnace, and warm the house sufficiently to keep the water supply pipes from freezing. After that I could finish the other loop in . . . well, comfort perhaps is not the appropriate term. But at least I wouldn't get frostbite.

Still, while I had a big-picture sense of where I wanted to go, I was resoundingly ignorant of the details. What's more, there was no one I could ask. Finding a male acquaintance who knew the basics of pipe soldering wasn't that difficult, but guy-knowledge

---

Admittedly that isn't much of an issue with radiator piping, where the same water recirculates year after year and the lime content isn't constantly replenished.

of hot-water heating systems had fallen to historical lows. The technology hadn't disappeared—the term used nowadays is "hydronic heat"—but it had become a specialized art, like rigging solar panels or rebuilding carburetors. I knew no one who had ever installed radiators, not counting my father, who with my grandfather's help had installed one in the rear addition in 1958, too long ago to count. Kent the engineer had some book knowledge of the subject, and could answer the occasional technical question, but for many practical details my best bet—often my only bet—was to study the antique hot-water system I already had.

I did have one odd nugget of knowledge that was to prove unexpectedly useful. Somewhere along the line I had picked up the idea that the pipes needed to rise continually (or, to use a term that hasn't come up since high school algebra, monotonically) en route from the furnace to the radiator. I wasn't sure why this was so—electric pumps made it unnecessary to depend on convection to circulate the water, and could push it down as easily as up. Nonetheless, I went to great trouble to ensure that the pipes sloped in accordance with what in retrospect seems an almost superstitious conviction, and for reasons that didn't become apparent till much later was fortunate that I had.

I'd gotten off to a modestly encouraging start. Having positioned the first radiator and gone mano a mano with the bushings, I'd established that I'd launched a project I had some prospect of successfully concluding. Now I girded myself for production. First I set up a work space. The previous owners had left a beat-up old wooden workbench in the basement. I dragged this up to the second floor and lined up my collection of pipe fittings, solder, propane torches, and other plumbing gear on top of it. Then I hung a fluorescent shop light overhead—the bright circle was cheering—and got ready to go to work.

It wasn't long before I ran into another obstacle. The short pipes dropping down from the radiator needed to make a ninety-degree turn and run about eight feet horizontally to the risers, vertical pipes running up through the walls from the basement. To enable the pipes to make the horizontal run, I'd have to drill holes through a series of joists, the long planks tipped on edge that held up the floor above. The joists were closely spaced and the pipe didn't have enough flex for me to shove in a single piece running from radiator to riser. Instead, I'd have to cut a series of short lengths, one per joist, slip them into the holes, then solder them together with couplings. Running two pipes eight feet would require fourteen couplings—twenty-eight solder joints. Progress would be agonizingly slow.

Another problem became apparent once I got started. Some of the joists were so close together, as little as ten inches apart, that it was impossible for me to fit an electric drill between them at the requisite angle—I couldn't drill the holes. I made repeated trips to hardware and home improvement stores to buy bit extensions, flexible shafts, right-angle jigs. Nothing worked. After three days I'd extended a pair of pipes approximately four feet. I could go no further without help. It was time to call the Chief.

The Chief's real name was John, but no one who knew him in high school ever called him that. He was a wiry little guy who played the tambourine and sang in the school folk group. I hadn't known him well in high school, but we'd become buddies while helping organize our fifteen-year reunion. He'd never married. He lived with his beloved West Highland terrier Duffee in a Chicago suburb called Westchester. At one time a branch line of the L had operated in Westchester. One day in 1951, while the Chief's mother was pregnant with him, his father had been killed in a head-on collision while working as a motorman on this line. I was born the same day. No significance is to be attached to this coincidence, but it lent the proceedings the shivery air of fate.

The Chief was a man of unexpected talents—in seventh grade he'd taken second place in a citywide math contest. After college he became the teletype operations manager for a brokerage house at the Chicago Board of Trade. The brokerage house had been sold after suffering financial reverses and eventually the Chief had been laid off. At the time that I knew him, he had no obvious means of support.

The Chief had two salient characteristics. The first was an inexhaustible ability to talk. Subject matter was incidental to these discussions. If the Chief had been held in a sensory deprivation tank for a week, he would afterward be able to spend two hours describing the fluctuations in his pulse. The second characteristic, which was closely tied to the first, was that he couldn't be rushed. If the Chief were talking and a ticking bomb thirty seconds short of doomsday were left in his lap, you could run in frantic circles begging and pleading all you wanted, and his only response would be to acknowledge the urgency of the situation and proceed as before.

The plus side of this was that the Chief never got flustered. He didn't always know the right thing to do, but he would approach a crisis in the same methodical manner that he approached everything, and at such times he could be very calming. In all the years I'd known him I'd never seen him at a loss.

The Chief had a vast fund of information on useful subjects, and many valuable skills. Provided there were no great hurry, he could rebuild an auto engine, repair a garage door opener, or remodel a bathroom. He took particular pride in being able to procure hard-to-obtain items. When we'd been working on the reunion and needed to find a caterer or a bartender or some such thing, the Chief always knew somebody. Every commercial establishment in North America seemed to have an outlet within ten minutes of his house, and if you needed some obscure part or product, he was happy to make the rounds and shop for it, presenting you in a couple days' time with a long list of possibilities neatly written on a sheet of yellow legal paper, complete with model number, availability, and price.

Notwithstanding the fact that he had no regular employment,

the Chief contrived at all times to be busy. I never called him that I didn't find him in the middle of some project, which always took longer than planned and entailed numerous setbacks and complications, all of which he patiently overcame, and all of which he described to me in meticulous detail. The first ten minutes of any conversation with him consisted of a detailed status report on tasks completed, work in progress, and prospects for the days ahead. The agenda was always long. But he had a good heart, and would help you with anything, especially if the project interested him.

I called him late in the day. I was in the dining room. The house was cold and dark, the only illumination provided by a bare bulb suspended overhead. I was feeling bleak. I looked at the ruined parquet floor. I had no idea how I was going to fix it. I explained my manifold problems to the Chief. "Chief," I concluded plaintively, "you gotta help me." I attempted to maintain my composure, but finished on what was closer than I would have liked to a wail.

There was silence on the line. Probably this was the Chief puffing on a cigarette. I wasn't an advocate of smoking, but there were times when the introduction of nicotine into the situation provided a certain baseline solace. "When I was out there I said this is a huge project," the Chief said finally—he had put in some time on the demolition crew. "Ed's never going to be able to finish it on his own. He's going to need some help." Another pause. "I got a couple things to do. But I can give you a hand."

Relief washed through me like some turbulent cleansing drug. There were a great many things I wanted the Chief's help with, and a great many other things I didn't yet realize I needed help with where his assistance would prove decisive. But all that lay ahead. Right now I wanted him to perform an essential comradely function: I needed him to buy tools.

The Chief knew about tools. These days not everyone does. Some years ago *Esquire* magazine, which has taken upon itself the formidable task of teaching the men of America how to be manly, ran a short primer on tools. Among the featured tools were—I'm not making this up—the hammer, the handsaw, and the electric drill. As one might expect of an article in *Esquire*, the focus was not so much on what one might do with these mysterious implements as on which brands to buy.[4] I was initially taken aback, wondering what sort of ninnies the editors of *Esquire* felt they were addressing that needed such matters explained. At the time I decided it was preppies—endearing tousled-hair youth with names such as Jock and Reggie and Tripp, whom I imagined earnestly studying up on hammers, in the manner of Boy Scouts learning the Morse code, in case Muffy wanted a towel rack hung in the bathroom on the super's day off. (Less the detail about Muffy, this was the example given in the article.) This was unfair, I now realize. The truth was that if you were born into the upper middle class, even in an old working-class town like Chicago, an introduction to tools didn't constitute an essential part of your upbringing, and it was possible to arrive at adulthood with no more thorough acquaintance with a pair of Channellocks[5] than you or I might have with the harpoon.

The Chief didn't have that problem. He wasn't, strictly speaking, a blue-collar guy—all his formal employment had been in office jobs—but he had the basic reservoir of tool knowledge that modern man doesn't perhaps require but could certainly stand to have. He owned a fair selection of tools, all bought for some project or other—the Chief wasn't one of those people who bought tools in the frivolous hope that a task requiring them might eventually arise.[6] That's not to say that he didn't enjoy buying a good

[4]Lest you think I hallucinated this article, it appeared in the issue of September 1984, pages 48 and 49. The mention of the handsaw was particularly odd—by the 1980s this tool had largely gone the way of the typewriter and the vinyl record. I still have a couple, but mostly for use by the kids.

[5]Channellocks are a type of adjustable wrench.

[6]The preeminent example of a tool in search of a project is surely the chain saw, which in my observation turns up surprisingly often in suburban garages—remember Mr. T?—but unless you're a lumberjack is to tools what the Hummer is to cars.

tool when he had the excuse—he was, after all, a guy, heir to 3 million years of accumulated mitochondria, whose Paleolithic predecessor had spotted an intriguing configuration of stone and thought, *Whoa, ax,* while the female of the species (you'll excuse the sexism, but one must call a spade a spade) mused, *Here is something for the knickknack shelf.*

I felt the same way myself. Already I'd purchased a reciprocating saw. A reciprocating saw—commonly but incorrectly called a Sawzall, a trade name of the Milwaukee Tool Company—is the machine pistol of power tools. It's unsuited to precision work, but rather is used chiefly to cut large irregular holes in things, or chop hunks off the end. I'd purchased it to help with demolition, in particular the cutting up of old pipes, with which the Barn House was crammed. (Each of the old apartments had been equipped with a sink, long since removed, but the pipes remained in the walls.) Mine, which I had purchased at the home improvement store on sale for $145, was a jaunty number with a yellow plastic housing, and I was as proud of it as my primordial ancestors had surely been of their clubs and spears.

Now I needed another tool—specifically, a right-angle drill, which would let me fit a bit into the narrow space between the joists and drill the holes. It was a specialized tool. The local home improvement store didn't carry it. Not a problem, said the Chief. A few minutes from his house was an establishment called Berland's House of Tools. Berland's was open late. He would go there and see what they had.

A half hour later he called back. "I'm calling from my cell phone," announced the Chief. Cell phones were not then common. "I'm in the parking lot in front of Berland's. This is an amazing place. They got all kinda tools here."

"That's probably why they call it Berland's House of Tools, as opposed to Berland's House of Pancakes," I said.

The Chief ignored this. "Get a piece of paper," he said.

"What do I need a piece of paper for?"

"Just get one."

"Chief. Tell me why I need to get a piece of paper."

The Chief sighed, as if dealing with a dim child. "I'm going to read you a list," he said. "You have to write it down."

"Why do I have to write it down? Just tell me if they have a right-angle drill."

"They got different kinds. You have to tell me which one you want."

"Tell me what they have."

"Get a piece of paper."

I'd been through discussions like this before. The Chief was perfectly willing to spend half an hour sparring over procedural details—he'd have made an ideal peace conference negotiator for the North Vietnamese. I got a piece of paper. Chief dictated model numbers, prices, and specifications. After some discussion I decided to get a unit with a three-eighths-inch chuck. (A mistake, as it turned out; the drill proved to be too fragile and was eventually replaced with a more substantial model.)

"You going to be there a while?" the Chief asked.

"Yeah, why?"

"I'll buy the drill right now and bring it out. You can pay me back later."

An hour and a half later Chief arrived at the Barn House with the drill. It was now close to ten p.m., and my only ambition was to go home, take a shower, and go to bed. The Chief, however, was just getting warmed up. I inserted a bit into the drill and got up on the ladder. The drill fit between the joists easily. In a few minutes I'd drilled a pair of holes, and in a few minutes more had fitted a couple additional lengths of pipe. We were on our way.

11

One cold Monday morning in mid-December I got a call from Tony. Bad news: The Barn House had been burglarized over the weekend.

I was annoyed but not surprised. Thefts from construction sites were common; tools and building supplies were easily fenced. The brazenness of these crimes was often astonishing. One night, Tony told me, thieves had stolen two gas furnaces from a two-flat he was renovating in Chicago's Humboldt Park neighborhood—and mind, the furnaces weren't just sitting in cardboard boxes on the job site; they had been *installed*, one of them on the second floor, with all the ducts, pipes, and wires connected. On another occasion one of Tony's men had been up on a ladder on the side of a house when he saw a van pull up next to his own vehicle on the street below. A man hopped out and began pulling tools out of the worker's vehicle and loading them into the van. When the worker began climbing down the ladder to put a stop to this, a second thief began shaking the base of the ladder, obliging the worker to hang on for dear life till the first thief was done.

Having your tools stolen was bad enough, but in the city you faced the additional risk that in the process you might get killed. Once robbers armed with handguns had entered a house where one of Jerry's crews was working, lined the men up against a wall, and taken their wallets and tools.

Now it was my turn to be a victim. I drove to the house and inspected the crime scene. I had secured one of the dingy rooms in the basement with an inexpensive lock and latch—the thief had probably needed all of five seconds to force it open. The room had contained such valuables as I had on the premises. The thieves had taken some copper pipe, the reciprocating saw—I had owned it for just five months—and a few other odds and ends. I guessed that the loss amounted to five or six hundred dollars. I went upstairs to dial 911.

The telephone at the time was located in the dining room; we had strung a long extension wire along the outside of the house from the interface box. As I waited for the call to go through I glanced at the fireplace. I noticed there was an outline on the wall where the paint ended. The shade beneath was darker and dirtier, making a scruffy silhouette. It took a moment for the significance of this to register. A carved oak mantelpiece had been bolted to the wall where the outline was. Now it was gone.

On hanging up after relating the essential details to the emergency dispatcher I was struck by a thought. There had been another mantelpiece upstairs in the front bedroom. It wasn't as elaborate as the one in the dining room; the wood was painted rather than stained. The mantel was of unusual though not unique design, with a full-length mirror along one side; I was to see a similar one at James's house in Kenwood a few weeks later. We'd removed it and stacked it with other salvaged woodwork in a room at the rear of the second floor.

I went upstairs for a look. The other mantelpiece was gone, too.

This discovery lent matters a different color. We'd been visited not by derelicts looking for drug money but by professional thieves who knew what they were after. The first mantelpiece had been displayed in a prominent place in the house; it had carved wooden pillars and a mirror, and was clearly an object of value. The second wasn't. It was covered with multiple coats of paint, the latest of which was a dingy salmon hue; there was little to distinguish it from the other jumbled woodwork with which it had been heaped. Yet these burglars had known that even relatively simple mantels commanded prices in the thousands of dollars at salvage dealers; they were by far the most valuable items then in the house.

The police when they arrived were efficient but unencouraging. They indicated a few additional points of interest. The burglars had yanked the electric meter out of its receptacle on the rear wall of the house; it lay a few feet away in the dirt. I puzzled about this at the time—if the house had been equipped with a typical burglar alarm with a battery backup, cutting the power would have automatically tripped it. But later it occurred to me that if the burglars were well schooled in their craft, they might have parked their vehicle (given the size of the haul, one assumed it was a truck) a block or two away, approached the house, pulled the meter, and strolled off. Had a siren sounded—generally there was a delay of a minute or two, to give the home owner time to disarm the system in the event of an ordinary power outage— they'd simply have kept walking. Since nothing had happened, they could be reasonably confident that the house was unprotected and return to conduct their business in peace.

The job must have taken quite a while. The cops deduced that the burglars had entered the house through a broken basement window but exited by the front door, since there was no other way to leave the building when encumbered with swag—the back steps had been demolished. The front door had been secured by a locked steel security door of the type designed to resemble wrought iron and look impregnable. Alas, this door was a fraud.

The thieves had pried it open, then carried the two mantelpieces (both close to six feet tall and perhaps four feet wide) out of the house, down the steps, and out to their vehicle, and in addition had taken the tools and copper pipe, which I knew from experience was capable of making a racket that would have rousted the deaf. Yet, I ruefully ascertained later, none of the neighbors had detected any sign of this protracted criminal adventure. We were surrounded by the soundest sleepers on earth.

By the time the police left, my initial anger had subsided, to be replaced by paranoia. You can imagine how I felt. Up to this point the project had been . . . well, fun is perhaps putting the issue a little strongly, but it had had its entertaining moments. Now matters had taken a decidedly darker turn. I imagined thieves lurking in every gangway, awaiting a moment's inattention on my part to infiltrate the premises and carry off such valuables as the first crew had overlooked. I knew too well that the best burglar alarm was the one thing we couldn't provide—human habitation. I'd read about buildings in crime-ridden parts of town that had been abandoned, or merely left unattended for a few days, and which had been descended upon by thieves and stripped of all saleable commodities, including appliances, cabinets, doors, electrical and plumbing fixtures, even pipe and wiring ripped from the walls. At the time I had been dismayed but detached, as though reading of a plague outbreak in Sri Lanka. Now those stories seemed more pertinent.

Previously innocent phenomena took on a sinister character. For many years in our old neighborhood we'd been accustomed to seeing scavengers prowling the alleys looking for discarded aluminum cans to sell at the recycling yards. We referred to these entrepreneurs as the metal guys. They used shopping carts piled to tottering heights with the day's take, which they'd stuffed in plastic bags. Some of my neighbors objected to the metal guys— in mining the garbage cans they had a tendency to leave the alley strewn with rubbish, after the manner of bears at national parks.

I took a more tolerant view—partly because of the metal guys, I was interested to learn, aluminum had by far the highest recycling rate of any commonly available consumer packaging material. Plus it kept them off the street.

In the Barn House's neighborhood the grocery-cart boys, who from a socioeconomic perspective one would have to categorize mainly as stumblebums, were joined by a more ambitious working-class type of scavenger who added a degree of mechanization to the program in the form of decrepit trucks. They cruised through the alleys looking for larger and presumably more profitable items, such as discarded washing machines, water heaters, bedsprings, and the like. In many respects these fellows performed a useful service. An appliance dealer commonly charged a fee to haul away your old refrigerator, but in the city you could leave it in the alley, confident that in days (or in one case less than an hour) it would be gone.

These operations were sometimes marked by an excess of enthusiasm. At an early stage of demolition we had hauled out a couple of ancient clawfoot bathtubs and dumped them in the backyard. I had no further use for the tubs, but one of Charlie's colleagues had expressed a mild interest in obtaining one—they'd become fashionable in some quarters. Before we could arrange the transfer, though, the tubs disappeared. I suspected a trucker who lived in the building behind us, but not knowing for certain (he professed innocence), and not being especially upset anyway about the disappearance of what I personally considered junk, I attempted merely to establish a few ground rules upon our next encounter—for example, no removal of items still attached to or clearly within the ambit of the house. The trucker took this well enough and I felt we'd reached an understanding.

The burglary obliged me to reassess the situation. I didn't suspect the metal guys, at least the ones I knew, but it seemed to me now that they were but one species of beetle in the larger urban habitat, not all denizens of which were benign. Previously I'd been in the habit of driving around with ladders and building materials casually roped to the roof of my car. Now this practice seemed unwise.

I considered my options. My basement storeroom was still full of building materials, mostly electrical supplies. On a per-pound basis they were worth less than the copper pipe, but all told the stuff had cost me close to fifteen hundred dollars. There was no point in buying a bigger latch; the closet's wooden walls were flimsy and easily breached. I walked down to Mike's house and asked if I might store my supplies in his basement. He consented at once. I spent well over an hour moving boxes of fittings and bundles of conduit. The day was cold and dry, a little above freezing, the sky an expectant teal and gray—the kind of day that under other circumstances would incline one to inspect the furnace and check the rock salt.

By the time I finished, daylight was rapidly failing. I drove to the home improvement store and bought four pairs of spotlights. When I returned I nailed them high on the four sides of the house, strung wire back to the sole live electrical outlet remaining on the second floor, and switched on the lights. They illuminated the front, rear, and side yards with a concentration-camp glow. I asked my neighbors to keep an eye out, particularly if the lights went off; they promised they would. My anxiety abated only slightly. I couldn't think what else to do.

Over the next three weeks I piped all the radiators in the front of the house. The Chief came over when he could. The process was tedious. I had to change the fittings on each radiator, manhandle it into position, mark holes in the floor for the supply pipes, move the radiator out of the way, drill the holes, push the radiator back, solder a length of pipe to each brass radiator valve and return elbow, attach the fittings to the radiators, then go downstairs and plot out how to run pipe to the nearest riser.

Installing radiator pipes was far more nerve-wracking than

electrical work. For one thing, there was a much greater chance that you would burn down the house. With electrical work, this was largely a theoretical danger, since under normal circumstances you worked with the power shut off. But piping involved the continual use of open flame, produced by the propane torch used to solder the joints.

Some joints you could solder at the bench, and many of the others weren't close to combustible material, but inevitably a few required dancing the flame off some piece of unplaned lumber that had been drying out since the Garfield administration and seemed likely to ignite if exposed to a warm breath. I attempted to direct the flame away from flammable surfaces to the extent practical, but often it was impossible to avoid scorching the wood, and occasionally the ancient timber would catch fire. I frantically doused the flames when this occurred, having filled a spray bottle with water for the purpose, but the illumination was poor and it was hard to see what I was doing. I lived in dread lest I leave for the day and some overlooked ember flare up anew.

Not for the first or last time the Chief lent a steadying hand. One day he showed up a little later than usual. "I went shopping," he said. "I thought you could use some stuff." He laid his purchases one at a time on my workbench.

"Clamp lights," he said. He produced three incandescent work lights, each with a metal reflector, a long cord, and a clamp on a swivel. You clamped the light on a board or pipe near where you were working, and aimed it at the job. Better lighting would improve the safety factor by a considerable margin. Cost: about eight dollars.

"Rags." The Chief had gotten a bundle at an auto parts store. I was going through rags at a great rate, wiping excess flux off solder joints. I had nearly exhausted our household supply of old sheets and shirts.

"Lemon Gojo." It was a tub of hand cleaner. "When I'm working on a car I always wash my hands with this stuff," the Chief said. "Cuts through the grease, doesn't dry out your hands. After you spend all day on a cruddy job, use this and you'll feel like you're clean." It was true. Washing up with Gojo became an end-of-day rite.

Items of small consequence, you may think. They didn't seem that way to me. Overwhelmed by the job in those days, I had no patience for housekeeping. The Chief did, and his domestic contributions lightened a burden that, looking back, I wonder how I would otherwise have borne.

Over the ensuing weeks the front loop gradually took shape. I was self-employed and could work at the house when other business didn't press, but under the best of circumstances, what with the need of making a living and the bales of paperwork required by the bank, I could arrange to be there at most three days a week. Even with the proper tool, drilling holes through the joists and fitting the pipes was a slow job. The mild fall weather had now ended; it was cold in the house. One morning Tony's men had arrived to find a thin sheet of ice in the toilet bowl. They installed a space heater in the dining room, in the process, I noted with chagrin, drilling a hole through the much-abused parquet floor to bring a gas line up from the basement. The space heater kept the house's interior temperature above freezing for the time being, but it wasn't yet full winter. I was none too confident that we'd be able to avoid having the water supply pipes freeze in the event of sustained cold.

Meanwhile I fretted about the job. A problem only slightly less worrisome than the danger of fire was that I had no idea if my solder joints would hold water. On occasions when I could do a joint at the workbench, it was easy enough to see that a good seal had been made. But most of the time the pipes were soldered in place, often in tight spots where it was impossible to view the entire circumference of the joint. I bought a little inspection mirror mounted on a swivel rod to enable me to see the backside of a fitting, but lacking experience in such matters I was uncertain what to look for. I dreaded the prospect of filling the system only to have the joints spout leaks like my father's bathroom plumbing. A drawback of copper pipe was that, while a proper joint wouldn't leak and required no further attention, repairing a bad one was a bear. It was tricky enough to solder a joint when the pipes were dry; it was impossible when they were filled with water, which cooled the copper below the melting point of the solder. The system would have to be drained, and even then a residual trickle could dissipate the heat. Redoing a single joint could take an hour.[1]

Things got harder still when I got down to the basement. Here the tributaries of the system joined together, and the pipes got bigger. Three-quarter- and one-inch risers ran into inch-and-a-half collectors and finally into two-inch mains at the furnace. The bigger the pipe, the harder it was to heat the joints. In some cases Chief and I had to apply two torches simultaneously. But even multiple propane torches were useless for heating the two-inch joints. The only thing to do was call Kevin the plumber. He brought over a torch and a big tank of acetylene, which burned hotter than propane and pumped out a lot more flame, and soldered the remaining dozen joints. It took him maybe half an hour. The front loop was complete at last.

And none too soon. It was December 27th; several days of single-digit temperatures were predicted. Christmas had come and gone—I had eaten roast duck at my father-in-law's with an ineradicable rind of dirt under my fingernails. I arrived at the house early; the Chief had promised to come later.

All that remained was to fill the radiators with water and light the furnace. With the assistance of the Polish carpenters I'd moved the furnace to a new location in the center of the house, Paul the

---

[1] Having learned a few tricks—the handy item known as a repair coupling was a particular revelation to me—I can do it faster now.

fireplace guy had hooked the exhaust flue to the chimney, and Kevin's boys had run in a new gas line. But the burners had never been lit. I opened the water intake, filled the boiler, wired up a thermostat, then flipped the switch. The automatic pilot made a staticky sound. But the flame didn't light.

The furnace had been covered with grit; I wondered if dirt had fouled the burners. I poked around a while. I knew nothing about furnaces; I might as well have been inspecting an atomic pile. I called the gas company. They said they'd send someone out later that day. I decided to finish filling the system, a slow process that took several hours. I inspected the joints anxiously, looking for leaks, but no moisture appeared. By early afternoon the water had reached the second floor. I noticed a dripping sound. Water was leaking from a threaded joint on a brass valve in what would eventually be a bedroom. I tightened the fitting. The leak slowed but persisted. I tightened some more. The fitting cracked. Damn. I shut off the water intake and opened the furnace drain. The water had just reached the level of the broken valve; if I backed it down a few inches I figured I could reheat the solder joint and replace the valve. After a few minutes the leak stopped; the water had drained below the break. I waited another ten minutes, closed the drain, then applied the torch. The solder melted. I replaced the valve, then resumed filling. I'd lost an hour.

It was now late afternoon and the light was fading. The gas man hadn't yet appeared. The Chief arrived and I explained the situation. He inspected the furnace. "It's a new gas line," he said. "Maybe there's air in it." He tinkered awhile without result. "Quit messing around there, Chief," I said. "Let's let the professionals do it."

I called the gas company back. It was now close to five o'clock and fully dark. I was told the gas man had rung the front door-bell and, when he got no answer, concluded that no one was home and left. "The doorbell was disconnected!" I shouted. "The house is under renovation! Did it occur to him to come round the back?" Evidently not. The earliest they could get him out again was the following morning. I was furious, but there was nothing to be done. It was a bitterly cold night; the newspaper had predicted a low of 7 degrees. If I left things as they were the water would freeze and burst the pipes. I would have to drain the system, wasting all the time needed to fill it. I shut off the water intake and got ready to open the drain.

The Chief was back on his knees tinkering with the furnace. I could hear the staticky sound from the electric pilot again. I had no idea what this meant, but it sounded ominous—for all I knew the furnace was about to explode. "Dammit, Chief, get out of there," I said. "We've got to get this thing drained."

"Wait a while," said the Chief.

He continued tinkering for some minutes. The staticky sound persisted. Suddenly there was a click followed by a *foomp*, then a low noise that grew in volume to a roar. A flickering blue light reflected off the concrete blocks beneath the burners. The furnace had ignited.

"Air in the line," said the Chief.

I was ebullient. "Chief! You're the greatest! You did it! Unbelievable!" I shook his hand and pounded him on the back. The Chief smiled contentedly and ducked out for a cigarette—Mary would have none in the house.

All I had to do now was finish filling the radiators. I opened the intake valve. There was no sound of rushing water—not a good sign. I opened the vents on the radiators on the third floor. When I had done this previously there was a hissing noise, as the water pushing up from below forced air out of the system. Now I heard nothing.

"I think the water has frozen in the pipes," I told the Chief.

I now faced a dilemma. I'd been told that if the furnace were operated with insufficient water in the system, it could overheat and crack the firebox. But I didn't know what the minimum amount of water was. It seemed unlikely that the water had frozen solid throughout; I suspected that at most there were half-inch plugs of ice in the upper reaches of the pipes. But who knew?

I discussed the matter with the Chief. "I don't think we've got any choice," I said. "We just have to run the furnace and hope enough water circulates to keep the firebox from cracking and that it melts the ice." The Chief agreed. We let the furnace continue to run. After thirty minutes or so I heard a hissing in the vents again. The bottom couple inches of the uppermost radiators began to get warm. The water had resumed rising.

By nine p.m. the radiators were full and hot. There had been no other leaks. The cheap room thermometer I'd bought a few days earlier read 50 degrees. We wouldn't be able to get it any warmer than that for two months—only half the radiators were working. The house wasn't sealed, much less insulated; many of the window openings were covered only with blue plastic tarps. The cycling of the furnace was controlled not by the thermostat but by the thermal limiter on the boiler, which switched off the burners when the water got too hot.

But I had heat in the house. There was no danger now that the water supply pipes would freeze. I could work without gloves with no risk of having my fingers get numb.

I walked around the house and inspected the work. I tell you true: Few experiences in life are so satisfying as staking out a little patch of the earth and making it warm.

I was ready to head for home. Not the Chief. Holding the reciprocating saw—I'd purchased a replacement for the one stolen—he indicated the old steel radiator pipes that still hung from the basement ceiling. "Might as well get these out of here," he said. "They're in the way."

"Ah, jeez, Chief," I said.

"Come on."

We sawed pipes till one in the morning and stacked the pieces on the lawn. When I returned to the house the following day they were gone. The metal guys had visited us again.

A few weeks later while out doing errands in the car with the family I had an epiphany.

"Ah, *shit*," I said, slapping the steering wheel.

"What's the matter?" Mary asked.

"I'm a moron," I said. I'd just realized that I needn't have bothered drilling holes for the radiator pipes in the joists. The house had ten-foot ceilings—I could have run the pipes *below* the joists, then had the carpenters frame out a drop ceiling below the pipes. It would have cost maybe $300 and taken just eight inches off the ceiling. No one would have noticed. I'd have saved three weeks.

"I should tell people about this," I said morosely. "I should write a book." That was the genesis of the present work. Shakespeare may have had nobler motives for writing, but Shakespeare, at least to his biographers' knowledge, never rehabbed a house.

12

One recognizes that home improvement shows on TV aren't high on realism—that the charming young couple hosting the program can't possibly complete the construction of that acre-size redwood deck in a half hour's time; that in fact it would take a crew of three a week; and that in nine cases out of ten a couple trying to build a deck without professional assistance would never finish at all, because they'd have previously gotten divorced. Still, miraculous feats of construction aren't the most improbable aspect of the TV shows, in my opinion. Rather, it's that the programs give the impression that the home owner will spend the bulk of the project working on his house, instead of what he really will be doing—namely, assembling paperwork, calling up the contractor, and arguing with the bank. Admittedly such scenes don't make for gripping drama, but you might as well give a presentation on human reproduction that plays up the twenty minutes of entertainment while ignoring the nine months of grief.

By early January we'd finally succeeded in getting the last of the documentation together, enabling us to close on the construction loan. This entailed a moment of ceremony. We came into the bank to sign some papers, and did; then the clerical staff made way for Wayne. Wayne's role in the loan approval process had never been entirely clear to us. He was a vice president, but that meant nothing; as far as I could tell, everyone at the bank was a vice president. As now became plain, however, a key part of his job was to impart cautionary wisdom.

Wayne settled into his chair with the satisfied air of a man about to give a well-honed performance. Time has obscured some of the details, but the flavor of it was as follows:

"Let me tell you what's going to happen," he began. "You've got a lot of decisions to make. You're going to be picking out countertops, and one of you is going to say, you know, honey, wouldn't granite look nice instead of Formica? And the other one is going to say, sure, sweetheart, no problem. Then you'll be looking at bathroom fixtures, and you'll think, that steam shower, that would sure be nice—or what about a Jacuzzi? And you'll say, hey, no problem. That front hall. You'll want some nice tile there. A chandelier. A carpet upgrade. They're not that much money, and when will there be a better time? So you'll say, no problem." Wayne went on in this vein for some time. He was really quite amusing.

At length he roused himself for the big finish. "And then the bills are going to come in. And you know what? *Problems.*" We laughed. Wayne drew the appropriate moral about the importance of not getting carried away. We promised we'd be good.

Fact was, the bank wasn't going to give us many opportunities to get carried away. For starters, we didn't get a lump sum— anyone daffy enough to rehab a house in the city wasn't someone you wanted to entrust with large sums of cash. Rather, the contractor would submit a bill, usually once a month or upon completion of the work, and the bank, having satisfied itself that all was in order, would pay the contractor. First, however, the bank wanted us to sink enough of our own money into the project that we weren't likely to walk away. The amount required was 20 percent of the value of the work—about $60,000—and what's more, we had to prove we'd spent it. It was at this point that I learned that my days of document production had only just begun. I was about to be introduced to lien waivers.

It occurs to me that perhaps everyone else in America in those days knew about lien waivers, and I alone suffered from some peculiar disability that prevented me from grasping what was required. If so, please disregard the following tedious narrative—all I know is it was a slow job for me. The basic concept wasn't that complicated. The law in Illinois, and I imagine most everywhere else, allowed tradespeople who had worked on your house to place a mechanic's lien—a claim—against the title to the property if they felt they hadn't been justly compensated for their trouble. Thereafter the lien traveled with the deed. In theory, I guess, the lien was a noble thing—it ensured that humble artisans would get their day in court. But as far as the real estate industry was concerned the lien was the equivalent of cooties. It was to be avoided at all costs. If the property was sold, the lien either had to be settled or "insured over"—that is to say, the title insurance company had to agree it would pay the judgment if the lien was finally settled in the tradesperson's favor. This the title company wasn't eager to do. I don't know that anyone's house was ever sold at a sheriff's sale for failure to pay the plumber, but I guess from a legal standpoint the possibility was there.

In a construction loan, the property was the bank's security, and the bank didn't want to have its title encumbered by liens in the event of foreclosure. So the bank demanded that in making payments to tradespeople the owner obtain lien waivers in exchange, by virtue of which the tradespeople certified that they'd gotten what they had coming. With me so far? As I say, it wasn't a complicated concept.

The problem was that lien waivers had to be completed in precisely the right way. It was the Noh drama thing again. The person in charge of making sure I did this was Sonja, who worked at the title company, which made payouts to the contractor on behalf of the bank.

The main thing to know about Sonja is that she was beautiful. Probably she had been chosen for her job for that reason, on the argument that when, as undoubtedly happened two or three times a week, a home owner became so popeyed with rage at her endless demands that he leaped across the desk to strangle her, he would be so mesmerized by her striking physical presence as to allow her the necessary few milliseconds to make her escape. The strategy had obviously worked; she still looked pretty healthy by the time she got to me.

Sonja's title was escrow administrator, and her job was to make sure you filled out the paperwork right. I was, as I say, a slow student. There were two types of lien waiver forms. The pink ones, headed "Partial Waiver of Lien," were intended for interim payments; the blue ones, entitled "Final Waiver of Lien," were to be filled out when the job, or at least the subcontractor's portion of it, was complete. On the first go-round with my subcontractors I had gotten the forms mixed up. Oops. On the second try I neglected to get the papers notarized (nobody told *me* they had to be notarized). The third time I omitted the following magical incantation, which was to be printed on the affidavit at the bottom of each waiver: ALL MATERIALS TAKEN FROM FULLY PAID STOCK, DELIVERED TO JOB SITE IN OUR OWN TRUCK. ALL LABOR PAID TO DATE. PRINCIPAL SUPPLIER IS: [whoever].

There were other documents to be filled out as well—sworn contractor's statements, owner's payment authorization forms, materials waivers, W-9 forms. I messed those up plenty too, and the ones I didn't, Tony did. (Tony also was required to submit documentation out the wazoo.) Many times the mistakes were my fault, generally because I hadn't followed instructions, one of my many chronic failings. Other times, to be honest, I don't know what I did wrong, except that in Sonja's unappeasable opinion it *was* wrong, and neither I nor anybody else was going to get any money until I got it right.

Then again, it's not as though I were uniquely stupid. Sonja's practice, on initial receipt of a batch of paperwork, was to issue a "corrections letter," the purpose of which was to enumerate in exasperating detail exactly what you'd done wrong. Everyone with a building loan got these letters, I gathered; the main difference was how long they were—my first one ran to six pages. What's more, after I dutifully resubmitted what I hoped were properly filled-out documents—not easy, because arranging for yourself, a busy tradesperson, and a notary to be in the same place at the same time was no trivial task—I sometimes got a second letter apprising me of certain necessary corrections to my corrections, which as far as I was concerned was the equivalent of failing the fifth grade twice.

I plugged away as best I could, ranting periodically to the loan officer at the bank, a young fellow named Chris. (Wayne, his fiduciary duty fulfilled, had moved on to other things.) "This is a crazy lady!" I howled at one point. Chris found this amusing, which mitigated my irritation to some degree; bankers rarely found anything amusing. However, the entertainment value I evidently provided didn't prevent Chris from imposing still more requirements. One day, for example, it occurred to him (or to someone; one never knew who in the bank had had these inspirations) that the Barn House should be periodically inspected by a licensed architect other than Howard or Charlie to ensure that the work had been done properly. What's more, Chris informed me, I would be expected to pay for the privilege, at $300 a pop. *Fine*, I said. *Anything else? X-ray the solder joints? Bulls tickets? Hire your brother-in-law to guard the blue tarp?* Chris laughed. But others expected things from me and didn't find the matter funny at all.

The Chicago building department, and city inspectors in Chicago generally, have long been notorious for petty graft. "Petty" is the operative term here. Corruption-wise the serious money in Chicago, at least on a per-transaction basis, is made at the higher levels of government. Chicago aldermen are legendary for their industry in this regard—between 1972 and 1999, twenty-six were convicted of felonies, mostly involving bribes, with occasional instances of embezzlement, extortion, fraud, ghost payrolling, and other malfeasance thrown in. At least two other aldermen were indicted but had their trials halted or indefinitely postponed due to failing health; even if we cast those aside, 14 percent of the people who served as Chicago aldermen over a twenty-seven-year period, or roughly one in seven (fifty hold office at any one time), were found guilty of corruption. A statistic like that inspires a sort of awe.[1]

Even an alderman, if one judged from the newspapers, was unlikely to get rich from bribery alone. The typical aldermanic payoff was on the order of $5,000, which bought you a zoning change.[2] A few got more—I once had a pleasant lunch with a pair of disgraced ex-aldermen, one of whom had done time for pocketing $50,000 (the property involved was unusually large, and the

[1] I should clarify, perhaps unnecessarily, that 14 percent isn't the highest conviction rate for a class of public officials in the state of Illinois. Of the past nine individuals who have concluded terms as governor, four have been charged with felonies and three convicted, one admittedly for crimes committed after leaving office. The fifth, the notorious Rod Blagojevich, was impeached and removed from office in 2009, following his arrest on federal corruption charges.

[2] Chicago aldermen for many years have had de facto control over zoning changes within their wards due to a custom known as "aldermanic privilege," in which they automatically approve each other's zoning requests when they come up for a vote in city council. Some aldermen now decide zoning controversies based on straw votes at community meetings, but aren't required to do so, and accusations of shady dealing are often heard to this day.

recipient unusually influential), and an enterprising council member in the 1970s stole close to $100,000 from the federally funded jobs program he ran. As a rule, though, the truly life-changing boodle—the put-your-kid-through-college kind, as opposed to the week-in-Vegas variety—went to those who could influence the awarding of government contracts, where millions were at stake. In 1987, for example, a former Chicago Park District official who had been in charge of the city's lakefront harbors was charged with taking a $200,000 kickback for steering business to a marine contractor.[3]

In contrast, the amounts involved in inspector payoffs were often laughably small. In 1978, four Chicago building department supervisors were found guilty of taking $50,000 in bribes, a sum made more impressive by the fact that it had been collected in increments of $25 to $50 over a period of eight years. On the same day twenty-seven of the city's seventy electrical inspectors were charged with taking bribes ranging from a few dollars to $100. In 1985, eleven of the city's nineteen sewer inspectors plus three former inspectors were indicted for soliciting 1,287 bribes totaling $74,556 over the preceding fifteen years—an average of $58 per bribe.[4]

The mid-1980s were the high-water mark of small-time municipal corruption in Chicago in modern times, if one judges from the newspapers. While inspector busts continued to be re-

[3]The park district continues to be a rewarding place to work. In 2005, another parks official was indicted for accepting kickbacks worth $137,000 from a landscaping company.

[4]Too much of this can be tedious, but in the interest of completeness I should say that in 1986, as part of a long-running federal investigation of city licensing and inspection practices called Operation Phocus, more than sixty-five people were indicted, including (I quote from the *Chicago Sun-Times*) "consumer services and building inspectors, firemen, police officers, businessmen, lawyers, park district workers, an ex-alderman, a state senator, and a judge." The accused included thirteen of eighteen inspectors in the city's consumer

First day of exterior demolition, 1993.
Note the ungainly roofline, the result of a 1930s remodeling.

Construction gets under way, 1993. Tony the Polish contractor
is on the sidewalk; his brother Jerry is on the right side of the porch.

Kitchen eating area, 1993. Note the nonfunctional wooden beam at the top of the photo.

First floor rear bedroom, 1993. Note the collapsed ceiling due to a leaking roof.

Second floor rear porch, 1993.

Basement laundry area, 1993.

Second floor kitchen, 1993—a relic of the Barn House's
pre-WWII conversion to multifamily use.

Ani and Ryan Zotti in the Barn House's overgrown rear yard, 1993.

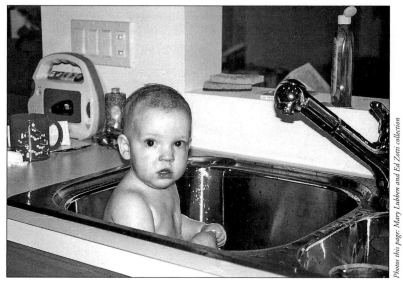

Andrew Zotti taking a bath in the kitchen sink, 1994.

Front porch, 2008.

Kitchen eating area, 2008.

Restored front hall, 2008.

Improvised railing at the top of
the front hall stairs, 1993.

New railing, 2008.

Family room (first floor rear), 2008.

Master bedroom (second floor rear), 2008.

Dining room, 2008.

Dining room fireplace following the theft of the mantelpiece, 1993.

Restored dining room fireplace, 2008.

Ed Zotti and Mary Lubben in the Barn House kitchen, 2008.

ported, mostly from that point forward they involved individuals rather than half the department at once. With a few exceptions, the amounts remained small. In 1990, one building inspector was arrested after soliciting a $50 payoff, another for taking $400 to overlook safety violations in an apartment building. In 1992, an environmental inspector was accused of accepting six bribes ranging from $10 to $25.

Compared to the epic thievery of previous decades, it sounds pretty nickel-and-dime, and it's possible that by the time we started work on the Barn House street-level corruption in Chicago was more the exception than the rule. But I wouldn't have put good money on it, and doubt most Chicagoans would have.[5] At any rate, I contemplated my upcoming dealings with city inspectors with apprehension.

My encounters with the city to that point had been relatively benign. In mid-summer the local ward superintendent, a good-natured but formidable woman of the sort one knows instinctively not to cross, had shown up at the house to chastise me for letting my contractor load the garbage carts with putrefying goo, to the distress of the garbagemen. In fact it wasn't the contractor who had ditched the goo, it was me—I had scooped it out from under the decaying basement stairs, the partially liquefied remains

---

services department, who were charged with shaking down small-business owners for amounts ranging from $10 to $2,500. Inspectors weren't the only city employees supplementing their incomes. During the late 1980s, thirty Chicago police officers pleaded guilty to dropping off corpses at friendly undertakers in return for payments ranging from $25 to $75.

[5]An indication of public expectations in this regard is the fact that during the 1990s a steady trickle of entrepreneurs was arrested for extorting payoffs from small-business owners, the catch being that the bad guys weren't city inspectors, they only claimed to be (one had worked in the city clerk's office for six weeks). One supposes the victims might have been a little more diligent about demanding identification, but come on, it was Chicago. A guy came in saying he was a city inspector and demanded a bribe. What more proof of bona fides did you need?

of leaves seemingly unraked since V-J Day. I professed shock and promised the ward superintendent I wouldn't let my guys get away with it again.

Then came Benny, the plumbing inspector. He was a hulking older man with a grim expression; he breathed with a rasp. He stopped by one afternoon to check progress to that point. He said little, glancing without much interest at the cast-iron soil stack and other pipework that the plumbers had installed.

On the way out he noticed a tangle of discarded electrical switchboxes and cabling lying on the floor. "You need those switchboxes?" he asked. I didn't. Benny wanted them for some project. The switchboxes were the deeper-than-normal kind you didn't see much in stores anymore. *No problem,* I said, *they're yours. Save them for me,* said Benny. He would stop by to pick them up.

The next morning I arrived at the house early. About eight a.m. there was a rap on the door. It was Benny.

"You got the switchboxes?" he asked, his tone suggesting I'd better. I was a little taken aback, having expected I might see him in a week. *Uh, sure,* I said. I hunted up my tools and set to work disconnecting armored cable while Benny watched grimly, breathing heavily all the while.

After a few minutes I handed the salvaged hardware to Benny. He grunted an acknowledgment and left. *Well,* I thought as I watched him go, *if that's all Chicago building inspectors are demanding nowadays, I've got no reason to complain.*

Others didn't get off so easy. Kevin the plumber told me Benny had instructed him to deliver a load of plumbing supplies, at Kevin's cost, to Benny's daughter's house in the suburbs. A neighbor who rehabilitated apartment buildings told me he'd had difficulty getting the plans for one of his projects approved. When he asked about the holdup, he received the cryptic response, "Oh, that's one of Benny's jobs." But I was lucky. I never saw Benny again.

13

One of the pleasures of renovating an old house is that, once a basic scheme of operation has been established, the work doesn't fully occupy the mind. You have to pay some minimal level of attention, of course, lest you slice off a leg or suffer some other disaster, but the essentials having been dealt with, you're free to ponder other things.

I'd now arrived at that point with the piping of the radiators. The work had become routine, although engagingly so. I was nowhere near as proficient a pipe fitter as I was an electrician, but I'd attained a certain threshold competence. I knew the system would work. I had to pause periodically to noodle out some knotty detail, but had no doubt I would.

In short, life had lightened up. Notwithstanding the edge of desperation that had come to be a constant feature of the project, there was something therapeutic about working with your hands, and it was in this moderately cheery state that I began to contemplate my surroundings. It was now possible to see the house's framing in all its unencumbered glory. Howard had been right: The house had good bones. Indeed, from the standpoint of scale, it had bones such as are to be found in no house built in the last half century, log cabins set aside. It was all very well to see balloon framing illustrated in books. The reality was more impressive.

During breaks I strolled around inspecting the premises. The house had been framed so that, except in the odd cranny (the joists I had to drill through for the radiator pipes were in one), the studs and joists were sixteen inches apart, measured centerline to centerline. The great majority of houses in the United States are built to this standard, which has prevailed since at least the Civil War.[1] That may seem unimportant, even obsessive, but in fact it's pretty handy. Because of it you can hang forty-eight-inch-wide sheets of drywall without having to custom fit each piece; you can run standard-width air-conditioning ducts between studs; you can install standard insulation, which is fourteen and a half inches wide, the distance between the facing sides of studs or joists. (Truth be told, insulation installed in an old house will be a little snug, because two-by-fours sawn a hundred years ago are three-sixteenths of an inch wider than those cut yesterday afternoon, but luckily the fiberglass readily compresses.) You can, in short, retrofit an old house . . . well, I won't say cheaply, but at least in a relatively systematic and predictable way. For this you can thank the standardization of American building practice ushered in by balloon framing.

Balloon framing is treated only briefly, if respectfully, in histories of architecture and construction because, frankly, there isn't much to tell. The technique was invented in Chicago in 1833 by

---

[1] Actually, there are two standard widths, sixteen inches and twenty-four inches, the former by far the more common. When exactly these spacings became routine practice I don't know. Howard told me he'd restored an 1869 house in Evanston that had been framed on twenty-four-inch centers, and for all I know they date from the introduction of balloon framing in 1833.

one Augustine D. Taylor, a carpenter from Connecticut who'd been commissioned to build the city's first Catholic church. The pastor of this church, it's safe to say, wasn't free with cash—the contract amount was $400, ultimately paid in the form of eight hundred silver half-dollars. The standard wood construction methods of the day called for a "New England frame" of heavy beams and posts held together with hand-hewn mortise and tenon joints, construction of which required a large crew of skilled carpenters. Undoubtedly realizing that if he built the church in this way he'd lose his shirt, Taylor devised a new method of framing using two-by-fours and nails, mass production of which had been perfected a short time before. His essential insight was that a building composed of many lightweight timbers was just as strong as one made of a few heavy ones, and was boatloads easier to erect. Taylor's approach had two advantages: (1) the materials were abundant and cheap; and (2) assuming you had one guy who knew what he was doing (presumably Taylor), you could get by with three carpenters, two of whom could be relatively unskilled helpers.[2] Balloon framing was quickly adopted for residential and other light construction throughout the United States and made possible the explosive growth of American cities during the nineteenth century.

Useful as balloon framing was, it had a significant drawback: Buildings constructed in this way were firetraps. Balloon-framed walls were hollow; wall insulation in those days was unknown. The space enclosed by the long timbers provided an unobstructed

---

[2]That said, let's not get ridiculous about it. Some historians—the late Carl Condit, for one—claim a balloon-framed house could be built by a single carpenter. It's possible, though in my opinion not easy, for an unassisted carpenter to erect a *platform*-framed house, to be described shortly in the main text. However, the longest wall in the Barn House consists of twenty-nine two-by-sixes each twenty-seven feet long. I suppose it could have been raised in sections, but I'd like to see one guy do it by himself even so. I'll bring the doughnuts.

passage—a flue, if you will—from the basement to the attic. If a fire started in the basement and reached the exterior walls, it would race up to the roof in minutes, and there went the house, and possibly the neighborhood. City houses in those days were built close together; firefighting methods were primitive. Not surprisingly, catastrophic fires in nineteenth-century cities were common. Everyone has heard of the Chicago fire of 1871 (300 dead, 18,000 buildings destroyed) and the San Francisco earthquake and fire of 1906 (498 dead, 28,000 buildings destroyed). But we've largely forgotten the Seattle fire of 1889 (29 square blocks destroyed, including most of the city's downtown), the Boston fire of 1872 (775 buildings destroyed), the Baltimore fire of 1904 (1,526 buildings), the St. Louis fire of 1849 (430 buildings), and the Pittsburgh fire of 1845 (1,200 buildings). Probably there are others, but those are the ones that came up when I Googled "great *xxx* fire," substituting for *xxx* the names of the first dozen large U.S. cities that popped into my head. As I say, they had a lot of fires in those days.

As it turned out, there was a relatively easy way to eliminate the flue problem, although it wasn't universally adopted for a hundred years. An example was then taking shape at the rear of the Barn House, where the carpenters were constructing the kitchen, the family room, and the master bedroom. It was called platform framing. Rather than heave up exterior studs extending the height of the building, the carpenters were building the addition one story at a time—raising the walls, decking over the result with floor joists and plywood (a platform), then starting the next floor. The platform prevented easy passage of flame from one floor to the next; fire-resistant fiberglass wall insulation filling the space between the studs provided an additional measure of safety.

Fire prevention wasn't the only reason carpenters abandoned balloon framing for platform framing, though. The other reason was perhaps more urgent, and not without some relevance today: They'd used up the wood.

Therein lies an instructive tale. The Barn House had been erected at the height of what may be unblushingly described as the golden age of wood construction in the United States. You may object: *The golden age of wood? That's like talking about the golden age of linoleum.* Wood is so . . . ordinary. Just my point. Wood was the default material for every application at the time of the Barn House's construction. It had been used not just for the framing—90 percent of American homes are still framed with wood—but for the siding (cedar clapboards over pine boards, in contrast to the vinyl or aluminum over waferboard sheathing commonly seen today), the roof (cedar shakes rather than asphalt shingles), flooring (oak or maple over pine planking rather than tile or carpet over plywood), even the wooden lath that supported the plaster. In the basement, six-by-six-inch pine posts supported eight-by-ten beams, which in turn carried two-by-ten floor joists. The doors were solid pine or oak, not the hollow-core wood or metal variety common now. The wooden baseboards were eleven inches high and topped with a formidable milled cap. Each window and door was trimmed with a five-inch-wide decorative wooden frame consisting of a finely milled casing surrounded by an equally complicated backband (to my ear the terms have a fittingly old-fashioned ring, though they're familiar enough to finish carpenters). Wood had been used for purposes for which it was patently unsuited, such as the tracks for the pocket doors, which in all likelihood due to friction and misalignment hadn't opened freely since the time the house was built. (We eventually replaced those on the heavier door with steel.) The only things not made of wood in the place were the foundation, chimneys, glass, plaster, wiring, hardware, tile, and pipes—and in old cities from time to time you heard of backhoe operators unearthing even pipes made of wood, usually cored-out logs or sometimes large-diameter tubes assembled from staves like a barrel.

The Barn House's profligate use of wood was typical of its era, when the American economy depended on wood to an extent that today we find hard to fathom. Wood was the country's principal building material and fuel source and easiest source of cash. In 1865, forest products accounted for half the internal revenue of the United States. True, the most prestigious buildings were constructed of masonry, and later masonry and steel; increasingly building codes in the larger cities required that permanent structures be made of fireproof materials, particularly after the 1871 disaster in Chicago. Nonetheless, wood remained by far the most common U.S. building material throughout the nineteenth century. Building styles originating in Europe and employed there largely in masonry buildings—the Greek Revival, the Italianate, the Gothic Revival, the Queen Anne—were imported to America and rendered in wood. The wide availability of machine-made wooden ornament from the 1870s onward made it possible to produce what now strike us as fantastically ornate buildings at modest cost. The wealthiest Americans built palatial country "cottages" out of wood, the most spectacular in what the architectural historian Vincent Scully has termed the Shingle Style, so called because they were covered in cascades of wooden shingles.

The significance of all this didn't fully penetrate till I got talking to Chester, the chief Polish carpenter. Chester was a big, friendly St. Bernard of a man with an extraordinary capacity for taking pains—I'd seen him spend hours after the other carpenters had gone home one afternoon shimming the family room floor joists till they were precisely level and true. One day I asked Chester whether carpentry in Poland was the same as carpentry in the United States.

No, he said. Houses in Poland were built primarily of masonry. Polish carpenters used wood mainly for interior work—trim, stairs, cabinetry and so on (one reason they did such beautiful work, it occurred to me—they'd been trained in the expectation that everything would show). Later I realized why Polish and American construction methods differed—the United States had big forests to supply the wood, and Poland didn't. What's more, when the Barn House had been built, the United States had had *really* big forests—so big that it's fair to say that at the time most Americans, certainly including the inhabitants of the upper Midwest, thought of the countryside not as farmland sporadically interrupted by trees, as now, but rather as a continuous carpet of forest at which civilization was slowly nibbling away. The Barn House's oversized timbers had been cut from the gigantic trees in this seemingly infinite expanse. This was the virgin forest.

I'm far from the first to marvel at the virgin forest, but it remains a topic on which it's worthwhile to dawdle. At the start of European settlement nearly half the land area of the future United States, 822 million acres, was covered with trees. Virtually all the country east of the Mississippi—the Illinois prairie was the major exception—consisted of a single uninterrupted expanse of timber. By 1920 it was mostly gone, felled in an orgy of tree-cutting the like of which hasn't been seen before or since. Today we scold the Brazilians for laying waste to the Amazon rain forest, but Americans a century ago cut more trees in less time with fewer people. By 2007, the better part of five hundred years after the start of European settlement, Brazilians had despoiled not quite 20 percent of the billion acres of Amazon rain forest under their control—195 million acres. (Admittedly most of the clearing has occurred since 1970.) By 1920, in contrast, Americans had cleared or radically disturbed more than 80 percent of the virgin timberlands of the United States—684 million acres.[3]

The trees of the upper Midwest, which supplied the raw material for the Barn House, were particularly prized. Mostly they

[3]Estimating the size of the primeval forest is an inexact art. Here I follow Michael Williams, *Americans & Their Forests* (1989). Lest I be accused of exaggerating, let me clarify that the original forest cover had been reduced to 470 million acres by 1920, of which just 138 million were primeval forest. Of the rest, Williams says, 250 million acres had been disturbed by grazing, cutting, and burning, and 81 million acres were "wasted"—that is, reduced to unusable stumps.

were white or Norway pines, part of the boreal forest known as the North Woods, which extended as far east as Maine and New Brunswick and as far north as Hudson Bay. White pines were straight and tall—some specimens reached a height of two hundred feet. The wood was strong, durable, largely free of knots, and easily worked. The lumber could readily be gotten out—the central part of the continent was served by a wide-reaching system of lakes and rivers that, with a few man-made additions, made it possible to distribute midwestern lumber almost anywhere in the eastern two-thirds of the country via the Great Lakes, the Erie Canal, and the Mississippi River and its tributaries. New technology—the circular mill saw, steam railroads, tractors—permitted the cutting and milling of lumber on an industrial scale. With the pine forests of New England depleted, loggers eyeing the upper Midwest thought: *Whoa.*

In 1898, a Chicago lumberman-turned-historian named George Hotchkiss estimated that the states of the old Northwest Territory (Michigan, Wisconsin, Minnesota, Indiana, and Illinois, although Illinois's contribution was relatively minor) had once been covered by a trillion board feet of commercial-quality lumber, the majority of it pine—enough to reach from the earth to the sun and back. He may have exaggerated, but not by much. Some 310 billion board feet of pine were cut and sold during the heyday of midwestern lumbering. The boom didn't last long. Commercial logging of the Midwest began in earnest around 1840, reached its height between 1860 and 1900, then entered a steep decline and by 1930 had all but ceased.

The process was appallingly wasteful. The circular saws of the day had such wide blades, typically five-sixteenths of an inch, that a mill sawing one-inch planks turned 312 board feet into sawdust for every thousand feet cut.[4] Logged-off stumplands full of pine

---

[4]The wide kerf partly explains why a two-by-four measures less than two by four inches. A typical framing member in the Barn House was one-and-

cuttings were subject to repeated wildfires. On October 8, 1871, one such fire destroyed Peshtigo, Wisconsin, and neighboring towns, killing fifteen hundred people—a catastrophe that went largely unnoticed because of the fire that leveled Chicago the same day.[5]

Still, the plundering of the forests had its benefits, the foremost being that it helped create, in addition to the Barn House, the country we now know. Tree clearance opened up 300 million acres of prime agricultural land. Midwestern logging generated more wealth than the California gold rush. The unavailability of heart pine flooring, it's true, wouldn't have appreciably altered the

---

eleven-sixteenths inches wide—the boards had been gang-cut, with the blades set every two inches on centers, and five-sixteenths inch had been reduced to sawdust. Two-by-fours today are even smaller, only one and a half inches wide, which has been explained away as shrinkage due to kiln drying, but inasmuch as blades are now thinner I think we can at least partly blame the lumber industry's predisposition to be cheap.

[5]The following story has little to do with the nominal subject of this book, but I can't bear to omit it. In the early hours of the Chicago fire, the wind was blowing out of the southeast, and the flames threatened Holy Family Church and St. Ignatius College, an impressive complex of buildings about a mile southwest of the Chicago central business district and five blocks from Mrs. O'Leary's barn. (Yes, there really was a Mrs. O'Leary, and the fire did start in her barn, although the bit about the cow and the lantern was a reporter's invention.) The founder, pastor, and chief fund-raiser of Holy Family and St. Ignatius was a formidable Dutch Jesuit named Father Arnold Damen. In the baroque version of the story, Father Damen stands on the porch of St. Ignatius and prays that his life's work might be spared. At the last moment the Almighty answers his prayers and causes the wind to clock around to the southwest. The fire, which till then has been driving toward the outskirts of town, promptly shifts direction, sparing the church and instead burning down the rest of Chicago, including the central business district and most structures of consequence constructed up to that time. For generations St. Ignatius alumni proudly told this story, illustrating, as others have pointed out, the somewhat narrow priorities of American Catholics at the time. The reality was slightly less dramatic. Father Damen was in Brooklyn at the time he made his prayer, and although the wind did shift, the fire missed the church and school by a fairly wide margin. But still.

course of American civilization. But balloon framing and cheap wood—in 1874, a thousand board feet of lumber could be had at wholesale for six dollars, one-sixty-seventh of the average price 125 years later—made it possible to populate a largely empty continent fast.[6]

Late Victorian wooden buildings like the Barn House—built from, say, 1875 to 1900—were the fullest flowering of this extravagant era. The larger examples, plus a few others built in the early twentieth century, collectively constitute the most elaborate wooden structures ever erected in the United States. Mainly they were built for pleasure, or the business of pleasure—suburban houses, summer homes, country estates and clubhouses, resort hotels (one of the largest still extant, the Hotel del Coronado near San Diego, extends over thirty-one acres and incorporates 3 million shingles). Wood let you do things that could be achieved with more durable materials only at vastly greater expense. Queen Annes in particular[7] were purposely built to be picturesque, full

---

[6]Chicago, if I may be permitted a bit of hometown pride, had played a central role in the reduction of the forest. It had been built where it was because the site was near the subcontinental divide separating the Mississippi and the Great Lakes–St. Lawrence basins. The term divide suggests a mighty prominence; the Midwest being what it is, the reality is less impressive—an imperceptible rise that separates the Des Plaines River, which flows south, from the Chicago River, which, when it flowed at all, generally during rainstorms, flowed east. (The rest of the time it stagnated—much of the low-lying region was a swamp.) In 1673, it occurred to a French explorer named Louis Joliet, who had portaged his canoe the short distance between the two waterways, that a canal would greatly simplify his life, not to mention inland commerce, and 175 years later one was built—the Illinois and Michigan Canal, which opened in 1848. The I&M made it possible, if not easy, to transport goods across the continent from the Atlantic Ocean to the Gulf of Mexico entirely by water. By 1856, Chicago had surpassed Albany to become the leading wholesale lumber center in the United States, and as much for that reason as any other became a great city. San Francisco, another nineteenth-century boomtown, became a great city, too, but San Francisco had gold. Chicago did it with cows, grain, and two-by-fours.

[7]Acknowledging again the murky state of the terminology for the residential

of turrets and balconies and sprawling porches (the Barn House's porch wasn't especially expansive, but those of many Queen Annes in the neighborhood and near my parents' house in Oak Park were). The style wasn't original—it had been invented in the UK, after all—and I suppose we'd have to concede it was sentimental. But it was fun and democratic in a way the more celebrated residential architecture of the period wasn't. My house and others like it had been the work of ordinary folk whose goal wasn't to awe but to delight—and how often, where the built environment is concerned, can you say that?[8]

It couldn't last. After the turn of the century the use of wood receded, partly because wood was becoming scarcer and the price was starting to rise, at least in the Northeast and Midwest. (The construction of enormous wooden houses persisted for some years on the West Coast, where large stands of timber remained and lumber prices presumably were lower.) Builders began substituting cheaper materials—stucco for cedar siding, asphalt shingles for wooden ones. Platform framing replaced balloon framing to some extent because the enormous timbers required for the latter were growing hard to come by. Per capita consumption of lumber plummeted, as did the use of wood for fuel, the coal in-

---

architecture of this period, I note that the term "Queen Anne" wasn't uniformly popular at the time—by the mid-1880s some considered it old-fashioned and preferred "eclectic." The Shingle Style has been described as an extension of the Queen Anne—certainly there's considerable overlap between the two. The Barn House, for example, though not a Shingle Style house by any stretch, had some features of the style, notably a pair of steep shingled gables.

[8]I'm not the first to think this. Vincent Scully has written: "No American . . . can look back upon those houses without some nostalgia, disappointment, or even sorrow. They promised a great deal for American life which has not been fulfilled. . . . They were the freest and, on the whole, among the most generous forms that the United States has yet produced, and . . . in their own way . . . also the gentlest." He was speaking of Shingle Style and earlier Stick Style houses, but no bright line separates these from most other high-end wooden residential building of the period, including Queen Annes.

dustry having taken over the market. Annual U.S. consumption of wood—and I mean the aggregate for the entire country, not per capita—peaked in 1907 and thereafter dropped by a sixth, not surpassing the earlier total until the 1980s, by which time the country's population was more than three times as large.

Depending on your point of view, therefore, you might regard the Barn House as either the gift of a lost age or a symbol of unsustainable recklessness. What you weren't entitled to do, in my opinion, was claim it represented some high-water mark of quality from which all subsequent home building represented a retreat. I knew this because I was seeing even then what the Polish carpenters could do.

At some point during the siege of the radiators—I don't recall exactly when, except that it was a sunny day and the house was silhouetted against a cloudless blue sky—I drove up to the Barn House, glanced at the roof, and realized immediately that something was wrong. Although only a couple of rafters were in place, I could see that the pitch of the reconstructed turret roof now beginning to take shape was too shallow. I went upstairs to consult with Chester, who showed me the drawings. They called for a 1:1 rise, and that was what he and the other carpenters were building—and from the standpoint of construction technique, doing an admirable job. Looked at from above, the turret roof was octagonal. This wasn't the sort of thing readily framed, and Charlie, at our direction (we were trying to save money), hadn't provided any detailed drawings of how it was to be accomplished, on the optimistic assumption that the carpenters could figure it out. Chester's solution had been to install an octagonal king post, or upright central timber, that as far as I could tell he had basically whittled out of a four-by-four. The base of the king post rested on what would eventually be ceiling joists in my third-floor office; a rafter from each of the eight corners of the turret roof was to rest against one of the eight sides of the king post, making a sort of teepee. (There were a few more subtleties, but that was the gist.) Though far from complete, it was already a pretty piece of work.

Unfortunately, through no fault of Chester's, it was wrong. The slope of the transept roof, which the turret roof had to match, wasn't 1:1 but 4:3—the turret roof looked squashed by comparison. I called Charlie. He was apologetic. The third-floor framing had been so butchered during the 1930s remodeling that there was no easy way to determine the slope of the transept roof—he'd had to estimate. I groused that this wasn't the sort of thing safely left to guesswork. He didn't argue, but there we were. I informed Chester. He didn't look happy, but recognized what had to be done—namely, take the whole thing apart and start over, including whittling another king post; the new roof would be higher and the first post was too short. The following morning he gamely began.

A few days later I realized we had another problem. Paul the solid-flue guy, once he'd rebuilt the buckled chimney wall, had rebuilt the chimney top, partly because it was crumbling but mostly because we needed some additional height to clear the rebuilt turret roof, as required by city code. Now the roof was to be taller still, which meant that the chimney needed to be so as well. Unfortunately, Paul, who like just about everyone who worked on the Barn House had a bit of the artist in him, had terminated the chimney with a corbel—which is to say, the top flared out, each of the uppermost half dozen or so courses of bricks extending a half inch farther into space than the one immediately beneath. It was a handsome piece of masonry, but now it needed to be about three feet taller. I called Charlie again.

"So Charlie," I said, "not to be critical, but not only is Chester tearing down the framing for the turret roof and starting over, at a cost of who knows how many thousands of dollars [in the event, two], I'm also going to have to have Paul tear off the corbeling and do *that* all over again. You know I have vast wealth, Charlie, but I was seriously not counting on having to rebuild this damned house twice."

Charlie was silent for a moment. "Well," he said, "you don't necessarily have to have Paul tear off the corbeling. He could just corbel back in, go up three feet, then corbel back out again."

I tried to envision this. "Let me see if I follow you," I said. "I zig out, then I zag in, then I zig out again. This is how they built the Leaning Tower of Pisa, Charlie."

"Nah, it'll look sharp. I'll do a drawing. You'll see."

The following morning the drawing arrived by fax. Charlie had provided front and side views. The side view showed the chimney guyed to the turret roof by what I took to be an ornamental wrought-iron strut—it looked like something out of *Mary Poppins*. I called Charlie and asked where he expected me to find a strut.

"Oh, that's optional," Charlie said. "Never mind that. The chimney looks cool, doesn't it?"

I studied the drawing. Charlie's proposal had its points, no question. When I showed the drawing to Paul, he thought likewise, although I suspect that's partly because he didn't feel like starting over. At any rate, we corbeled the chimney as suggested, less the strut. Charlie had been right—it was the handsomest piece of masonry in the neighborhood, which wasn't saying much, given that the chimney on the house next door consisted of a stack of concrete blocks. But it was considerably more impressive than the Barn House's original chimney.

That kind of thing happened a lot. The truth was, we were improving on the work of the house's builders, sometimes in unexpected ways. Many of the improvements were obvious, such as the new mechanical systems, the technology of which had evolved well beyond what had been available in 1891 and a lot of which hadn't been available at all. The radiator pipes now would be hidden rather than exposed. With its ten-foot ceilings, the house would never be cheap to heat, but the two-by-six exterior studs would allow us to install thick R-19 insulation, reducing heat loss. (New houses increasingly are being built with two-by-six outside walls for just that reason.) The new windows were double-glazed with nonstick vinyl sash glides (the sashes themselves were wood). We installed fire-stops—horizontal two-by-sixes nailed between the studs at floor level—to forestall the fire-racing-up-the-flue scenario.

Some of the improvements, however, were purely aesthetic. The upper third of the house had been finished in cedar shakes, which initially had been nailed flat, so that they lay in the plane of the wall. Charlie had decided the shakes ought to flare out in the front of the house, and that the flare should be carried around to the sides, under the eaves of the transept, to make what I thought of as a skirt. The idea was to lend a little flash to the house's silhouette. The drawings showed the flaring extending to the rear of the house, but didn't explicitly say that the existing shakes had to be replaced. Our understanding all along had been that, in the interest of economy, the contractor would salvage as much of the old work as possible. One might have made the argument that the shakes at the back at the house, assuming they were intact, could remain as they were.

The carpenters were having none of that. One day I arrived at the house to find them industriously working away on a scaffold toward the rear of the house. On inquiry I learned that they were extending the flaring unasked. Many of the shakes had to be replaced anyway due to sun damage, and as long as they were going to all the trouble, they felt, they might as well do the job properly. There was no additional charge. I watched for a while in admiration. The Barn House when it was done wouldn't simply be restored; it would be materially improved.

14

I mean no disrespect to anyone involved, but it tells you something about our situation, and what it was like renovating city houses in those days, that a trumpet-playing homeless guy with two big dogs moved into the basement of the Barn House and that we were grateful he was there. His name was Tom S——; he'd been living on the streets for years. One day he'd shown up at one of Tony and Jerry's job sites and offered to keep an eye on things if they'd allow him to live in the house while work was under way. The project was one of a series of jobs Jerry had lined up under a city-funded neighborhood improvement program; the buildings were mostly in tough neighborhoods and had been plagued by thefts and vandalism. Tony and Jerry readily agreed to Tom's proposition. He'd watched a couple of houses for them; work was nearing completion on the second when the Barn House was burglarized.

How many homeless people live in Chicago or any big U.S. city has long been a matter of debate. During the 1980s homeless advocates had claimed enormous numbers, and in the early 1990s the newspapers still sometimes reported that Chicago was home to as many as sixty thousand. The figures arrived at by actual count were much lower—the 1990 census had turned up sixty-eight hundred, of whom around sixteen hundred lived on the street, with the balance in shelters. Whatever the number, they were a conspicuous feature of the urban landscape, most visible at the time on Lower Wacker Drive, a below-grade service road girdling the Loop, where many camped out on the loading docks of office buildings. Most subsisted on handouts, but a few earned a marginal living—I've already mentioned the metal scavengers who pushed old grocery carts through the alleys collecting discarded aluminum cans.

Tom had contrived his own method of getting by. I went out one cold January morning to meet him at a job site on the west side, only a few blocks from the neighborhood where I'd grown up. The project was a small single-family house. Expecting a shuffling derelict, I was surprised to find an alert-looking fellow with glasses and a salt-and-pepper beard wearing a sporty muffler and a plaid bucket cap. He was quite thin. He supported himself by playing the trumpet on street corners. For company he had two enormous dogs named Layla and Oscar. I wondered: *What is this guy doing living in basements?* We agreed that he would watch our house for the duration of the project.

Tony's guys moved him in a few days later, building him a bed in the front of the basement and hauling down the gas space heater previously installed in the dining room. He had a hot plate, a coffeepot, some utensils, and a few other odds and ends. I wouldn't describe the room as cozy—it was the sort of rough-hewn place where you expected to meet people named Igor and Trogg—but it assuredly beat the streets.

Tom went out to play his trumpet mostly in the afternoons; he was usually on hand when I arrived in the morning. He was often chatty and eager to be of help. Some weeks earlier I'd brought over an unassembled workbench, the kind you saw in home improvement stores with a smiling do-it-yourselfer in a spotless work shirt depicted on the box. My mother had given it to me for a Christmas present, thinking I might find it handy at the Barn House. I thought it a silly thing and hadn't gotten around to putting it together. Tom proceeded to do so, unasked by me. The workbench had jigs and vises—it was handy, I had to admit.

A few days later I mentioned that I needed to rig up a support rack in the basement for the furnace expansion tanks—they needed to hang clear of the air-conditioning ducts I was about to have installed immediately above. The following day I found the tanks suspended from a neat piece of apparatus fashioned from a length of gas pipe, scrap lumber, and metal strap. Tom had done it. I was delighted. I had a hundred such chores on my list; if I could delegate some of them to Tom, my burden would be greatly eased.

I mentioned this to Tony, who looked skeptical. "Just don't give him any money," he said. *Eh,* I thought, *the laborer is worth his hire.* I gave Tom twenty dollars.

I was curious how this seemingly capable fellow had wound up on the streets. "So tell me your story," I asked Tom as I washed up that night. He embarked on a complex narrative, the thrust of which was that he didn't get along with his father. The hour was late and the tale obviously long, so after a time I asked for a postponement. I had more urgent business: another assignment for Tom.

The next day Pete the sheet-metal guy was to arrive with his crew to install the ductwork for the first-floor air-conditioning system—a second set of ductwork would later be installed upstairs. In my ceaseless drive to save money I'd agreed to cut holes in the plywood subflooring at points where the ducts for the walls would angle up from the basement. The work wasn't difficult and I had much else to do—was Tom game? *Sure,* he said. I gave him the reciprocating saw and indicated the locations for the holes.

Tom was hard at work when I arrived the next morning, but his manner was odd and got odder. Initially I detected a touch of sway as he leaned over a spot on the kitchen floor, sawing away, though the resulting hole was competently done; then it seemed to me that as he moved to the next hole he waved the saw with more bravado than was wise.

"Tom, you okay?" I asked.

"I'm fine," he said. His tone was belligerent. My suspicions belatedly aroused, I checked his corner of the basement and found a partly empty half gallon of vodka on the bed. When I returned upstairs to confront him he was unmistakably drunk.

"Tom, give me the saw," I said. He refused. I yanked out the plug and after a bit of shuffling and bad language succeeded in extracting the tool from his grip.

All of this played out in full view of the sheet-metal workers, five sturdy suburban lads. I was acutely embarrassed, and in my opinion I had every right to be: I'd given an alcoholic the where-withal to buy booze, equipped him with a dangerous power tool, and invited him to cut holes in my house. What's more—this was the part even I couldn't quite believe—I'd put myself in the position where continuing to employ him as chief guardian of my principal lifetime investment was pretty much my only choice.

I finished sawing the holes myself. With the fading of the light the sheet-metal workers departed; Tom fell into a drunken slumber on the bed. Chief arrived and began sweating pipe; I returned to drilling holes with the right-angle drill, using an unorthodox arrangement of bit extenders in one particularly intractable location. As the bit broke through the bottom of the hole it caught and stalled; a snapping sound issued from the drill, followed by a grinding noise. I'd stripped the gears.

The next morning when I awoke my left eye was burning—I had the sensation that something was trapped beneath the lid. The usual first-aid measures were unavailing. I headed out to the house and attempted to work but the pain was not to be borne. I feared that a piece of metal or other debris had become embedded and would scratch my cornea or otherwise impede progress on the pipes, which had been plenty impeded already. I drove to the emergency room at Northwestern Memorial Hospital on the near north side.

You never knew how much time you'd spend in Northwestern's ER waiting room owing to the fluctuating volume of trauma patients, which on the near north side generally meant people who'd been shot, stabbed, or beat up. Although the neighborhood encompassed East Lake Shore Drive and other precincts of idle wealth, it was also home to Cabrini-Green, a public housing project notorious for snipers and random violence, as well as Rush Street, an entertainment district that in prior decades (it was then in transition) attracted a good many habitués of the Chicago demimonde, which was larger than you might think.[1] If you weren't in imminent danger of death you could find yourself hanging out in the ER waiting room for hours even if, as I had once learned from experience, it was Saturday afternoon and there didn't appear to be many people ahead of you, because "ambulances keep pulling up out back," to quote the triage nurse.

Luckily, it was ten thirty on a Sunday morning, when gang violence in Chicago was normally at a low ebb, so when I turned up with my injured eye that day I was seen with lightning speed

[1]You saw all kinds of things on the near north side. In the mid-1970s, during a brief stint as a police reporter, I'd seen two men whom I took to be a couple walk into the Eighteenth District police station, where I was then loitering. One appeared to have been painted red, owing to a profusely bleeding scalp wound inflicted by the other (weapon uncertain, although I'm guessing a bottle) in the course of an argument that was still in progress. This was a sight you didn't see every day, even in the Eighteenth District, and the cops behind the counter were briefly agape before scrambling to arrest the perp and call an ambulance for the victim, who despite the fact that a considerable fraction of his blood was then external to his person seemed more pissed than hurt. Another time I was the night foreman at a typesetting shop just off Rush Street. After work one night, maybe around one a.m., I was getting a burger

by city ER standards—certainly less than an hour. The preliminaries out of the way, the doctor examined my eye by placing
what I conceived to be a luminous sterilized golf tee on its surface. He found no agonizing granules, only a generalized bruise.
"It's what we see when mothers get poked in the eye by babies,"
he told me. A realization dawned—Ani, two and a half at the
time, was accustomed to crawling into bed between my wife and
me at dawn; she had a tendency then to flail. The pain subsided
without treatment after a few days.

---

at a local coffee shop when I noticed an attractive, well-dressed young woman
sitting alone a couple booths over. A few minutes later an odious lounge-
lizard type sat down across from her and attempted to make conversation.
With an expression of terror the woman looked around for the waitress, who
strode over briskly. "The lady doesn't want to be disturbed," the waitress told
the lounge lizard. The man made some comment to the effect that the woman
could speak for herself. The waitress repeated that the lady didn't want company and that if he didn't bail she would call the police. The lounge lizard
grudgingly exited. A short time later the waitress returned to take the young
woman's order. The woman pointed at the menu and made inarticulate bark-
ing noises. Evidently she was what in crueler times was known as a deaf-mute,
although without apparent cognitive difficulties.

15

The events of the next few months, I confess, are mostly a blur. The only reason I can tell the tale at all is that I kept a diary of sorts, but it's none too coherent. Typically I tapped it out late at night on the computer after I'd returned from the Barn House. Often I was exhausted. What notes I took on the job site were scribbled with a carpenter's pencil in the margins of receipts and to-do lists. Much of the diary is cryptic or fragmentary and parts of it make no sense. I have vivid memories of certain episodes during this time, and between them, copies of faxes to Tony, and my midnight journal I've tried to assemble a reasonably linear account of this busy period. If the result seems jumbled or confusing in places, well, that's how it felt at the time.

Thursday, January 27, 1994. Spent morning at house discussing change orders with Tony and Jerry. Extent of work required now being evident, have asked Tony to quote on additional projects. Price $48,500, more than we can afford. Decide to omit all but essentials—more drywall and insulation, new roof, new basement floor slab (old one an inch thick, crumbling). Cut and fit pipes in afternoon. Tom apologetic about recent untoward episode; I emphasize need for sobriety. On return to house this evening, though, he's noticeably listing, wants to get into conversation while I teeter on ladder. Can see drinking will be constant thorn.

Friday, January 28. Bob calls—trying to replace three-way switch but has mixed up wires, now frustrated. At family gathering over holidays gave me static about foolishness of reinstalling Barn House radiators. No matter, I explain how to fix switch. Doesn't make Bob happy. "Ed, quit laughing so much," he says.

Sunday, January 30. Beautiful snowy day, maybe 25 degrees. Go sledding with kids, then spend rest of day on paperwork— first more "corrections" on forms for Sonja, then first pass on income taxes. Discover I haven't paid enough estimated tax on freelance income, owe nearly $20,000.

Monday, January 31. At house with Chief to work on pipes. No carpenters today, Tony says too cold. Ice in basement sink despite radiators; thaws once propane heater started. Tom says cold water froze briefly Sunday. Sonja making me crazy, wants me to reorganize "owner's statement"—basically spreadsheet showing amounts budgeted, previously paid, now owed, and remaining, broken down by trade. Insists I follow inexplicable system of organization she learned as child on Neptune. Matters complicated by my idiosyncratic approach, with general contractor paying some subcontractors while I pay others.

Chris from bank calls—more problems. They just read title report on town house, proceeds from sale of which to be applied to construction loan; noticed two mechanics' liens from 1987. Call Bob to see if he can make liens go away.

Tuesday, February 1. Sonja tells me everyone I plan to pay must submit federal W-9 form. Spend most of day on paperwork.

Wednesday, February 2. More paperwork. Sonja wants me to get blank forms notarized; feel this defeats purpose of notarizing but ain't arguing. Get food for Tom. Mary, in advanced stage of pregnancy, accompanies me to house, solders joints at workbench. Spud wrench not working right.[1] My sister calls to tell me she has shingles.[2]

Thursday, February 3. Frantic faxing all day. Bring papers to Tony's office, have him notarize. Various transactions involving attorneys, Mary, town house management company, Kevin the plumber, Sonja, bank. Architect visits Barn House to inspect work to date, unseen by me. When not diverted by house work, try to do some work work—namely, magazine column, newspaper column.

Friday, February 4. Working at house, try to install bushing in basement radiator but it cracks, can't back out. Tom comes over, suggests using reciprocating saw to slice bushing into wedge-shaped sections, then chip out. Works like a charm. Mary meets with Sonja; all paperwork finally in. Tom goes out around three, returns in evening drunk; playing a few squeaky notes on trumpet as I leave.

Saturday, February 5. Chief late getting to Barn House; discover he has put bushings in backward. Can't get solder to melt; hand torches don't put out enough heat in cold. At night Tom returns drunk and plays "How Much Is That Doggy in the Window" on trumpet while dogs howl. "Nothing like fun at the old ballpark," says Chief.

Sunday, February 6. Good day—buy new tip for torch that delivers more heat, get all piping for mudroom radiator cut and soldered. One problem: three-eighth-inch right-angle drill, which Chief has had repaired, breaks again. Admit defeat, tell Chief to

---

[1]On returning to the subject fourteen years later, at first I couldn't remember what a spud wrench was, but now recall it's used to screw a fitting into a radiator bushing.

[2]The skin condition, not the roofing material. I assure you it's 100 percent cured now.

get sturdier half-inch model. Mary brings kids to house briefly; Ryan wants to stay and help Daddy. Next weekend, I say.

Monday, February 7. Get call at Barn House—Ma has fallen, broken femur, in hospital. Talk to Pops, seems pretty helpless. No carpenters; Tony says waiting for me to finish. Do much piping. Light snow; sit on radiator eating pizza, admire pretty view of jungle backyard. Snow thicker after nightfall; three inches predicted tonight, four more tomorrow. Can't get windshield unfogged till halfway home. Snow driving hard at midnight.

Wednesday, February 9. Tom calls; on returning to house last night found footprints in snow leading to rear—someone tried to force back basement door. Call Tony to see about getting dead bolt. Sonja calls to say check ready but she's still waiting for architect's report.

Friday, February 11. Been going to twenty-four-hour diner at end of block for eggs, sausage, and hash browns in preparation for sweating pipe. Today sit next to talkative Irish drunk with bad teeth, what look like cigarette burns on lips, who announces he's from County Clare. Feel as if surrounded by derelicts. Talk to Ma; she's upset with hospital, weak due to combination of broken leg plus multiple previous broken bones. Some hospital staffer giving her grief. Call doctor, nurse; they say they will see about Ma. Tell Pops to help more with Ma. Get into argument with my sister about Pops.

Sunday, February 13. More pipes. Somebody blocks Barn House driveway with his car.

Monday, February 14. Visit Ma at hospital; doing better. Different guy blocks driveway.

On Wednesday, February 16, the Chief and I finished sweating the rear radiator loop. It's unnecessary to recount this struggle in detail. The molten globule of solder on my kneecap—that had no permanent consequences, other than the scar. The fifty-odd joints the Chief was obliged to sweat while contorted in anatomically impossible positions with the ambient temperature at 3 degrees Kelvin—eh, all in a day's (okay, a week's) work. Placing the system in operation was no longer fraught with drama. Having become confident of our plumbing skills, we were more casual about filling the pipes with water and no doubt in consequence the process was more eventful, the high point being our discovery of a joint we'd neglected to solder when water sprayed across the basement. That oversight having been addressed, we got both loops operating, and that plus the reconstruction of the exterior walls and winter's retreat sufficed to raise the house's interior temperature to 64 degrees.

That night the Chief and I stood in the basement drinking celebratory beers and admiring our handiwork. Even if it offered no operational efficiencies, a copper-plumbed hot-water heating system would be worth having on aesthetic grounds alone. The pipes ramified in all directions from the aorta at the furnace, the copper gleaming softly in the light of the scattered bulbs. The routing had been accomplished exclusively with right angles and forty-five-degree bends, as though the London Underground diagram had been rendered in 3-D, with air-conditioning ducts running through it in place of the Thames and a leaky gate valve at Charing Cross. It was gorgeous, in any case, and we felt pretty satisfied with ourselves. The thing worked—that was the central fact. We'd fabricated a system out of salvaged parts and a pile of pipe, with no prior knowledge and minimal assistance, and now it just hummed away.

Thursday, February 17. Awakened after midnight by phone call from Tom to tell me no replacement filter for shop vacuum cleaner. Groggy on rising at four a.m. for flight to New Jersey on business. Must have returned Friday but can't remember.

On Sunday, February 20, I got into an argument with Mary—she was upset because we'd spent little time together and I hadn't done much for her birthday, the seventeenth. She was now in her eighth month of pregnancy. The plucky Jacki, an art history grad with a nose ring[3] living in Wicker Park, provided child care on workdays, but most other times Mary was home alone with the kids, now four and two. I admitted I'd been a little distracted but pointed out that I was in the midst of a major construction project that was way behind schedule—by now we'd abandoned any hope of finishing before the baby was born—my mother was in the hospital, I was trying to make money to fill the gaping hole in our finances, and between trying to keep the bank happy and the situation at the house under control I was feeling more or less constantly harassed.

The argument ended inconclusively, as it was bound to do. If I'd been out chasing floozies or Mary had been running up big bills at the spa—here at least we might have assigned blame. In marital difficulties arising from fixing up an old house, however, no one was at fault. Your problems stemmed from your virtues, or so it seemed to me. I was single-minded, sure, but the job demanded single-mindedness, and if in pursuit of it I neglected the candy-and-flowers end of things, well, I was about at the limit of what one man could do. Mary, on the other hand, could say with perfect justice that a house in the city was my idea (for that matter, so was having a third child), and if that left me no time for the customary niceties, I was hardly being fair to expect her to just suck it up.

The crux of our difficulties, as I think back on it now, was that, like the house, I was a throwback to a departed age. Some guys might feel the need to buy oversized vehicles or go shirtless at football games to demonstrate their manliness; I wasn't one of them. I knew my calling in life—to bring order out of chaos. True, our present circumstances involved a little more chaos than I felt altogether comfortable with, but you played the hand you were dealt. I had gotten us into this fix and I would get us out; I

---

[3]A commonplace now, I realize, but notable at the time.

just needed some space. In that respect I was my father's son. When I was growing up, my old man had worked on the house and my mother took care of the kids—that was the natural order of things, and neither in my hearing had ever complained about it.

But that was then and this was now. One big difference was that, whereas my mother had stayed home during my earliest years (she returned to teaching when we were older), Mary worked throughout—in fact, though I made a good buck by writerly standards, as a bank executive she reliably earned more than me. Another difference, already alluded to, was that our project was far larger than either of the home renovations my parents had taken on. Work on their houses had been intermittent, with long pauses between stages, and they'd never had to move out; however annoying the sawdust, my father at least had been on the premises most of the time. Furthermore, my father's job (he'd been a railway clerk) involved set hours—when he was done for the day he was done. Not me. When I wasn't at the Barn House, I was holed up in my office at our town house working on paperwork or freelance writing assignments. Finally, and I concede this was a purely personal quirk, I had a tendency to get lost in my own little world. All of this meant that for long stretches Mary was essentially alone and increasingly resentful. Still, while all this is clearer in hindsight, even now I'm not sure how much more I could have done.

Monday, February 21. Bank still not happy with fricking town house title. Confer with Bob. Chief calls—haven't heard from him in a while. Turns out the day after we got rear radiator loop operating he went back to Barn House to pick up tools, then on way home lost control of car on icy patch on Lower Wacker Drive, crashed into pillar at thirty miles per hour. Vehicle totaled, wrist and ribs broken, in cast for six weeks. On leaving hospital returned to Lower Wacker to see about car, found windshield smashed, belongings stolen, including tools, cell phone, car stereo, jacket. Thief left his hat, though.

Tuesday, February 22. Spend day at Barn House finishing odds and ends so carpenters can work while back in Jersey City on extended business. Bob calls, downtown getting town house title straightened out. In bed at midnight, up at three to finish work work; can see I won't get done in time for 6:30 a.m. plane so postpone flight till 9:30, which is delayed till 11:45 due to heavy snow. Twenty inches in Chicago after I leave.

Friday, February 25. In NJ; Mary tells me loan payment to Tony finally went through after month of paper shuffling.

Thursday, March 3. Back in Chicago ten p.m.

Sunday, March 6. Invoice NJ work—$12,000. Mary says will pay off recent debts but still no money for taxes.

Monday, March 7. Take kids to visit Ma, now in rehab facility.

Tuesday, March 8. Car fails state emissions test. Must have done something to get fixed but notes don't say what.

Wednesday, March 9. Tony says carpenters starting on roof today. Mary says between us we make good money but can't afford clothes, vacations, or dinner out and drive eight-year-old Toyota. Clean up town house for showing to prospective buyer.

Thursday, March 10. Go to Chief's house to help him install modem in computer. Mary getting worried—I haven't been to Barn House in days.

Sunday, March 13. At house for first time in more than a week. Roof looks great, as does house in general.

Tuesday, March 15. Talk to custom stair guy to get estimate to replace balustrade and other parts missing from front-hall staircase. Cost: close to $2,000. Tony and Charlie come over; we argue about base for porch columns, conclude carpenters haven't followed plans.

Wednesday, March 16. While walking to house from diner, hear bang, commotion behind me; turn to see high school–age kids bolting down street. Evidently trying to break into car trunk.

Saturday, March 19. Warmer. Start insulating attic.

Sunday, March 20. Sheet-metal guys start on upstairs AC ducts. Toward end of day watch rain out rear attic door.

Wednesday, March 23. Beautiful weather, close to 70, sunny.

Mary brings kids to house; crawl all over, have great time. Tell Tom he needs to clean up dog poop in basement. Carpenters working on siding this week. Do more attic insulation.

Saturday, March 26. Start repairing decrepit attic floor. Many boards loose; Ryan put leg through gap earlier.

Sunday, March 27. Mary due any day, having rough time—tired, kids demanding, laundry, and so on. Stress giving her contractions. Stay home.

On Thursday, March 31, at 2:15 a.m., Mary started having serious contractions. We called the babysitter and arrived at the hospital at 4:30. Andrew Jeffrey was born at 9:20 a.m. Once he was cleaned up and deposited on Mary's chest, the obstetrician, a jovial, no-nonsense woman, stood at the foot of the bed flanked by two nurses, all in long smocks splashed with the mess of childbirth, looking as satisfied with a job well done as I'd ever felt after a day hoisting radiators. Mary told me later she was surprised I stayed at the hospital for several hours afterward and didn't rush back to the house.

Friday, April 1. Take kids to visit Mary at hospital, do work work rest of time.

Saturday, April 2. Pick up Mary and Andrew at hospital. Tony sends flowers. Beautiful day; people stop by.

As had been our custom with our first two, Mary breast-fed Andrew except at eleven p.m., when I gave him a bottle and walked him to sleep so she could get a few hours' rest. I loved walking babies, having spent hours at it with Ryan, who was the Swiss watch of infants, sleep-wise, and required a good forty-five minutes of swaying ambulation before I felt sure enough of his having drifted off to lay him in his crib, stealthy as a burglar. Half the time he promptly woke up anyway, whereupon the process started all over, but it was one of those patient tasks to which I was well suited. Andrew presented a different problem. He would nod off quickly enough but then wake up later and fidget, which meant more walking, adding sleep deprivation to a list of challenges that was already long.

Sunday, April 3. In-laws come over, make Easter dinner. Afterward go to library, work.

Monday, April 4. Meet with Tony and Jerry at house to review progress. Exterior pretty much done but back door a nailed-up sheet of plywood. At first thought this temporary, but after passage of considerable time and still no door I ask Tony, who says carpenters waiting for me. I sputter: *Me?* Where does Tony think I'm going to get door? He points to passage in contract saying owner responsible for doors. Says *interior* doors, I retort; this is *exterior* door. We inspect relevant opening; exteriorness beyond dispute. "I guess we make a little boo-boo," says Tony, shooting look at Jerry. Door appears in due course.

Tuesday, April 5. Spend most of day nailing down attic floor planking. Tom hovers; says woman yelled at him because he told her she was beautiful.

Wednesday, April 6. More planking. Tom tells me about bar fights in tavern at end of alley.

On Thursday, April 7, I started on the electrical work. In contrast to the heating, this presented no technical challenges of moment; the main problem was that there was an enormous amount to do, since you couldn't just tack up plastic cable in the slapdash manner countenanced pretty much everywhere but Chicago—you had to use conduit, as I say. I didn't mind; I liked bending conduit—it was an esoteric skill, like blowing smoke rings or twirling a lariat. More important, I felt conduit was better fitted to the gravity of the task—namely, keeping people and electricity separated, in contrast to plastic cable, an inherently flimsy material that to my mind didn't foster the appropriate attitude of respect.

A friend in California once told me about his house, which I imagined (never actually having seen it) to be a typical West Coast mountain domicile equipped with a hot tub and redwood deck. Like every other house in California it was wired with plastic cable. Some item of electrical apparatus in the house had ceased to function, and my friend ingeniously isolated the fault to a length of plastic cable running through the crawl space beneath the house. Hoping to ascertain precisely where the juice had hung up, he inserted himself beneath the house, scraped the insulation off the conductors with a knife (the cable was stapled to the underside of a floor joist, and I had the impression loomed perhaps a foot above his nose), and confirmed the presence of 120 VAC with a meter. "You did *what*?" I exclaimed, explaining that scraping the insulation off live wires was never smart, and doing so while lying on damp earth in a confined space was about as stupid as it was possible to get and still have a nervous system. Conduit, in my view, would have more successfully conveyed what the plastic cable hadn't—that is, *Muy peligroso, dumbshit. Mitts off.*

First task: mounting boxes for outlets, switches, and light fixtures, which I'd later connect with conduit.

Saturday, April 9. Up early, work on house paperwork. Feeling harried—been staying up late with fidgety Andrew. In effort to share kid-watching duties take Ryan to house; he's sweet but wants me to look at something every couple minutes—don't get much done, distracted, make mistakes. Tell Mary we need to rethink this or won't finish till December. She says she'll take kids full-time again. Up till twelve fifteen a.m. working on fax to Tony about changes.

Monday, April 11. At client's all day. Mary calls; Andrew sick. Take to hospital; they both stay overnight.

Tuesday, April 12. Tony calls to discuss Tom. Carpenters need to move him upstairs so basement floor can be repoured, but Tony doesn't want dogs to accompany him because of smell— they produce voluminous waste; he doesn't want it soaking into floorboards. We agree carpenters will build kennel for dogs in backyard.

Thursday, April 14. Mail in federal tax return. As expected, owe $20,000 we don't have. Enclose note saying we'll pay soon. Chris from bank calls; architect inspecting house noticed owner's statement shows plumbing work as complete but obviously isn't. I freak—if project total increased by amount actually required to finish (as opposed to amount we told bank), we must come up with another $14,000 in owner's equity. Kevin the plumber calls looking for $2,200; I ask what he thinks it will cost to finish job. Says $4,500. Ask him to give me lowball estimate for $2,000 to keep bank happy. Feel as if organizing drug deal.

Friday, April 15. Tony tells me Stefan, one of carpenters, who previous year had nearly sliced off thumb, fell four feet off ladder, shattered upper right arm, needed surgery to insert ten-inch pin.

Monday, April 18. Town house showing in morning; at Barn House by two to do more electrical boxes. In evening drunk shows up asking for Tom; staggers down front steps when I say not here. Leave at eleven p.m., then up with Andrew till one thirty a.m.

Tuesday, April 19. Meet Chief at house—down to plastic restrainer on arm but can't work yet. Discuss electrical.

Wednesday, April 20. Real estate agent calls. City home sales slow; would we consider lease for town house? Not enthusiastic.

Sunday, April 24. Warm day; Mary and I take kids to Fullerton Avenue beach. On return talk to Katie, one of town house neighbors, who says she and husband have sold unit, moving to North Shore with their two kids. Two other couples in development with small children also heading for burbs. "This is a great place for kids, but everybody with kids is moving out," she says. People in our circle experiencing rash of petty crime—Jacki the babysitter has been burglarized four times in eighteen months in two different city apartments. Eventually she moves to California.

———

That evening I went to the Barn House to inspect progress in the basement and was joined there by Tom. In preparation for pouring the new floor, the carpenters were demolishing the ancient partitions and carting out the debris. "Lotta history being hauled away here," he observed. Tom was never so annoying as when he was right, and this was one of those times. It wasn't that the repulsive basement contained anything I cared to save—on the contrary, it was a collection of scabrous junk, and the practical man in me felt righteous for causing it to be expunged from the earth. At the same time, I recognized that I was erasing part of the history that was one of the reasons I'd bought the house—a record of futility and half-assedness, to be sure, but a record just the same. Twenty-four hours later there was no sign it had ever been.

Saturday, April 30. Out of town on business. On return Tom calls, says dogs back in house—carpenters haven't put up chain-link fence in backyard as promised to keep them from running loose; doesn't want to chain up for fear they'll get tangled. Also, Layla pregnant. Insist dogs remain in kennel, go out to house to put up chicken-wire fencing. Oscar easily digs beneath, so demand Tom chain him; he reluctantly agrees. Carry pregnant Layla out to kennel; clearly close to giving birth. Tom says he was arrested for not having performer's license.

Sunday, May 1. Work work all day. Feel overwhelmed.

Monday, May 2. Spend couple hours hassling with Sonja over next payout. Chris agrees if project amount bumped up $2,500 to cover remaining plumbing and electrical, all salubrious, no additional money from us required.

Tuesday, May 3. Cabinet guy arrives at Barn House to measure kitchen. "You've got yourself a project here," he says. Thanks, Einstein. Tom says Layla gave birth to nine puppies yesterday, seven dead by this morning. Remaining two whimpering in cardboard box on his bed. Tony says Jerry mugged yesterday while sitting in car talking on cell phone near west-side job site—guy put knife to his neck, demanded wallet, got $90, credit cards. "When I get done with this house, I'm getting out of here," Tony says. More complications with Sonja; Pete the sheet-metal guy hasn't filled out lien waiver right. Forge changes so Tony can get paid. Mary tells me she's stressed—home all day with three kids including newborn; I'm seldom home and when I am I'm working. Agree but don't see much alternative.

Saturday, May 7. Minimal house work all week. Tom says all puppies dead. Oscar in family room; tell Tom to put in kennel. Layla all skin and bones.

Sunday, May 8. Forget to wish Mary happy Mother's Day.

Tuesday, May 10. Mary prices new woodwork—$10–15,000. Will have to salvage old stuff, although in bad shape.

Saturday, May 14. On arrival at house, Tom says Layla dead. Find emaciated corpse on back porch, legs stiffened in air, eyes half open. Mary calls; planned to take kids on outing, but as soon as she started car temp gauge redlined. Tell her to stay home. Gabe's wife complains guys pouring new basement floor have wrecked her fence, chipped masonry; apologize, promise we'll fix. Need hacksaw blade; Tom volunteers to get at hardware store, but on way back Oscar attacks neighbor's cocker spaniel, bites him (spaniel) in side. Owner, already unhappy with Tom, demands Oscar's medical history. I think: *My next house will be in the suburbs. It'll have eight-foot ceilings and wall-to-wall carpeting and vinyl siding and I'll spend my weekends on the couch watching sports.*

Sunday, May 15. Mary has 101-degree fever. Car redlines when switched on; probably bad sensor (not serious) but take cab to house, install 270 feet of conduit.

Monday, May 16. Plague of locusts descends on house, soon our bodies covered with boils. Ha, just kidding. But it's time for a little break.

16

Prior to Daniel Burnham, who in the *Plan of Chicago* cheerfully contemplated a city of 13,250,000 by 1952 (along
with several other key assumptions in the plan, this estimate over-
shot reality by a generous margin—metropolitan Chicago's population in 1950 was just 5.5 million and is 9.5 million now), no
utopian or urban planner to my knowledge had proposed as a
desirable form of human habitat a city of a million or more.[1] The
closest I could come up with in an admittedly unscientific survey
(I read a bunch of books) was Idelfonso Cerdá y Suñer's 1859
plan for Barcelona, which had that city topping out at 800,000,
considerably shy of the 1,670,000 who live there now.

[1] I should clarify that Burnham wasn't advocating that Chicago be enlarged to
this size, merely acknowledging that if the rapid growth evident in his day
continued, the city would arrive at that number by 1952. His chief departure
from earlier urban visionaries was in proposing no limits to expansion, with
a few exceptions a characteristic of planning in the United States and particularly in Chicago to this day.

Most ideal communities were much smaller. In his dialogue *Laws*, Plato envisioned that the population of the planned city of Magnesia would be fixed at 5,040 families, which modern commentators estimate would mean about 50,000 people. In Thomas More's *Utopia* (1516), cities were limited to 6,000 households of ten to sixteen people, for a population of maybe 80,000—a respectable-sized town for the era, I suppose. But ideal cities thereafter didn't get markedly larger even as real ones grew vast. The "garden cities" proposed by the English planner Ebenezer Howard a century ago were to have a total of 250,000 people, mostly distributed among satellite communities of 32,000—this at a time when the population of greater London exceeded 6 million.

After Burnham a few planners proposed cities of bolder scale, the most famous of whom was the Swiss architect Charles-Edouard Jeanneret, better known as Le Corbusier, whose proposed-but-not-built La Ville Contemporaine (1922), a stark essay in high-rise modernism, was to have 3 million inhabitants. This scheme, now generally acknowledged as mad, became the model for disastrous public housing projects in Chicago and throughout the world, in the process largely extinguishing any budding enthusiasm for planned megacities. (Unplanned megacities, of course, have continued to grow explosively, whether anyone was enthusiastic about them or not.)

Instead, the preference for communities of modest size became if anything even more pronounced—community here being understood in the narrow sense of a municipal corporation having defined borders. The average Chicago suburb has just 18,000 inhabitants—the region, in fact, has the most independent municipalities of any city in the country, an oddity I once heard an urban expert attribute to the racist citizenry, who presumably figured it was easier to keep troublesome minorities out of small, homogenous towns. However true this may have been (I don't claim racial views in postwar Chicago were especially enlightened), a simpler explanation is that most people prefer suburbs because they find it easier getting their hands around a small community than a large one—most people but, as we shall see, not all.

I spent a good deal of time that winter and spring trying to get the insurance company to reimburse me for the December break-in. Obtaining estimates for the stolen mantelpieces proved to be unexpectedly difficult. The first couple salvage houses I contacted couldn't be bothered trying to assign values to these unusual items. The woman answering the phone at the third salvager was likewise dubious, but agreed to check with the boss. She asked my name; when I told her, she asked whether I was the same individual who edited a certain newspaper column. I admitted that I was. "We *love* that column," she said, and after a moment of off-line consultation invited me to come on over—the boss would be happy to accommodate me.

The firm, located in an old brick loft building only a few blocks from the Barn House, turned out to be one of the country's largest dealers in antique mantelpieces. The owner, a ponytailed fellow named Stuart, had become something of a wheel in the architectural salvage business, spending his days traveling to demolition sites and extracting picturesque fragments of buildings otherwise bound for landfill or the scrap yard—elevator grilles, stone lions, terra-cotta ornaments. He had chunks of structures designed by Louis Sullivan and Frank Lloyd Wright. A few items he'd kept for himself (eventually he opened a museum to display it). The rest was for sale.

Stuart invited me to inspect the premises. Most of the mantelpieces were stored on an upper floor—the space was impressively large. How many items were stacked there I can't say, but the number was surely in the thousands, each representing a building now dust, or anyway a room now dust, or remodeled beyond recognition. I wandered up and down the aisles, the photos of the mantelpieces taken from the Barn House in my hand. Not all the assembled woodwork had come from Chicago (and from what I could see, none of it had come from my house), but a lot of it

had, and much more from towns elsewhere in the Midwest—
places whose moment of glory had come and gone, and whose
antiquities, if one may use the term, were now being stripped for
export. (Detroiters were especially bitter on the subject.) A lot of
the salvaged goods wouldn't wind up in Chicago, the region, or
even in a city. Some friends had a Louis Sullivan rosette in their
powder room in suburban Atlanta; I'd heard Texas was an enthusiastic importer of Chicago common brick.

Yet I can't say I found the scene bleak—the stuff was being
recycled rather than simply discarded, after all—nor (the initial
shock having passed) had the experience of being victimized left
me personally all that upset. Truth was, the thieves had done me
a favor—I hadn't really liked the mantelpieces they'd made off
with, two fussy Victorian relics, and at the moment, to be candid,
I had more use for the insurance money. Although I wouldn't care
to advertise the fact, there was something to be said for an occasional encounter with chaos, assuming it didn't entail bodily injury or leave you stuck for the loss. My friend Hank had come to
a similar conclusion years earlier. He was initially dismayed when
his house was damaged by fire, but when he realized the settlement would allow him to modernize his outdated kitchen . . .
well, I'd be exaggerating to say he'd become an advocate of arson.
But he could see it had its points.

I went back downstairs, my due diligence complete. Stuart
wrote up a generous estimate of my mantelpieces based on the
photos, which I subsequently submitted to the claims adjuster. In
the fullness of time the insurance company deducted a trifling
amount and sent me a good-sized check.

I'd gotten another break. At first I chalked this up to the fact
that I was in a high-profile line of work, but in time I realized
there was more to it than that. Fact was, I'd gotten a lot of breaks
on my project, foremost among them the intervention of Charlie,
Tony and Jerry, and the Chief. Eventually I realized a larger force
was at work: I was a beneficiary of the city-guy mafia.

Anyone who's lived in the same place for an appreciable length of time recognizes the web of relationships in which he's become enmeshed. I was periodically reminded of this by my Irish Catholic mother, surely one of the most social beings on earth. Anyone who knew my mom could claim at most one degree of separation from the rest of humanity, because she knew everybody else. One evening in a hotel in Jerusalem (I'd accompanied my mother on a trip to Israel with a church group following the demurral of my father, who figured there wouldn't be anyone to talk pigeons with), we shared a dinner table with an older couple neither of us had ever laid eyes on before. Within twenty minutes my mother had established that the woman had grown up on the west side of Chicago in the house next door to the childhood home of her (my mom's) sister-in-law—my aunt—from which said sister-in-law had departed in, oh, maybe 1941. "Ma," I said as we left the table, "sometimes you scare me."

From ancient ties like that certain advantages easily arose. You knew people, they knew you—or if not you, then your mom, your neighbor, or your best friend's sister's ex. If you needed help or advice . . . well, if you were a knucklehead like me, you could just start calling people out of the phone book, only to discover that the party on the other end of the line was a pigeon-racing buddy of your dad's.

The city-guy mafia was a special case of these ordinary social networks. For the most part it wasn't so different—on the contrary, inasmuch as a considerable fraction of the Chicago contingent consisted of graduates of the University of Notre Dame (about which more later), it could be as tribal as the best of them. It merely included a few extra nodes. In addition to the usual connections through family and friends, city people knew each other, or anyway knew *of* each other, by virtue of certain urban pursuits: writing for the newspapers, say, or belonging to civic or professional associations, or—let's not be too hifalutin about this—hanging out at the same bar in Wicker Park.

However you gained admittance, the city-guy mafia, in the

manner of all networks, opened doors and made urban life less intimidating. This had two important consequences, both of which I grasped only in retrospect. The first was that, in contrast to suburbanites, city guys were comfortable with big-city scale— the city was their natural home. The second was that, once stirred to action, the city-guy mafia was a formidable engine for change, as we would shortly see. And so back to our story.

Wednesday, May 18. Laryngitis in the morning, followed by shivers. Do financial projection; optimistically $16,000 in hole for year.

Thursday, May 19. Get notice from city saying Oscar must be impounded for ten days. Can't reach Tom.

Saturday, May 21. Work on conduit. Tom says he'll take Oscar to pound.

Monday, May 23. Work work all week. Write pessimistic magazine column: "I like the city and hope that people like myself can work out a way to stay in it, and I think there is a reasonable chance we will. But I wish I could be more certain than I am."

Saturday, May 28. Ani's birthday party. Pleasant day.

Sunday, May 29. More conduit. Despite repeated admonitions, Tom still hasn't brought Oscar to pound, but says he has arranged with Tony to do so.

Saturday, June 4. Oscar still hasn't gone to pound, crapped all over second floor.

Sunday, June 5. Working late at house when Tom arrives, drunk and morose: "I have an IQ that's tested out between one hundred and eighty and two hundred, depending on what scale was used, and I can't figure out why people do these things to each other." Turns out alley kids have been throwing stuff into yard at Oscar and won't stop when asked. Still hasn't taken Oscar to pound. "What if it were your wife they wanted to examine? Not that Oscar is my wife." Tell Tom not interested in pursuing this discussion.

Thursday, June 9. Do electrical work at house till eleven p.m.

Tom arrives late, drunk as usual. Decides to change burned-out basement lightbulb, but it's stuck and shatters as he tries to turn it. Wearing gloves so not hurt, but I shout at him to stop—fear he'll electrocute himself, don't want his death on my hands.

Saturday, June 11. Oscar in house again. Floorboards in dining room reek of urine, will have to be replaced. Chew Tom out. "But I have emotional needs," he says. Call Tony, say we needed to start thinking about getting Tom out.

Monday, June 13. Tony's fireplace installer calls, says can't fit flue pipe into wooden chimney chase carpenters have constructed without having it jut into family room. Upon consultation, problem apparently that Charlie has designed offset into chase at point where pierces roof. Call Charlie, ask why offset. "We wanted to engage the rail," he says. I love Charlie, but can be such an architect sometimes. Eventually conclude chase must be dismantled, rebuilt two feet east. Going to cost. Tony's guys take Oscar to pound at last.

Tuesday, June 14. Lee over, finishes installing new main electric panel. Decide to have him help me finish electrical in interest of concluding job before heat death of universe. Chief installs 250 feet of coax for cable TV.

Wednesday, June 15. Lee calls to say we have problem—inspector says two-inch conduit from electric meter to main panel can't run through crawl space beneath family room, as now; code requires cutoff switch within five feet of meter. We must run twenty-five feet of pipe with three right-angle bends along outside of newly re-sided house—will look hideous. Decide to appeal to chief electrical inspector.

Thursday, June 16. Temp 98 degrees. Lee works on electrical with son Gordon while pregnant young woman watches. Lee's supervision of Gordon consists mainly of screaming at him. Gordon not happy. During break ask how he likes being electrician. "Gotta be an easier way to make a living than this," he says. Later tell Lee Gordon doesn't see much future in electrical business. Lee agrees: "He says I work too hard and don't charge enough." Gordon pursuing other ventures with assistance of "his wife or girl-friend or something" (pregnant young woman) but has had problems. I ask: Legal problems? Yes, says Lee. Gordon has been in jail on drug charges.

Gordon is right about one thing, though. Lee charges only $150/day for Gordon and self, less than $10/hour.

Saturday, June 18. Still very hot. Chief reports hearing two gunshots near Barn House previous evening; remarks on trash on nearby lawns.

Monday, June 20. Mary wishes me happy (wedding) anniversary. I'd completely forgotten.

On Saturday, June 25, Lee, the Chief, and I spent the day pulling wire through conduit. Lee knew his business and from time to time instructed the Chief and me on fine points.[2] In odd moments he revealed a little about his background. His father had been the first black electrician in Cook County. Now he lived with his family on the west side, where life evidently hadn't been easy—his truck had been repeatedly broken into and his tools stolen. Concluding that he resided in a desolate ghetto neighborhood, I was surprised to learn on further discussion that his home was just a block or two across the city line from Oak Park, the middle-class suburb where my parents lived. It was a different world wherever it was, but I was only fitfully reminded of it. Lee was a craftsman, a member of the brotherhood, and that was bridge enough.

Sunday, June 26. Finish pulling wire, get all outlets, switches, and pigtails (temporary bulbs) hooked up. House blazes with light.

Wednesday, June 29. Tony's guys put up insulation while Chief and I string telephone, intercom wires—gentlemen's work compared to previous. Take break to admire house from sidewalk. Provided inspection limited to exterior, place is stunning. For-

[2]One such point is described in Appendix D.

merly most decrepit structure on block; to my eye now handsomest. Passersby stop to compliment.

Thursday, June 30. Tony calls—front door frame totally shot, should be replaced. Cost: $900. Noticed same thing, say okay.

Saturday, July 2. Fax Tony saying my alarm guy will soon have burglar alarm operational; we should get Tom out before drywallers start.

Sunday, July 3. At house doing odds and ends. Tom chatty: "By 2010 there will be ten billion people in the world. That's a lot of folks. Of course by then we'll be harvesting krill from the oceans and serving it at McDonald's. Maybe we'll be eating bugs, too. Fortunately by then our extraterrestrial efforts will be removing a sizable portion of the population from the planet."

Monday, July 4. Supposed to go to John's for holiday but Ryan has hacking cough so stay home.

Tuesday, July 5. Get letter from IRS—going to put lien on house for back taxes. Mary in panic.

Wednesday, July 6. Mary calls IRS—they won't put lien on house if we pay $11,000 by July 23. Around ten p.m. Tom calls; wants to know if I left used diaper in bathroom. Say no, kids hadn't been out there. Subsequent remarks stranger than usual: "I am not prepared to deal with . . . here I am and there you are . . . I expect to find things a certain way . . . in the capacity I am providing I have an enormous degree of insecurity. I feel it's important to maintain . . . please understand where I'm coming from." End discussion with some effort.

Thursday, July 7. Pete returns to finish upstairs AC. Duct routing simplified by my drawings, but still more complicated than new house. Drawbacks of hiring low bidder now apparent. I stare at knotty problem in master bedroom ceiling muttering, "I don't know," only to have Pete say he doesn't know either. After study, figure if I can get forty-five-degree whatsit to hook onto ninety-degree thingamajig, can get around funky framing without ducts protruding into room. Pete not seeing it. Say I'm certain parts exist, although as usual no definite knowledge of this. Pete says if I get he will install.

Sunday, July 10. Have to redo radiator supply piping to Ani's room, forget why. Job takes three and a half hours; first time around took three days. Call Mom, who inherited money from frugal spinster schoolteacher aunts, arrange to borrow $11,000 to pay IRS.

At some point in mid-July I needed Lee to sign a final lien waiver, which as always had to be notarized. He insisted we drive out for this purpose to a currency exchange in a tough west-side neighborhood called Lawndale, which still had vacant lots dating from the riots of the 1960s. On arrival the stocky man behind the counter greeted Lee familiarly. "This came for you," he said, handing a piece of mail past me to Lee. It was a compact window envelope containing an official-looking document; I couldn't help noticing the return address. It was a welfare check.

Lee and I concluded our business and returned to the car for the trip back to the north side. We drove in silence for a time. "I guess you saw I was on relief," Lee said finally. I said nothing. We never discussed the matter again.

Friday, July 15. Porch balustrades finished, look fabulous. Go to building supply store for duct parts for master bedroom, find what I want in ten minutes. Back at house lay out pieces, write detailed note to Pete explaining how to install. Call city about request for waiver on electrical work. Inspector says he talked to boss: "At first he said, 'That's not how we do it.' But then he said, 'Ah, hell, give it to him.'" Convey gushing thanks.

Sunday, July 17. Stop at house in afternoon to see how Pete doing. Unbelievably, still doesn't have master BR ducts right, defying expectations of male superiority in spatial reasoning. "Gimme the nut driver," I say, show how supposed to go. Leave on errand; when get back still isn't right. Get up on ladder and fix myself; while at it redo several return ducts where Pete's attention apparently drifted. "Huh," he says later.

Saturday, July 23. Arrive at house to find Chester has propped up front porch roof with two-by-fours, disassembled fabulous balustrade, taken down pillar, sawed six inches off bottom. "Chester, what are you doing?" I shriek. He says blueprints showed railings thirty inches high; as installed only twenty-four inches. Ask to see prints. Drawing of entire house in fact shows thirty-inch railing, but refers to detail drawing further back in sheaf. Thumb through drawings, now bedraggled after months of use, discover detail drawing torn out. Retrieve my copy of prints, show Chester detail drawing—indicates twenty-four-inch railing. "You got it right the first time. If it were wrong we would have said something," I say. Chester looks stricken. "My head is cabbage," he says. Puts porch back like it was, although line on pillar six inches from bottom shows where reattached.

By the end of July we'd finally sold our town house and had to be out by early September. We now turned to postponed details such as woodwork. We'd saved the house's original trim during demolition, thinking we might be able to clean and reinstall it, and in fact the doors, magnificent multi-paneled affairs that looked like they belonged in an English country manor, had come out of the dunk tank looking pretty good. But the baseboards and window trim, I realized on close inspection, were hopelessly splintered—we had no choice but to buy new. We might have used stock molding, I suppose, but never seriously considered it; we hadn't come this far to cheap out on the finishing. On the other hand, we also had neither the time nor the money to get new woodwork milled and installed before move-in day. I decided that once the drywall had been hung, I'd have the interior painted white to seal the walls. We'd get to the millwork when we could.

Monday, August 1. Chief and I work at house till late. On way home tire goes flat on Lake Shore Drive. Pulling over I discover two problems: first, flat; second, seriously low spare. Past midnight, nearest gas station half mile away. Car pulls in behind mine—it's Chief. Gets out silently, forages in trunk, then approaches with grin, carrying flashlight and battery-powered air pump, come to save my sorry ass again.

Wednesday, August 3. Chief and I finish last of intercom cabling, other odds and ends before drywall. Tony has moved Tom to different job site. "It's kind of strange with Tom not being here," Chief says. "Then again, a lot of times it was kind of strange when he *was* here." Air of constant crisis has subsided in any case. Take numerous photos of electrical conduit, of which very proud. On arriving home discover no film in camera; by time I return, drywallers have covered everything.

The Mexican drywallers had made an initial appearance in early August and shown up in force a few days later, the empty bottles of Woda Sodowa seltzer water left in odd corners by the Polish carpenters giving way to the tamarind soda preferred by the Mexicans. I'd long since come to terms with drywall. In my youth, no doubt influenced by my father, a self-taught plasterer, I considered it emblematic of shoddy construction and the decline of the West. However, my sense of the rightness of things had had to adjust to reality: Drywall, done properly, produced work not easily distinguished from plaster (ignoring the occasional nail pop), with the decisive advantages of being cheap and fast.

The Mexican drywallers now proceeded to demonstrate how it was done. As a kid I'd helped my dad hang gypsum board as an underlayment for plaster; it'd take us an hour to cover perhaps thirty square feet. In that time the Mexican drywallers would have finished half the house. There were two crews—the hangers (who affixed the drywall to the studs), followed by the tapers (who covered the seams between boards with paper tape, then ladled on copious quantities of joint compound, commonly called mud, which they troweled smooth and sanded flat). None of the hangers was taller than five feet eight or weighed more than 160 pounds, yet they tossed around four-by-ten-foot pieces of drywall as though dealing cards.

Saturday, August 13. Ricardo the taper starts. Explain major challenge, replacement of curved ceiling in service stairwell—basically quarter-toroidal helix. No idea how to accomplish using flat drywall. *De nada,* says Ricardo.

Monday, August 15. Hangers conclude their part of stairwell ceiling—soak quarter-inch-thick drywall in water to soften, slice at one-inch intervals so will bend, then mount to ceiling with one million screws. Still pretty lumpy.

Wednesday, August 17. Don't arrive at house till five; Ricardo and helper still there, work till eight. No ladders, walk around on stilts. Helper muds seams with ten-inch-wide applicator. Ricardo says planned on staying in Chicago six months, still here after eight years. Now buying house in suburbs. Ladles vast amounts of mud onto stairwell ceiling. I ask, you sure this will work? *De nada,* he says.

Monday, August 22. Upstairs AC not cooling, although compressor and air handler running constantly. Take cover off air handler, find giant block of ice. After study of manual, deduce Pete has run returns into side of air handler, not bottom as specified, so air isn't drawn past cooling coils, allowing condensation to form ice. Splice two more returns into bottom of air handler, solves problem once ice melts, though takes all day.

Wednesday, August 24. Meet with painters at house about spray-painting interior. Hoped to pay $1,000; after haggling agree on $3,400.

Friday, August 26. Ricardo finishes mudding in A.M.; do a little touchup. Staircase ceiling a work of art.

On the last Saturday in August, we left for Door County, Wisconsin, on a brief low-budget vacation, stopping at the Barn House en route. The floor guys were installing oak flooring in the master bedroom using sleepers (crosswise strips) rather than ply-wood underlayment, which I knew would be trouble and would eventually necessitate my having them tear the floor out and do the whole thing over—but we'd worry about that another day. Right now life at the Barn House was about to enter a new phase.

17

We moved in on Labor Day weekend. The three-man moving crew was supervised by a wiry, long-haired young guy who drove his crew hard. I wasn't on hand for most of the work—I was engaged in last-minute preparations at the Barn House while the movers loaded the truck, then cleaned up at our old home while our possessions were off-loaded at the new one. Mary told me it had been a long day—at the end of it, one exhausted mover refused to take another step. The unforgiving foreman had fired him on the spot, which was all very well, but we were left with our piano sitting under a tarp in the backyard.

That night after we were in bed Mary jabbed me awake—she thought she'd heard a noise coming from downstairs. I groggily roused myself to investigate. After shuffling to the top of the stairs and flipping on the light, I looked over the railing into the beady eyes of what was surely the ugliest creature on earth, which crouched on the landing below. It was roughly the size of a rabbit, with gray fur, a narrow ratlike face, and an obscenely long, hairless tail.[1] I had no idea what it was, but it clearly had teeth, no doubt sharp. We stared at one another for a long while without moving. Finally I called to Mary in a low voice and asked her to bring any weapon she could put her hand on, which turned out to be a fireplace poker, plus my work boots—I figured if I was going to take this thing on, no sense losing a toe. Thus prepared, I advanced on the critter, which retreated into the narrow wall cavity for a long-gone pocket door. Cornering it there, we called the police. Two uniformed patrolmen arrived by and by.

Peering into the creature's hiding place, one cop informed me that it was a possum. I was nonplussed. I was a city guy; my experience of possums to that point had consisted of reading Walt Kelly's comic strip *Pogo*.

"You should call animal control," the cop said.

"When does animal control open?" I asked. We were now about a half hour into Saturday.

"Monday morning."

"That doesn't seem like a practical plan."

Just then two plainclothesmen arrived from the tactical squad. Unlike the beat cops, these were men of action. One of the tactical guys directed the available adults to arrange packing boxes in a sort of gauntlet leading from the possum's lair to the front door, then waved a two-by-four at the animal in a manner calculated to alarm. The possum promptly scooted out the door and down the front steps.

The incident epitomized the first few months following move-in, during which we didn't so much reside in the house as camp in it. The place was at best 60 percent done. It lacked the most basic amenities, including a complete bathroom or kitchen. The

---

[1]Well, I thought it was hairless. Subsequent discreet inspection of the animals in question—they turned out to be fairly common in the neighborhood—established that the tail did in fact have hair, albeit quite short.

rooms (including the bathrooms) lacked doors or woodwork, the openings merely framed with construction lumber. Most of our household goods were stacked in cryptically labeled boxes in what would someday be the living room. There were no window coverings of any kind; the lighting consisted of a few $3 fixtures and bare bulbs. We slept on mattresses on unfinished floors; Mary rose early each morning to take a shower at her sister's apartment two neighborhoods north before heading off to work. Her tolerance of disorder had never been high and she was in a perpetual low-grade froth. I, on the other hand, had adopted the put-one-foot-in-front-of-the-other mind-set of a refugee fleeing the Khmer Rouge: First we'll do A, then we'll do B and C and so on in the bleak expectation, or anyway hope, that somewhere in the vicinity of step quadruple-Q we'd achieve normality.

We told ourselves the kids were too young to grasp the rudeness of their surroundings. However, one Saturday night after his bath, Ryan, now almost five, observed while getting toweled off that the bathtub (which had no faucet, only a length of half-inch copper pipe projecting from the wall) was in one room, the sole operating toilet was in a different room downstairs, and the house's only sink was in a third room, the kitchen. "Dad," he said, "that's *weird*."

It turned out the possum wasn't the only variety of wildlife to have found its way into the house. We also had mice, who presumably had taken up residence at some point during the long interlude when the principal barrier to intruders was the blue tarp. At night we heard them scampering in the walls; I looked up from the table one evening to see a little gray head peering out of an electrical-box opening in the kitchen wall. The following evening Mary spotted a mouse darting across the kitchen floor and, moving at an impressive percentage of the speed of light, squished it against the wall with a board. Later I regaled friends with this tale at dinner: "You should have seen it. That mouse was *two-dimensional*." Mary didn't find this funny.

———

Notwithstanding my preoccupation with the house, ordinary life proceeded in its inexorable way, abetted chiefly by Mary. Our older two kids had now entered preschool, a momentous event. School had always been a concern for us, as for most city families. In 1987, then-Secretary of Education William Bennett had described the Chicago public schools as the worst in the nation, which was easy to believe; in my recollection they hadn't been all that hot in 1965. The city's Catholic elementary schools, once a mainstay, were in decline due to sharply rising costs and falling church attendance—enrollment was down 60 percent, and half had closed. Middle-class Chicago parents typically moved to the suburbs once their kids reached school age.

To counter this trend, the church we attended, Old St. Patrick's, had started a new school. The parish was one of the few in the city undergoing a resurgence. Located in a decaying old building on the edge of downtown, Old St. Pat's had had only four registered parishioners in 1983, but its energetic pastor, Jack Wall, had boosted attendance through outreach efforts, such as the "world's largest block party," an annual summer event that drew thousands.

I had nothing to do with the block party, but I knew a few of the people involved in organizing it. Many were graduates of the University of Notre Dame or St. Mary's College, its neighbor in South Bend, Indiana.

Growing up, I confess it had never quite sunk in that Notre Dame was in Chicago's orbit.[2] I realize this bespeaks a certain

———

[2] South Bend is outside metropolitan Chicago as officially defined, but it's the last stop on the South Shore commuter line, and is roughly as far from Chicago as Poughkeepsie is from New York. The South Shore Line, as rail fans know, is the passenger-carrying successor to the Chicago South Shore and South Bend Railroad, the last U.S. interurban, interurbans being the glorified trolleys that flourished briefly in the early twentieth century before succumbing to the automobile.

obliviousness on my part. I had of course heard of Notre Dame, Ara Parseghian, and the golden dome; I'd seen *Knute Rockne: All-American*, with Pat O'Brien and Ronald Reagan. Just for that reason, I thought of the school as a remote national icon, like the Washington Monument or Fort Knox. This impression was undoubtedly reinforced by the fact that Notre Dame was in Indiana, which Chicagoans from childhood (to be precise, from their first car trip to Michigan) regard as a primitive backwater on a par with Chad or, perhaps more aptly, the desolate reaches of eastern Germany—a wilderness of swamps, rusting industrial infrastructure, and deserted towns, overhung by a stench that would kill a goat.[3] South Bend, it's true, was a pleasant enough hamlet well beyond the most toxic industrial zone, but that only heightened the sense of antipodean isolation. My mother had taken me on an excursion to Notre Dame when I was nine or ten; it might as well have been on the banks of the Seine.

I was obliged to take a different view of things on graduating from college and settling on the north side. Domers, as Notre Dame alumni called themselves, were an inescapable part of the Chicago social scene—far more so than graduates of my alma mater, Northwestern, or the University of Chicago. This stemmed in large part from their indomitable will to party, which Lord knows wasn't a major motivator for the U. of C. Maroons.

Sociability, of course, isn't unusual among the collegiate set; what distinguished the Domers was their ability to put it on a commercial basis. At some point during the 1980s I became acquainted with what I thought of as the boat people, the nucleus of which consisted of two Notre Dame graduates who shortly

[3]In fairness, the far south side of Chicago was no garden of paradise either. In 1970, the electrical contractor by whom I was then employed asked me to make a delivery in the company pickup to a job site near Lake Calumet, then a center of the steel industry. I was startled to discover on arriving that virtually the entire district—buildings, trees, and for all I could tell the people— was tinted reddish brown, presumably due to iron oxide from the mills.

after moving to Chicago had begun entertaining themselves and their many friends by organizing parties. Several of the more memorable events were held on rented boats, which spent the evening plying the local waterways. Cruise boats in Chicago were not then numerous. As I heard the story, which may have been colored a bit by beer, the principals found themselves beneath a table toward the end of one of these revels and vowed to establish a boat company so they could have waterborne junkets whenever they felt like it. A week later, sobriety evidently having done nothing to diminish the charm of this notion, they flew down to Florida to inspect a boat they eventually bought. A year or two after that they commissioned the construction of a custom party . . . well, yacht would be putting things too grandly, but it was a nice little craft. In 1987, Mary and I, by no means party people, nonetheless thought it would be a hoot to get married on this vessel.[4] Today cruise boats in Chicago constitute a sizable fleet.

These were the people Jack Wall had enlisted to help revive his tumbledown parish. They were well suited to the task, and not just because of their proclivity for parties. If gays and artists were the shock troops of gentrification, Domers were the occupying army. They filled entire apartment buildings in downtown Chicago. (Well, maybe not entire buildings, but I know of one where they were so numerous it was commonly known as the dorm.)

A few Notre Dame alums didn't merely live in downtown apartments, they built them. In the mid-1980s a large downtown housing project had been constructed a couple blocks from Old St. Patrick's by a team of local developers, one of whom was a former Notre Dame football star. The venture was a typical

---

[4]It was, too. Not to brag, but ours was by far the most entertaining wedding I have ever attended. We said our vows while passing beneath the Madison Street bridge at the edge of the Loop on a busy Saturday afternoon. One passerby leaned over the railing and shouted, "Mazel tov!" while another advised, "Don't do it!"

Chicago production from beginning to end, involving massive public subsidies, a mortgage default, and years of protests after the developers tried to evade federal rules requiring that some apartments be set aside for low-income tenants (they coughed up a few in the end).

But eventually the buildings filled up. Virtually no one had lived in the area previously; now it was home to several thousand people, at least a few of whom were children. In 1989, Father Wall hired a Roman Catholic sister named Mary Ellen Caron to begin preschool and kindergarten classes for thirty-five young-sters in two rooms in one of the apartment towers. The school grew with surprising speed. By the time we enrolled our kids just five years later, more than four hundred students attended and classes were being held in multiple buildings—some preschool classes were conducted in a former Catholic high school on the near north side that had shut down a few years previously. Start-ing a few days after we moved into the Barn House, Mary had been taking Ryan and Ani there each morning on the L, after which she continued downtown to work.

The school was everything we could have hoped for, with a bright, enthusiastic staff, a well-thought-out curriculum, and an exemplary commitment to diversity. Though the majority of chil-dren in the school came from upper-middle-class families, the most popular kid in preschool was Francisco, whose parents were cops—the dad, a mounted patrolman, rode over on his horse one day and let the kids pet it.

I ought to emphasize that Father Wall, a deeply religious man, was trying to attract people back to the church in organizing the school and other parish programs, and hadn't had as his primary aim the resuscitation of Chicago. That was just how it worked out. I should also clarify that not everyone who played an impor-tant role in the resurgence of the parish and its school was a Domer, Irish, or in some cases even Catholic. (The original group organizing the world's largest block party, for example, had gone to Marquette University, a Jesuit school in Milwaukee.) Better simply to credit the city-guy mafia. The essential fact remains that, at a time in our lives when our children's education had become a matter of urgent concern, and the thought of the suburbs might have wafted through our minds, a first-class school had materialized out of thin air. The speed with which things had come together evidently surprised Father Wall, too. Without really meaning to, and with no scheme of empire in mind, he had tapped into Chicago's formidable Irish Catholic–dominated establishment. An early effort to attract young adults involved asking prominent Chicago Catholics to speak on the role of faith in their lives; you can guess where that led. The mayor and his wife became supporters of the school at an early stage, sent their kids there, and were honorary cochairs of the school's annual fund-raiser—we watched with fascination during the silent auction as a clutch of real estate developers outbid one another to join the mayor's foursome for a round of golf. (The winning bid, if memory serves, was upwards of $10,000, a small sum in some circles but impressive in Chicago.)

The school, eventually renamed the Frances Xavier Warde Schools and popularly known as FXW, was the first real indication we had that trying to raise a family in the city might not be the nightmare we had feared. We became friendly with the parents of our children's classmates. Some were rehabbers like us; others lived downtown, either in lakefront high-rises or new close-in residential developments, many built on old railroad yards. Some were professionals; one couple owned a legendary Italian lemonade stand on the west side not far from our old town house. Quite a few, it occurs to me now, were traders.

We were fortunate the school thing was working out, because the house still monopolized much of my attention. In November the floor finishers showed up. We moved out while they were at work, having been warned that the noise and dust were intolerable, but I returned each day to the house to move radiators and such and keep an eye on things. As always, the workers were Polish, although these men weren't the same breed as the carpenters—anyway, the firm's owner wasn't. He showed up on the first day accompanied by a much younger blonde in a fur coat, tight jeans, and high-heeled boots, evidence to my eye of a different set of priorities. He spoke minimal English, but his manner suggested that a certain amount of time had been allotted for the project and delays wouldn't be cheerfully brooked.

It was my project and my money, of course, and I indicated via Tony, who was on hand to translate, that certain repairs were essential. Assurances were duly made, but after the bosses departed it was just me and four men whose English was mainly limited to *okay* and *reparation*, which I took to mean "repair." With hand gestures I managed to communicate with the group's carpenter, who turned out to be an adherent of the right way—one learned to recognize the brethren through secret signs, in the manner of early Christians—and we got as much done as we could.

It helped that I'd planned ahead. In the front hall, for example, there were those two large holes cut in the handsome heart-pine flooring for heating registers, then inelegantly patched with mismatching wood after the registers were removed. Early on I'd noticed that a peninsula of heart-pine planking extended from the front hall a few feet into the rear hall, presumably a vestige of some forgotten room reconfiguration. Soon after the commencement of work I'd had the peninsula sawed off even with the hall doorway and the excess planking removed and stored. Now I had the flooring-crew carpenter use the salvaged material to replace the ugly patches, which he did with admirable precision. When later refinished, the patched sections were indistinguishable from the rest of the floor.

Once repairs in a given room were complete, sanding immediately commenced using massive floor sanders having the appearance of vacuum cleaners designed by the Russian army. Fat cables sprouting from the handles trailed across the floor and down the basement steps. A friend experienced in such matters had warned me not to inspect the electrical hookup: *You don't want to know.* But of course I did. I found that the floor guys had removed the front cover from the main electrical panel and jammed giant screwdrivers into the 240-volt terminal blocks above the main breaker; the sander cables were hooked to the screwdrivers with enormous alligator clips. The nearest circuit protection was in the alley; an accident would not only vaporize one or more floor guys, it'd kill the power to half the neighborhood. I retreated back up the steps.

The final step in finishing was applying stain and varnish. I'd selected a common stain called golden oak. Calling me over to consult, the floor guys gave me to understand that they thought the color was a little dark—they wanted to know if I wanted to dilute it with mineral spirits. *Sure*, I said. They mixed up a batch and poured some on a section of newly sanded floor. It looked like India ink. Did I approve? They might as well have been brain surgeons asking my opinion of the sutures. *Go ahead*, I said, hoping not to be appalled. Once rubbed in—the process was extraordinarily fast—the stain proved to be indeed dark, but not objectionably so. Charlie, who visited later, went further: "It's perfect," he said. Though I had had the impression of having narrowly avoided disaster throughout, when the job was complete I had to confess the workmanship was impeccable.

Y ou'll excuse me, but we have a few practical matters we need to discuss before proceeding further:

■ Something we didn't realize till too late during our work on the radiators was that there had been a simple solution to our problem heating up the larger pipes, had we been alert enough to notice it. MAPP gas—the letters stand for methylacetylene-propadiene—is a hydrocarbon mixture with a higher combustion temperature than propane, making it much easier to sweat a joint. Cheap and safe, MAPP gas is sold in the same aisle in the home improvement store as propane and comes in bright yellow cans—they could scarcely have been more conspicuous if I'd tripped on one. I'm consoled by the thought that, had I known about such things at the outset and so avoided the trials here described, this would be a pretty boring book.

■ Admirer of radiators though I am, I admit they have a significant drawback: They make for a dry house during heating season, which among other things manifests itself in staticky rugs, dry skin, gaps in the floor planking, and pianos that go quickly out of tune. When I was a kid my mother sought to rectify these problems by hanging humidifiers behind the radiators in our house, skinny open-topped metal tanks filled with water that evaporated when the radiator heated up. How well these worked I can't say, because we never remembered to fill them. Portable electric room humidifiers have the advantage of bright lights and noise to remind the forgetful but still need refilling at short intervals, making one long for the simplicity of the auto-filling humidifiers used on forced-air systems. I've read about auto-filling ductless central humidifiers that supposedly work on the basis of Dalton's law of partial pressures, which is a grandiose way of saying the humidity spreads around the house on its own, but I can't say from personal knowledge that it actually does. All of which is to say I don't have a solution for this vexing issue, so be prepared to deal.

■ Two things you need to know about paint. First, only the uninformed, or those without children, use flat interior paint, because while it may initially hide the defects of your lumpy and irregular walls, it shows every fingerprint thereafter and can't easily be cleaned. Paint having a slight sheen to it—one manufacturer calls its semi-shiny finish "pearl"—washes up much more readily. Second, for exteriors you want 100 percent acrylic paint. Painting your wooden siding won't be any cheaper, but at least you won't have to do it every three years.

▪ I'm not saying it ought to be a major design driver, but home appraisers often have the idea that a room must have a closet for it to count as a bedroom. In fact there's no national standard and many older houses have closetless rooms where people routinely sleep, but if you don't put in closets when you have the chance, don't be surprised if you get an argument later.

▪ I've intimated this a couple times already, but now state it as scientific fact: Whereas everyone notices the difference between an eight-foot ceiling and nine-foot ceiling, thinking the former ordinary and the latter luxurious, hardly anyone notices the difference between a nine-foot ceiling and a ten-foot one. This means you can drop a ten-foot ceiling ten or twelve inches to accommodate pipes and ducts in the serene confidence that no one will know. I acknowledge this falls into the category of things most people don't need to be told. I just wish someone had told me.

18

I

t's a commonplace to say of old houses that they don't build 'em that way anymore, and in fact they seldom do, but that's not because the skills are lost or the materials can't be obtained or even, in the last analysis, because the cost is too high. The main reason they don't build 'em that way is that nobody asks. I had worked on old houses most of my life, but even so there were things I didn't know to ask for and consequently didn't get—for example, quartersawn oak flooring, which sad story I'll relate a couple chapters hence. But I'd learned I could get custom millwork, and meant to, since few interior features so palpably distinguished an old house from a newly constructed one as the elaborate wood detailing commonly found in the former. I was in the happy position of not having to design the woodwork from scratch, although no doubt Charlie could have worked up something suitable if asked; I simply needed to copy the resplendent molding I already had. Duplicating old woodwork wasn't difficult—all you had to do was give the mill shop a few representative pieces, and of course a wad of cash.

I'd made arrangements in this regard with a young mill shop owner named Guido. His prices were reasonable, but at this point that was immaterial—we'd spent our savings, maxed out our credit cards and could barely afford a cup of coffee, much less a truckload of custom millwork. I'd gone ahead and ordered the stuff anyway, hoping something would develop. The millwork arrived one morning; I opened the mail while the workers piled it in the hall. In the stack I found an envelope from a publisher—a book I'd written had unexpectedly gone into royalties and they'd sent me a good-sized check, which would cover Guido's bill and leave us a little for groceries. For all the unseen forces watching out for us, we had our share of just plain luck.

A staggering number of tasks remained to be completed in addition to the woodwork, many of them made more complicated by the fact that we now lived in the house. A bathroom, for example, required a good deal of intricate finishing under any circumstances, with a long series of tasks that had to be accomplished in a certain order, but attempting to schedule the work, which often involved lengthy delays for processes such as curing that couldn't wisely be rushed, became positively nightmarish once the bathroom was in regular use. I found myself making timelines and checklists worthy of a missile launch, and about as prone to mishap.

Some setbacks were of the more mundane variety. While lowering an old washing machine down the basement steps—we hadn't made up our minds to discard it, and it looked a little rummy rusting in the yard—I lost my grip on the dolly. The washing machine bounced down the steps; I fell on top of it at the bottom. An X-ray established that I'd only suffered contusions, but for a good two weeks afterward my ribs hurt like hell.

After the usual false starts and distractions, we'd assembled the finishing materials for the bathroom walls—tile for the showers, wooden wainscoting elsewhere—and one day Tony sent a carpenter named Mirek over to install them. I was downstairs that afternoon when I heard a splashing sound in the walls, and on investigating found water pouring from the basement ceiling. I ran upstairs to find Mirek pounding nails into the wainscoting in the bathroom directly above. Mirek spoke no English, but by means of frantic gestures I persuaded him to stop. Seeing the alarming cataract downstairs, he pulled out a carpenter's pencil and began writing on the wall, the first instinct of all tradespeople in times of crisis. It was an equation—I realized Mirek was trying to persuade me on mathematical grounds that his nails weren't long enough to cause the leak. I warmly replied that the lack of dripping water antecedent to his hammering strongly argued for his involvement. We pulled off the wainscoting and were doused by spurting water. Acknowledging the reality of the situation, Mirek disappeared briefly to scare up the necessities to put the matter right, my plumbing inventory being momentarily depleted. The repair concluded—Mirek was one of those dependable sorts who might not do everything right, but at least lost minimal time fixing what he'd done wrong—it was back to the wainscoting. A week later I got the shower door and shower head mounted, plus a spout for the half-inch copper pipe, and after that a toilet and sink.

In early November Tom K— the finish carpenter and his helper Frank arrived to begin installing the woodwork. Tom was Greek and retained a heavy accent despite long residence in the United States; Tony had warned me he could be temperamental. He was, but that posed no great difficulty; he was a member of the brotherhood. Early on I learned that when Tom was especially proud of some bit of craftsmanship he announced, "You no like it, I tear it out," whereas if he had his doubts he said, "You can't do nothing, forget it." When the latter occurred I gazed mournfully at the item in silence, then offered a modest suggestion about whatever defect had caused Tom pain. Invariably after some coaxing he relented and did it over.

Few such occasions arose, though. Tom's work was exquisite— "like furniture," he declared periodically. It was hard to disagree.

He and Frank built what amounted to a picture frame around the doors and windows, each an elegant composition of casing and backband plus a sill (in the case of the windows) or high flanking baseboards (in the case of the doors). They did one room at a time. The change in appearance was extraordinary—the finished rooms seemed positively palatial. "Looks rich," Tom agreed. We at last had tangible evidence that the house's interior would some-day match its now-handsome exterior.

Like the framing carpenters before them, Tom and Frank took it upon themselves to rectify occasional weak points in the house's original construction. The closet under the front hall stairs had the tiny window of which we've already spoken—the glass mea-sured just twelve and a half by sixteen inches. Originally it had been surrounded by the massive five-inch-wide casing used else-where in the house—beautiful there, but in this context absurdly overscaled. Tom and Frank sliced the casing down to three inches wide—the result looked much better. Once again the brother-hood had improved on the house's original design.

One may ask: Was *every* tradesman who ambled into the Barn House a member of the Brotherhood of the Right Way? The answer manifestly was no, but I do have to say we encountered quite a few more than might be expected in a random sampling of the population, especially considering the lamentations about declining craftsmanship and incompetent contractors that one routinely hears. To a large extent, I concede, that was Tony's doing, because he hired the bulk of the subcontractors, but even in projects in which he had no involvement the brothers turned up far more often than not. I could claim I had a gift for spotting talent, but that would be like saying I had a knack for picking people who spoke English—assuming you had the eye, about which more in a moment, no special skill was required to detect members of this scorned cult.

Which, frankly, is what it was. In reality, I think, the Brotherhood of the Right Way was respectably numerous; its members just kept their heads low lest they attract unwanted attention, like the Huguenots or fans of the White Sox.[1] Fact was, the brotherhood coexisted uneasily with the bottom-line crowd, who recognized that the profit lay in knowing when to say: *good enough.* (Not a problem confined to the building trades, incidentally—ask any software developer.) You were an artist in a world that didn't reward artistry—I knew that from my own experience. As a writer I occasionally got compliments for a well-turned paragraph— people expected such things of writers. But rare was the electrical job at the end of which people came up to me and said: *Hey, nice pipes.*

I think the main reason so many craftsmen worked on the Barn House, and we got such a beautiful job as a result, was simply that I recognized them when they showed up. The Brothers of the Right Way liked having their work appreciated, and would go to a great deal of trouble for anyone who acknowledged their efforts. For all that you heard, standards of craftsmanship in the United States hadn't deteriorated to any remarkable extent that I'd ever noticed. The real problem, it seemed to me, was with those who did the hiring. A lot of people wouldn't know quality work if it came up and introduced itself. They lacked the critical eye.

A good eye wasn't a matter of being hard to please. Any contractor can tell you stories about clients who thought they knew more than the tradesmen, asked for impossibilities, and got thrown off job sites. That wasn't the mark of a good eye; that was just being obnoxious. Nor was it merely a knack for judging level, straight, and true, although that was an essential skill. The real trick lay in the ability to give intelligent direction to the project.

---

[1] I speak as a north-side White Sox fan in a town where feelings about baseball run deep. A well-known tune in Chicago called "South Side Irish" concludes, "And when it comes to baseball / We have two favorite clubs / The go-go White Sox / And whoever plays the Cubs."

That meant knowing what the job was supposed to look like when it was done, and equally important, what was achievable and at what cost.

No question it helped to have some basic familiarity with the trades, and for that matter with manual labor. I'd had the advantage of having grown up watching people work on houses and doing a fair amount of work myself. I'd also had the good luck to come along at a point when my family wasn't so far removed from its working-class origins to have decided this kind of thing was beneath them—if my father had been a stockbroker I'd likely have been as adrift as the next guy. One of my fears, in fact, was that I'd fail to transmit the principles of the right way to my own children, a matter I'll return to. But first, if you don't mind, a few more practical tips:

▪ Anyone who gazes upon a deft piece of finish carpentry (or sometimes even framing carpentry, as happened a few times with us) will marvel at the beauty of the wood in its natural state, which is an understandable reaction, and may conclude it's his duty to leave the wood exposed or otherwise inadequately finished, which is foolish. You see evidence of the latter tendency most conspicuously in the treatment of new cedar siding. It's possible to leave cedar unpainted, and if the cedar-sided object in question is a tool shed on the Maine coast, in a quarter century or so it will weather to a lustrous silver-gray. In the city, on the other hand—and here I speak from the evidence of my own eyes—in ten years it will look like hell.

Despite urgings to the contrary we were steadfast regarding the painting of our cedar (typically nowadays new cedar is stained, but we had to match the painted original). However, we waffled on the matter of interior trim, much of which frankly is also better off painted. Most rehabbers believe they owe it to posterity to strip away the thick encrustation of paint with which previous generations have befouled the woodwork, and doing so in fact often reveals details that the accretion of years has obscured. It doesn't follow that you're obligated to leave the uncovered result forever bare. Oak, of course, stains handsomely, and old pine often does so as well (good luck with new pine—although I realize stained pine furniture is fairly common, I've never seen a house with new stained-pine trim that rose above the level of a summer cabin). However, poplar, Tom's species of choice for trim intended for painting (hard, fine grain, no knots), won't take stain worth squat.

After I'd proven to my satisfaction that my collection of old pine doors would stain beautifully, I tortured myself for months about what to do with the surrounding poplar trim, thinking I needed to stain it as well. Charlie finally persuaded me to relinquish this misguided notion, and I can report with confidence that a stained old-pine door surrounded by painted poplar (and further set off by oak flooring, a rich wall paint color, and other details) produces as agreeable an effect as one could want.

■ While we're on the subject of exterior work, I may as well say that if you're going to go to all the trouble to have your house sided in cedar, make sure all the other exterior trim is cedar, too. For some reason nobody involved with the restoration of the Barn House thought there was anything odd about using trim made of pine, which predictably proceeded to rot. We patched the trim, but eventually had the decaying front and rear porch steps rebuilt of cedar.

■ Should the opportunity arise—and consider yourself lucky if it doesn't, since the project isn't practical unless you've gutted much of your house—you'll want to equip your hot-water supply with a recirculation pipe. The concept isn't widely known even among plumbers, and I had to thumb through a stack of home improvement books looking for an explanation of how it was done, but the idea isn't complicated. At the top of your hot-water riser, you connect a half-inch pipe run that descends to the basement monotonically (again that wonderful word) and splices into the drain tap at the bottom of the water heater, thereby forming a loop. The idea is that, even with all the faucets closed, convection will keep hot water circulating steadily, drifting upward in the riser when warm and buoyant, then returning via the recirculation pipe when cool and dense. Turn on the second-floor shower, therefore, and you'll have hot water in seconds, without the usual frigid delay. I embraced the idea as Parisian youth embraced socialism—thinking it an ideal worth pursuing, but having doubts that it would actually work. I was gratified to discover on taking my inaugural shower that it worked just fine, and have enjoyed prompt hot water ever since. One concedes that a recirculation pipe slightly enlarges one's carbon footprint, since convection depends on constant discharge of heat to the void, but since I assiduously recycle and am otherwise virtuous, I figure I can indulge myself this once.

■ The following information will be useless to anyone not installing a hot-water radiator system (which is to say, pretty much anyone), but in my opinion significantly advances this ancient art. I wanted to install radiators in the basement of the Barn House, since we planned to use part of it as a rec room. Plumbers whom I spoke to on this subject seemed to think the job would be indescribably difficult, and admittedly in the days of gravity-fed systems it was something of a trick, since the exigencies of convection required that all the radiators, including those in the basement, be above the level of the boiler. For this reason, the radiators in basement apartments, including the one formerly at the Barn House, were flat units suspended horizontally just below the ceiling. Since heat rose and cold sank, basement apartments were usually cold in winter. I didn't propose to put up with that nonsense. I'd read in the *McGraw-Hill Encyclopedia of Science & Technology*, in which I reposed great trust, that in a pump-fed hot-water heating system the water could be forced in any direction, including down, which I considered license to put the basement radiators on the floor where they belonged. As I say, plumbers (including the legendary Polish plumber Boniek, of whom unfortunately we will have no occasion to hear further in this book[2]) were certain this wouldn't work, and that at minimum I needed to install a separate basement loop with a separate pump and for all I knew a separate furnace.

Paying these warnings no heed, I installed the basement radiators according to my own lights, then was mortified, and frankly mystified, to find they didn't always work. Sometimes after the system had been drained, refilled, and restarted due to some project or other, a couple of the basement radiators would remain cold, although for no apparent reason they might resume operation without human intervention after some months. I spent years trying to noodle out what was up, removing pipes, looking for blockages, and so on. Finally, in a flash of insight that in my estimation ranks with Newton's apple, I realized that (a) sometimes air got trapped in the pipes serving the basement radiators, blocking the flow of hot water, and (b) to avoid this problem, I simply needed to repipe both supply and return lines for said radiators so that they provided

---

[2]Just one story about Boniek, whom I called in when our toilets backed up due to failure to replace the root-filled sewer pipes when we had the chance. Boniek's English was limited and he often brought his wife, Alice, along to translate. When he proposed replacing some pipe, I asked whether it would be wise first to inspect the pipe by threading a small TV camera into it catheter-style, as I had seen other plumbers do. Alice translated Boniek's reply. "Boniek doesn't need camera," she said, trilling her *r*s gravely. "Boniek has *experience*." The repair solved the problem; the toilets haven't backed up again.

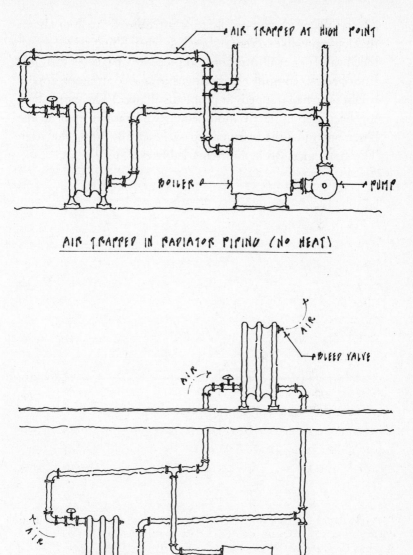

AIR TRAPPED AT HIGH POINT

BOILER ▸ ◂ PUMP

AIR TRAPPED IN RADIATOR PIPING (NO HEAT)

AIR ▸ ◂ BLEED VALVE

AIR ▸

BOILER ▸ ◂ PUMP

AIR ▸

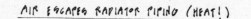

AIR ESCAPES RADIATOR PIPING (HEAT!)

a route rising monotonically to a radiator on the floor above, making it possible to vent trapped air when filling via the upper bleed valves—see illustrations on preceding page. (In fact, had I not been so compulsive about ensuring a continuous slope, I might have had trapped-air problems all over.) The piping having been appropriately modified, I was gratified that all the basement radiators warmed up satisfactorily from the start. The system has worked unremarkably ever since.

19

In the seven months between Labor Day and April Fool's Day, which seem like appropriate bookends, we succeeded in establishing a basic level of livability in the house. We installed the doors and woodwork (I first stripped the paint from the ancient lock sets and hinges, which Tom and Frank then mortised into place); finished the floors; tiled the bathrooms, the laundry room, and front and rear entry hall floors; mounted the kitchen cabinets and bathroom vanities and installed the countertops; hooked up the appliances, plumbing fixtures, and numerous electric lights; rebuilt a couple of fireboxes for future fireplaces; installed a shower door; put up closet shelves, clothes and towel hooks, toilet paper holders, and other fixtures; replaced the useless 1890s-vintage wooden track on the living room pocket door with a proper steel one; installed a new balustrade, indistinguishable except in minor respects from the original, to replace the one missing at the top of the front stairs; hauled an enormous mound of trash out of the backyard; and in the remaining time, ate, attempted to earn money, tended to sick or crying children, and every so often slept.

The Chief assisted when he could. Once again we were obliged to learn new trades, or at least enlarge our knowledge of old ones, such as how to glue PVC pipe together. The Chief approached all these projects with his customary optimism.

"This plastic pipe is the greatest," he said one evening as we rerouted a two-inch drain in the basement. "It's cheap, easy to cut, no threading."

"I guess," I said. "The only drawback is it'll give you lung cancer."

"Lung cancer?"

"Yeah, smell this stuff." I waved the glue applicator in his direction. The fumes were overpowering.

"Smoke a cigarette and you won't notice the smell," said the Chief.

By the time spring arrived the Barn House's residents could use the toilet, take a shower, and brush their teeth at a sink without having to change rooms, much less go to somebody else's house. We could cook a meal and wash and put away the dishes. In short, we could lead, by city standards, normal lives.

We'd turned an important corner. One indication of this was that the laboriously refinished floors now seemed ordinary. I wasn't disappointed with the work; on the contrary, I'd come round to Charlie's view that the floors were just right—but they'd passed from the realm of the heroic to the everyday. Not three months previously men operating heavy machinery and making God's own din had struggled mightily in this confined space—now children played on the result without a thought.[1] The floors

---

[1] At times one wished they had an occasional thought. Hearing loud bangs one day, I ran to the front hall to find Andrew, then one year old, sitting cheerfully on the floor surrounded by wooden pegs that Ryan had been dropping over the second-floor balustrade above, mercifully missing his brother

in my mind's eye had receded from the foreground into the background; they looked as though they'd always been that way.

That was the idea. I wanted everything to seem not bright and shiny and new, but timeless—a common enough ambition, I suppose. But it's trickier than you might think.

There are several schools of thought on how to modernize an old house. The first is to pay no attention at all and buy whatever they're pushing this week at the home-improvement store. Happily those taking this approach aren't so numerous as formerly.

The second school consists of the historical purists, who attempt to re-create the house as it stood at a particular moment in time. Mary and I had visited a few homes redone along these lines on neighborhood house tours, most of them magnificent exemplars of late Victoriana with ceiling medallions and period antiques and sometimes operating gas fixtures. Some might object that these places were more like museums than homes, which I don't think was necessarily the case, but they required more time and money than we had.

A third group consists of persons of artistic inclination who use home remodeling as an opportunity to make a design statement. We had a number of friends and acquaintances in this category. I remember one gay couple who created a series of rooms so brilliantly conceived and executed you felt you ought to take off your hat on entering—among other things they'd rebuilt a closet, and I mean a closet-sized closet as opposed to the larger walk-in variety, as a library complete with floor-to-ceiling built-in shelves, what I recall as walnut crown molding with indirect lighting, and a rolling wooden ladder with brass fittings on a (very) short track.

I admired these efforts, but they weren't what I wanted to do, even if I'd had the resources and talent. For one thing, the arty

---

but impressing a series of smile-shaped dings into the newly refinished heart pine.

types often produced bits that were first-rate considered singly but incongruous taken together, lacking a common thread. More important, they were too clearly the product of an individual rather than of their time, whereas we wanted a house rooted in history.

I'm not sure if I picked up this idea working in the trades, but that reinforced it. Once an old electrician, seeing me crank down a fitting with what he considered excessive force, commented, "I'd hate to be the guy that comes after you." I thought that was an interesting way of looking at things. You weren't the first person to work on the project; you wouldn't be the last. You were appreciative if your predecessors had done their work competently and so made your job easier; by the same token, you didn't want to leave a mess for the next guy. The project—any construction or remodeling job, really—was a sort of serial collaboration.

I'd come to think of an old house in the same way. You owned it temporarily. In the rare case you might find the place such a shambles that the only sensible thing was to start over, but more commonly you'd discover well-crafted elements that needed only a little repair and buffing up. Other parts of the house might require rebuilding, and naturally you'd want to install modern mechanical systems and amenities. But the place had been built in a certain style, and it seemed perverse simply to ignore that style in constructing new. What's more, I thought it self-evident that all the parts of the house ought to exhibit some unity of design. The result if skillfully done would be a modern house that retained its original character while reflecting at least in small ways the times—and not necessarily just the good times—through which it had passed.[2]

That was my goal, and by now I felt some confidence that we'd

---

[2]One such sign in the Barn House was its old interior doors. They cleaned up smartly when I refinished them years later, but if you look closely you can see the neatly patched holes left by apartment dead bolts.

at least partly achieved it. In the spring of 1995 my brother John, standing on the front sidewalk during his first visit in close to two years, stared at the top floor of the house with its turret and dormer and asked, "So what did you do up there, anyway?" I was delighted—I'd wanted no one to be able to tell what we'd done. We'd demolished and rebuilt the roof; what John saw now bore only a faint resemblance to the house when we'd bought it. But it likely approximated the building's appearance as originally constructed, and more important looked right, to the point that it was hard to imagine the place having looked any other way.

Still, the house was far from complete. We'd done no decorating. The woodwork, however comely, was unpainted, and the walls were uniformly white. We had no curtains, no rugs, not even closet doors. We had fireboxes built into the chimneys but no mantelpieces—the fireplaces were mere holes in the walls. We had no garage and no landscaping. Barely half the house's interior space was usable in other than the roughest sense. The "office" where I did my writing was an unfinished (and more pertinently, uninsulated) attic—my computer perched on cardboard boxes; over the winter I'd pecked away at the keyboard in my parka, warmed mainly by a space heater. The living and dining rooms weren't finished either—the floors had to be rebuilt, and having exhausted our funds, I was the one who was going to have to rebuild them.

That was the project to which I turned next. By now I'd abandoned hopes of restoring the dining room's intricate parquet veneer (too far gone) or installing walnut inlay as a replacement (too expensive). I'd learned enough to ask how much more quartersawn oak would cost compared to plainsawn—don't worry, the distinction will be explained in due time—but the price we'd been quoted was $5,000, which was out of the question.

Instead I settled for getting the floor level. I mentioned earlier that the floors in the front of the house had buckled after someone's misbegotten experiment in bricking up the foundation wall below—you'd think a mole had tunneled around the perimeter of the rooms. Having first removed the boxes piled in the living room by the movers, I gingerly extracted what remained of the parquet, pried up the subflooring, removed the bricks, then reinstalled the planks. Determined to avoid the squeaks endemic to wooden houses, the Chief and I then fastened all the planking in both rooms to the joists below with drywall screws—fifteen hundred in all. That done—the preparatory work took nearly three weeks—we called the floor guys back to install and finish new oak flooring. While they were in the midst of this, a fill-in mailman stuck his head through the living room window and asked, "Does anybody live here?" But we wound up with a helluva floor.

Construction on the first and second floors was now more or less complete, but Mary remained unhappy—though she'd made things reasonably homey, there wasn't a room in the house that was anywhere near done, done here defined as all work finished and the rooms decorated. Experienced rehabbers will recognize the great perceptual divide these words signify. Some may call it a male-female thing, but that's apt to lead to bitter remarks. Rather, let's say it springs from the division of labor.

Typically in any home rehabilitation project you have the construction department and the ministry of interior design. The construction crew thinks it is carrying a good deal of the load and can point to indeterminate but certainly large quantities of plans drawn, dust swallowed, earth moved, pipes run, large and intransigent objects transported, nails nailed and screws screwed, wires pulled, risks taken, injuries sustained, subcontractors set straight, paperwork submitted and submitted again, crud shoveled, mistakes corrected, complex and dimly understood systems successfully installed, disasters averted, difficult persons dealt with, and withal a host of troubles patiently borne. The decorating unit thinks this is all very well, but we still don't have a front-hall rug.

Moreover, from the standpoint of bringing matters to a conclusion, the renovating moieties often have radically different ideas on how to get from point A to point B. The construction crew believes, and is confident any reasonable and practical observer would agree, that one ought to stain all the woodwork, then refinish all the doors, then paint all the radiators, and in general perform the many tasks that need doing in a global and systematic manner, whereas the decorating lobby thinks we should finish (and I mean totally finish) one room at a time. I make no attempt to judge the wisdom of these disparate approaches, or to recount the outcome of every step in the decision-making process. Suffice it to say that one or both of the participants spent much of their time mad.

Mary had other complaints, too. Her commute downtown from our old town house, which was only a mile or so from the Loop, took fifteen minutes door to door; now the trip, consisting of a circuitous L ride plus a few blocks' walk on either end, took her forty-five minutes. She also didn't like the walk to the L station, which took her down a dreary commercial street. I couldn't do anything about the long commute, but I thought maybe I could brighten up the walk. The commercial street had a wide paved median formerly used for streetcar tracks—why not plant trees in it? When we got a flyer announcing a meeting to reestablish the local community association, I saw my chance. I decided I'd help get things organized, then lobby the alderman and the city to landscape the median.

Things began promisingly. At the initial meeting, held in the basement of a nearby church, I learned that the community group had been quite active at one time—they'd been the people behind the nightly CB patrol—but had fallen dormant once crime became less pressing. I volunteered for the bylaws committee, figuring once we got our paperwork in order (legal issues required that the organization be essentially created afresh), officers elected, and other busywork dispatched, we'd be ready to take on city hall.

It didn't work out that way. Here again I'll omit a great deal of dispiriting detail, but basically the bylaws committee, having cooked up a serviceable document, prevailed upon party A, who had a history with the prior organization and thus some stature, to chair a meeting of the membership to push through the bylaws without unnecessary ado. However, despite the fact that the necessary parliamentary maneuvering had been reviewed with some care beforehand, party A on taking the gavel ignored these preparations and let the debate drift, with the result that the meeting sputtered out and the participants scattered with essentially nothing resolved. Many more meetings were required to get the organization reconstituted, by which time another resident, an eccentric older man, had sent around flyers for a competing organization he claimed was the rightful heir to the dormant group (and more significantly, to its bank account), confusing everyone and requiring much tedious sorting out. By the time all was settled—believe me, I spent months at this—many had lost interest and turnout at meetings was poor.

In the end it didn't matter. Although we hadn't done any lobbying, local officials a little later announced they were going to landscape the medians of the nearby commercial streets as part of a city beautification program, which in due course they did—an indication, although I didn't see it that way at the time, that we were being swept up in a larger tide.

None of this happened quickly enough to relieve the tense domestic situation. Mary and I had an argument that spring—I don't remember much about the timing or the circumstances, except that we were driving somewhere on an errand. She'd been grousing off and on for months about how miserable our life was. I hadn't had much response up till then; the point was tough to dispute. What set me off on this occasion, I think, was what I took to be the implication that, whereas she lived an existence of unrelieved pain, I occasionally enjoyed myself. Looking back on it now, I concede there was some truth in this. I always enjoyed myself—I found points of entertainment in a root canal. What's more, if we may resort once more to the out-of-control car meta-phor, I at least had the benefit of being at the wheel, while she was screaming in the backseat.

Still, objectively speaking, I was absorbing a lot of punishment, for which I figured I deserved a little credit. "I live in filth!" I yelled by way of opening statement. I exaggerated slightly, but for the most part this was true. Though we were now years into the project, I wound up covered in dust and grime just about every time I worked on the house, the kind that sifted into your hair and wound up in the handkerchief whenever you blew your nose. I offered a few other remarks in this vein, then launched the blockbuster of marital arguments:

"You're just like your *mother!*"

Understand that I get along fine with my mother-in-law, al-ways have. She had certain idiosyncrasies, some of which, consid-ered in isolation, Mary could be said to share, that's all I was saying. Regardless, the shot had the desired effect. The argument continued in a desultory way for a while; Mary may have said I was just like my father. But her bunker had been knocked off its foundations. As we pulled into the driveway she said in a quiet voice, "Am I really just like my mother?" I doused my fuses im-mediately. "Aw, no, babe," I said, putting my arm around her, and the argument was over. But I'd be lying if I said it was the last one we had.

Toward the end of March 1995 I got a bill from Tony and Jerry for extras. I'd expected the bill but wasn't sure of the amount. At the outset I'd been fastidious about requesting a price in ad-vance for this or that modification—a concrete floor in the crawl space here, a dropped ceiling to conceal radiator pipes there. But I became more casual about such matters as the project wore on. There didn't seem much point—whatever the price, I realized after the first couple outings, it would likely be reasonable, and I was certain to say go ahead. As a result I'd lost track of the total.

Some changes I knew were going to be expensive. Rebuilding the turret roof because Charlie had indicated the wrong angle in the plans, for example—that was definitely going to cost me. Even so, I was taken aback when I opened the bill and saw the bottom line—$19,000. That night I sent Tony a long fax disputing a number of charges. He called the following day, quite upset. We needed to have a meeting.

Anyone who has worked on an old house, or been involved in a construction project or for that matter a complex contract of any kind, has had such a meeting. I'm certain tense words were exchanged upon completion of the great pyramid at Giza. The difference was that in the old days these disputes were settled by having the contractor put to death. Our prevaricating age didn't countenance such expedients. You had to argue endlessly about assumptions and technical terminology and standards of work-manship, and who said what to whom.

The major sticking point in our case had to do with moving the chimney chase for the fireplace in the family room. Tony had billed me $5,000 for it. I was exasperated. True, Charlie's plan was the proximate cause of the problem, and I'd hired Charlie. But, I reasoned, I'd hired the whole damn bunch of these guys. Tony had been responsible for constructing the roof and furnishing and installing the fireplace. Surely as an experienced contractor he ought to have realized during initial construction (if not sooner) that no flue was going to fit through that opening, and advised me to come up with a plan that would actually work. I rehearsed the matter with friends at a party, who were happy to see it my way. "This is why you hire people who know what they're doing," I argued. "What do I know about offsets? I'm the fricking *home owner*. I don't know *jack*. I'm looking for *expert advice*."

Tony arrived with Jerry one morning a few days later. We sat at the kitchen table—light poured in between the trees through the double windows; it was really quite pleasant—and debated for four and a half hours. I was subtle. I was eloquent. I pro-pounded arguments that at least should have gotten a special prosecutor appointed. However, a Polish guy is a tough nut. Tony didn't budge from his insistence that he was just following the plans. In the end Jerry suggested we split the difference, which seemed fair under the circumstances, so that's what we did.

The news didn't cheer Mary. Even with the reduction, we still owed thousands of dollars we hadn't counted on paying. That night she reported that our monthly expenses exceeded our income by a considerable margin. "I feel like we're destitute," she said.

That overstated matters, but we were house poor, no question. Truth was, fixing up an old house in the city was an extraordinarily expensive proposition, even setting considerations of speculation and profit aside. We had purchased the Barn House for $250,000 (which at the time seemed high, considering its sorry state, but nonetheless was cheaper than virtually everything else we'd seen), then spent at least $350,000 renovating it—I say at least because after a while we quit adding up the bills lest we make ourselves sick.

Granted the $350,000 included a few nonessential items, as Wayne had predicted it might. We'd spent two grand on a granite countertop in the kitchen. This was frivolous, I acknowledge; Formica would have done just as well. We had blitzed through $30,000 restoring the cedar siding. Another indulgence—I'm guessing $10,000 tops would have gotten the place clad in low-maintenance vinyl, at the cost, it must be said, of obscuring many of the house's distinguishing architectural features, limiting the choice of colors to the dozen or two the siding company felt like selling, and generally making the house as ugly as sin, but think of the money we'd have saved on paint. Nix the copper gutters, out with the fancy faucets, to the devil with . . . well, to be honest, there wasn't much else we could have easily dispensed with. I suppose we might have used half-inch drywall instead of five-eighths, and substituted stock moldings for custom millwork. Conceivably—one shudders—we might have repaired the venerable oak balustrade with stock pieces from Menard's.

But that was about it. If the job was to be undertaken at all, there was work that had to be done. It was customary in our coddled age to provide a house with running water and electric lights. Likewise a steel beam that actually supported the floor above, as opposed to merely seeming to, couldn't be considered a silly whim. One wanted a roof that didn't leak, windows not shedding parts, a porch on which one didn't set foot at peril of one's life. In a house of comparable age in the suburbs (my parents' home, for example), one might have expected repairs on this scale—some of them, anyway—to have been undertaken serially by a succession of previous owners, none of whom would have come close to bankrupting himself in consequence; in the city, by and large, it was all up to you.

My point is that while we might have cut the odd corner, nothing would have changed the fundamental fact: If you wanted to fix up an old house in the city, you had to drop a ton of cash. This needs to be borne in mind when considering the extravagant sums for which city houses are sometimes sold, which give the impression that windfall profits are easily come by and that the participants are cleaning up. Not so—certainly not in the early going, anyway. Our middle-class home in the city had set us back more than $600,000, which had gone toward a house purchased relatively cheaply and renovated by nonunion labor working for a contractor who had trimmed his profit margin. The $600,000 figure bore no necessary relation to what the house would actually *sell* for, you understand. That's what it actually cost.

The matter is worth enlarging on. In the midst of one anxious financial consultation, when the depth of the hole we had dug for ourselves had become inescapably plain, Mary had asked, "Did you ever think you would own a six-hundred-thousand-dollar house?" "Babe," I said, "we don't own a six-hundred-thousand-dollar house. We own a five-hundred-thousand-dollar house that cost six hundred thousand dollars."

Even the lower number for a long while was a stretch. Later in

1995, while we were in the process of arranging a new mortgage that would pay off the original mortgage plus the construction loan and put the financing for the house on a long-term basis, the Barn House was appraised at $470,000. This figure had been computed on an impressive-looking form, based on comparable sales with additions for this and subtractions for that, and purportedly reflected what the place would honestly fetch. The fact remained that no house in the immediate vicinity had ever sold for that much money. Somebody had to be at the high end, of course. The difficulty for us was that anyone willing to pop for the priciest house in the neighborhood would have wanted it more or less finished, which ours demonstrably wasn't. We had no intention of selling—I was stubborn, as I say—but it rankled that we didn't have the option of doing so unless we wanted to take a catastrophic financial bath.

All that having been said, I don't honestly think the biggest drain imposed by the Barn House was money. One day I mentioned to Mary that I always told myself the same thing at trying moments during the project; the only thing that changed was the emphasis. At first I mostly said, "It's just a house." But as the project wore on I found myself moaning, "It's just a *house*," as opposed to a cancer cure, the next *Huckleberry Finn*, or, to put the matter in practical terms, more vacations with the kids. My point was that the one unrecoverable asset you poured into a house wasn't cash. It was time.

Toward the end of June we began preparing for our final city inspection. Two things had made this urgent. First, in order to pay off our construction loan and secure a new mortgage, we had to get an official city signoff. Second, we needed the space. I wanted an office so I didn't have to spend another winter freezing in the attic, and we also needed a room for an au pair—that would be cheaper than hiring babysitters to watch Andrew while Mary and I worked. But we couldn't legally finish the third floor without a second fire exit. I intended to install an exterior spiral staircase, but that would be a complex and expensive project. One step at a time: first the inspection, then the finished attic, and last the spiral stairs.

We removed my temporary office and other signs of habitation from the attic, then called the city. As expected the inspector headed straight for the third floor and nodded approvingly when he saw the unfinished framing. He noticed the rear attic door, which now opened onto nothing. *Going to bring some stairs up there?* Yes, I said—someday I wanted to finish the third floor. *You're doing this the right way,* he said. *Yup,* I thought, *just not in the right order.* He jotted on some papers and we were done. Two days later I cleared out the attic so I could start the finishing work. I discovered a considerable amount of dirty cellulose insulation remained. It was July 1, 1995; I'd been hauling this stuff out of the attic off and on for more than two years.

20

Surprisingly little of a systematic nature is known about cities and how and why they grow and decline. No doubt that's an impertinent thing for a nonspecialist to say, but I suspect many who make their living studying cities would privately agree—some not so privately. In 1986, I wrote an article marking the twenty-fifth anniversary of the publication of Jane Jacobs's *Death and Life of Great American Cities,* a famous attack on the bulldozer-style urban renewal programs of the 1950s. The book struck a chord with the public, and largely because of it the late Ms. Jacobs (she died in 2006) remains widely revered today. But professionals were less impressed, as I discovered when I called up George Sternlieb, then director of the Center for Urban Policy Research at Rutgers University and a prominent figure in the field, to ask for a comment. "I don't think much of her work, and I think it's a sad reflection on the field that they're taking her stuff seriously," he said. "It's by default of other insight. On a flat plain, pimples begin to look like the Rocky Mountains."

Professor Sternlieb's view of Ms. Jacobs, I think, was harsher than she deserved, and in fact her reputation among scholars has grown in recent years, a matter I'll return to. But it's hard to quarrel with his larger point. It's not that cities are a complete mystery; to the contrary, in the big-picture sense—the orbiting-ninety-miles-overhead view, as it were—we know quite a bit. It's at the street level that things fall down.

We know, for example, that the world is currently undergoing an urbanization boom unlike any yet seen. In 1800, 3 percent of the world's population lived in cities; as of 2007 half did; and 60 percent are expected to do so by 2030—almost 5 billion people. In 1950 there were 67 cities with a population of a million or more, in 2000 there were 387, and by 2015 the United Nations expects there to be 554.

It's commonly assumed most cities in the developing world are gigantic slums, and many are indisputably squalid; the UN estimates that more than a billion people live in shantytowns or worse. But quite a few cities have acquired the accoutrements of modernity. Of the one hundred tallest buildings in the world as of 2007, fifty-six were in Asia or the Middle East, including eight of the top ten. (The tallest as I write is the Taipei 101 building in Taipei, Taiwan, which is more than two hundred feet taller than the biggest U.S. building, the Sears Tower in Chicago.) In 1950, twenty cities in the world had rapid transit systems; today 165 do. China, one of the most rapidly urbanizing countries, had only a handful of airports with scheduled service in the 1950s; as of 2005 it had 135, and within five years it expects to have 186.

At the same time, however—I venture to say few other than specialists have grasped the extent of this—many cities are declining in size, and not just in the United States. According to the *Atlas of Shrinking Cities*, a fascinating volume produced in 2006 by a consortium of architects and others based in Berlin, 350 major cities throughout the world saw their populations drop a tenth or more between 1950 and 2000, and a quarter of all large cities lost population in the 1990s.[1] In the UK, Liverpool, Manchester, and Glasgow have lost roughly half their people. The populations of Lisbon, Leipzig, and Brussels have fallen by more than 30 percent, that of Copenhagen by 40 percent. Venice remains one of the world's most popular tourist destinations, yet only sixty-two thousand people still live there. The causes of the downturns are varied—deindustrialization, suburbanization, the occasional signal disaster. The *Atlas* cites post-Katrina New Orleans, whose population has fallen by nearly half, as well as post-Chernobyl Pripyat, Ukraine—population loss 100 percent. To be sure, fewer people aren't always a sign of decline; in cities such as Paris and San Francisco, they reflect the fact that small affluent households are replacing large poor ones.

Another thing we know, or think we do, is that the last great era of city-building is now upon us—arguably it'll conclude by the end of this century. Two factors contribute. The first is that the world's population will be close to stabilizing at between nine and ten billion. (That's another little-appreciated development—the population of most developed countries will soon level off or decline due to falling birth rates, with the United States one of the few exceptions thanks to immigration. Even in developing countries like India the growth rate is falling.) The second and more important factor is that the global migration of people from the countryside into the cities, under way since the early nineteenth century, will be coming to an end. By 2050 the United Nations estimates the world will be 70 percent urbanized and the developed countries 85 percent, the latter figure presumably approximating the end state. As urbanization winds down, the worldwide boom in city construction will taper off as well. That doesn't mean individual cities will necessarily stabilize. Judging from the experience of the present day, some will thrive while others wither away.

[1]Oswalt, Philipp, and Rieniets, Tim, eds., *Atlas of Shrinking Cities* (Ostfildern, Germany: Hatje Cantz Verlag, 2006), p. 6.

Which ones? Who knows? That's where we get into unknown country. Social scientists have struggled for much of the past century to explain the sharp turns of urban fortune, and for that matter the most basic mechanisms of urban growth, with decidedly mixed success. In the 1920s, researchers in the so-called Chicago school of sociology, many of whom were on the faculty of the University of Chicago, took the then novel step of venturing out into the city around them to search for patterns of neighborhood change—what some called urban ecology. Chicago was a promising laboratory for this project because: (a) for the U. of C. researchers at least, it was just outside the door; (b) it lacked topographical features (Lake Michigan chiefly excepted) that would distort the pattern of settlement; (c) like many American cities at the time, it was growing rapidly, offering a chance to observe the process of development within a compressed period of time; and (d) it wasn't New York—which is to say, it was a fairly typical (if big) U.S. city. As a result, it's been said, Chicago during the twentieth century was the most thoroughly studied city in the world.

An influential product of this work was an evolving theory of urban development, or to use the textbooks' grander term, urban spatial organization. In 1923, a U. of C. sociologist named Ernest Burgess proposed what became known as "concentric-ring theory," illustrated with a famous diagram (it consisted of concentric rings), which held that cities naturally developed outward from the initial point of settlement, with the central business district at the core; then the "zone of transition," a euphemism for the slums; and after that the zone of workingmen's homes, the "zone of better residences," and farthest out the commuter zone—the suburbs. A defect of this scheme, obvious from the start, was that it was too simple even for Chicago's relatively blank slate. In 1939, the land economist Homer Hoyt, who'd spent many years in Chicago, proposed a refinement known as sector theory, which held that transportation routes emanating from the city center tended to become development corridors, helping to establish one side (or sector) of town as the affluent part while another was stigmatized as the poor part. This pattern persisted as the city expanded into the hinterlands, with the result that in Chicago, for example, the south side has remained for well over a century the baddest part of town.

You may say: *It took sixteen years to figure out* that? But of course scientific progress is often slow, seldom more so than in the case of cities, where the research subjects are scattered around the globe. Hoyt, demonstrating exemplary thoroughness, based his theory on an analysis of 142 cities throughout the developed world, doubtless running up some serious frequent-railroad-passenger miles in the process. Despite his hard work, just six years later sector theory had to make room for the "multiple-nuclei" model proposed by former University of Chicago students Chauncy Harris and Edward Ullman (Harris spent his career at the U. of C. as a geography professor). The multiple-nuclei model acknowledged the fact, evident even in 1945, that with the increased mobility made possible by the automobile, in many metropolitan areas the traditional downtown was but one of many commercial centers, and not necessarily the most important. Suburban decentralization is now recognized as a worldwide phenomenon associated with increasing affluence.

But the suburbs weren't the last word in urban spatial organization either. The latest development to stump researchers has been gentrification. First widely evident in the 1950s—if you buy the argument that artists and bohemians represent the first wave, you can make the case that gentrification was under way in Greenwich Village, and possibly the near north side of Chicago, in the 1920s—the phenomenon had attracted scholarly notice by the 1960s. Forty years later experts still don't agree on what it is, what causes it, or whether it's good or bad. (Indeed, as that value judgment suggests, the debate has become highly politicized.)

One school of thought—the "production-side" theory, advanced by the geographer Neil Smith—holds that the forces of capitalism realized there was money to be made in buying cheap inner-city property and fixing it up for yuppies. No disrespect to Professor Smith, but from personal experience I can attest that profit doesn't enter the picture till the late stages of the process. Another school, the "consumption-side" hypothesis associated with the sociologist David Ley, proposes that—I omit a few subtleties—yuppies think cities are fun. (A late addition to consumption-side theory is globalization, which has increased the supply of yuppies.) Far be it from me to take sides in a dispute of such long standing, but the odds favor Professor Ley.

We'll get back to the broader implications of gentrification later. At the time we worked on the Barn House the subject raised a more pressing question, which was much debated then and is no less controversial now. It took one of two forms, depending on where you were: (1) *How can we halt this oppressive plague?* or (2) *How can we get it to start?* Had I spent my early adulthood in Boston, New York, or San Francisco, possibly (1) would have seemed more salient. Inasmuch as I'd slugged it out in Chicago, (2) loomed larger in my mind.

The truth is, nobody in Chicago in those days knew what it would take to get a declining city turned around. In college I'd read with great interest Jane Jacobs's book, which, notwithstanding the conceptual and methodological lacunae to which Professor Sternlieb presumably was adverting, seemed (and still seems) a shrewd description of city life. In it she enumerated what she felt were the essentials of a successful city—namely, mixed uses, short blocks, a diversity of new and old buildings, and sufficient density. Anyone with some experience of cities will grant that this is a plausible prescription. But it didn't fully address the situation in Chicago, where we seemed to have the requisite density, mixed uses, and so on, but neighborhood improvement remained elusive. There had to be more to it, I thought, and at an early age I developed my own theory of what it took for a down-at-heels part of town to revive: It had to look urban.

This requires some explanation. While driving taxicabs as a college student in 1970, I'd stumbled on a number of ramshackle Chicago neighborhoods that nonetheless were unmistakably city-like in appearance. One was a section of town known as Wicker Park. Though its fortunes have improved a good deal since, Wicker Park in 1970 was known chiefly for hookers and drug sales—it had been the setting for *The Man with the Golden Arm*, Nelson Algren's 1949 novel about a morphine addict. As late as 1992, the owner of a coffeehouse in the neighborhood was telling me the space occupied by his establishment had previously housed an illegal drug factory.

But it looked cool. The heart of the community, Milwaukee Avenue, one of Chicago's great commercial diagonals, was narrow, lined by three- and four-story buildings, and paralleled by an L line; the Loop rose like the celestial city at its foot. The houses on the side streets were attractive if weather-beaten exercises in red brick dating from just after the fire. A couple streets consisted mainly of mansions, reportedly built by German brewers who'd been the district's original settlers. I knew little about the neighborhood, but I thought: *This will come back.* I wasn't the only one who thought so; rehabbers were hard at work by the late 1970s, although it was fifteen years—some would say twenty—before they had much to show.

In the end, of course, their work paid off—the neighborhood became one of the most popular in the city, and the chief struggle now is whether rising rents and corporate tenants (for example, those Bank of America slimeballs) will dull the urban edge. Many people and organizations contributed to the neighborhood's revival, but without wishing to deprecate the importance of the Busy Bee restaurant and the Around the Coyote festival and other local institutions Chicagoans know well, I don't think there's any disputing that what got things off the dime was the neighborhood's striking physical appearance—it looked urban.

I'll have more to say about all this later—I certainly didn't understand it in 1970. Even then, however, I could see that my city-spotting instinct had one conspicuous weakness: There was no telling how long revival would take, except that it would assuredly be longer than you thought.

On a smaller scale, that was the problem we now faced at the Barn House. Finishing the attic—one project on a seemingly endless list—took nine months. There was an extraordinary amount of work to do, some of it complicated, a lot just tedious, and in the early stages I had to do most of it myself, with occasional assistance from the Chief. At best I could devote two or three days a week. I wangled some work out of Tony under our existing contract, but I couldn't afford to hire him to do more— our credit card debt was brushing up against six figures. The only way we avoided crushing interest payments was that Mary routinely flipped debt to whichever card issuer (the credit card companies were having a price war at the time) was offering the lowest introductory rate.

No doubt my insistence on doing things the right way prolonged matters, but I expected to spend a lot of time in the office, and in my experience I was more likely to regret things I wished I'd done and didn't than wished I hadn't done and did. Anyone in my shoes would have felt the same. The cantilevered "bench" where one attic gable extended out over the driveway—no sensible person would have left that sagging five degrees out of true, and a couple dozen precisely sawn wedges were all that was required to make it level and square. Similarly, the oddball jogs in the framing were easily concealed with furring and a false wall. The floor that sloped so steeply as to verge on requiring a tow rope— okay, I grant you that meant pulling up all the subflooring and notching the planks at one side of the room and shimming them at the other so as to feather the rise to the point of imperceptibility. But I'd have had to open up the floor anyway so I could stuff insulation in the joist ends to avoid drafts. The electrical work, the ductwork, the remainder of the insulation, truing up the ceilings, screwing down the subflooring, gluing and screwing half-inch plywood underlayment on *top* of the subflooring . . . why, anybody would have done those things. They needed to be done.

By September I was far enough along to start thinking about drywall, so I got on the phone to Jesus, the head of the drywall-hanging crew. I braced myself for a hefty quote—what with the turret and dormer, the walls and ceilings in the attic had all sorts of exotic angles that were sure to require fancy trimming. What's more, the heavy sheets of drywall were in the basement, and had to be hauled to the top of the house. Sure enough, when Jesus dropped by, he made frightful grimaces as he considered the complexities of the job. "I gotta tell you, man, you gotta lot of work here," he said. "This is gonna cost you a lot of money." He paused and screwed up his face again. "I'm gonna have to charge you seven hundred dollars."

I'd been expecting two thousand. "Whoa," I said weakly. I agreed to rent a scaffold so Jesus and his crew could throw the drywall up the side of the house, and two weeks later that's more or less what they did, hoisting the massive sheets effortlessly in a sort of vertical bucket brigade. Moving forty or fifty sheets of drywall plus a couple dozen more sheets of plywood (the afore-mentioned carpet underlayment) took them till mid-afternoon, whereupon they set about the work of hanging. If cutting the drywall into precise trapezoids and half octagons gave them pause, I detected no sign of it. By the following afternoon they were done.

Next came Ricardo, the mudder. I pointed out the angles—the ceiling looked like a geodesic dome. All the lines need to be straight, I said. *De nada,* said Ricardo. He charged me $750. I did a little touching up when he was done, then applied a coat of white primer. The effect on a bright day was remarkable. I felt as though I was standing inside a Platonic solid. "It's not the Barn House anymore," Ani announced, inspecting the job. "It's the house."

The day before Thanksgiving I took the sawhorses downstairs

to the dining room and set up a couple sheets of plywood on them; Mary spread a cloth to make a table for Thanksgiving dinner for my extended family—the first time we'd had everyone over since we moved in. At mid-meal my brother-in-law Tom (the piratical one) paused to gaze around the room. Though there was still much to do, a fancy brass light fixture with etched glass globes now hung from the ten-foot ceiling. "This place makes our house seem small and out of date," he said.

The remainder of the work we may pass over lightly. The stair guys installed a nicely proportioned balustrade on the service stairs. Tom spent a week or so installing the trim. My brother John helped me paint. The final step was carpeting the attic and the service stairs down to the first floor. The installers were a couple young guys in T-shirts who looked like slackers but did an exemplary job with no visible seams. We finished in mid-March. We moved in Petra, our Swiss au pair, and I set up my office. The trees outside the window were starting to bud; I saw robins and blue jays. Though some details were still missing, the attic was the first part of the house's interior to be reasonably complete, a couple months shy of three years after we'd purchased the house.

All fixer-uppers of old houses know theirs isn't an entirely sane pursuit, and that they must remain constantly alert for signs that flinty resolve has degenerated into obsession, for fear they'll next start counting sidewalk squares or keeping too many cats. I knew I'd crossed the line in the summer of 1996, when I took to sieving the yard.

As with many Barn House projects, straining the dirt wasn't what I'd meant to do originally. My initial thought was simply to get the property cleaned up to the point that it didn't look like hoboes lived there. That meant hauling away a considerable volume of accumulated junk, such as the scrap lumber and other debris I'd tossed out the back of the attic to the yard three stories below, where it had been festering in a vague pile for close to a year. As it turned out, that defined the outer limits of the gestation period of a now-familiar nocturnal mammal. Mary and I learned this when, on approaching the mound one evening (the day had been busy), we were greeted by a possum with bared teeth. This proved to be a mama guarding her young, whom we discovered jammed together like sausages beneath a tented heap of boards. We withdrew long enough for her to relocate the family, then finished hauling the junk to the trash.

The question, once we got down to bare ground, was what to do next. Owing to years of neglect, the press of piled-up rubbish, and the tramp of a thousand passing feet, the earth around the house had been compacted to the density of lead. After a half hour's ineffectual scratching with a cultivator—I might as well have tried to carve stone with a nail—I decided to rent a rotary tiller. Progress subsequently was faster but not fast. The whirling blades gnawed away slowly at the dense soil; I felt as though I were mining coal. Worse, every few minutes the tiller would buck and lurch in unexpected and often terrifying directions, signifying that I had struck some immobile subterranean mass. The tiller quieted, I'd commence excavating the obstruction with a spade. I unearthed a bewildering variety of objects in this way, possibly remnants of an ancient civilization, or maybe just an ancient interstate. There were lots of pieces of concrete, anyway, and quite a few plain old rocks. I set them out on the garage slab and later secreted them in the trash carts one at a time, so the streets and sanitation guys wouldn't beef.

But a lot of the crud didn't lend itself to efficient spadework. For one thing, there was an extraordinary quantity of broken glass, not to mention rusty nails, furnace slag, crumbled bricks, anonymous pieces of plastic, and a good deal else, most of which, I knew objectively, I should have simply let lie. I wanted it gone, though—it betokened a dark and benighted age, of which I wanted for some ineffable reason to purge every trace.

Thus the sieve. I fabricated it out of two-by-fours and quarter-inch wire mesh, as always using drywall screws for the frame plus roofing nails to batten down the mesh. The carpentry done, I set the sieve on a thirty-three-gallon plastic trash can and ladled in a couple shovelsful of contaminated earth, which I then proceeded to shake. This method lacked grace even by my low standards. The weight of the dirt was considerable at the outset, and to apply sufficient force one had to engage one's entire being in a sort of spastic rhythm, as though having a seizure, albeit of a slow and wearying sort. Eventually the sieve would empty out and I'd find myself staring at the leavings, faintly hoping to spot the Kimberly diamond or at least another 1891 dime but condemned always to disappointment, although I have to say that after a few repetitions a rusty nail became an object of consuming interest. Then I'd dump the refuse into a plastic grocery bag and start again.

After I'd been laboring in this manner for a day or so the Chief came by—he hadn't been to the house in a couple weeks. Heaving to a short distance off, he stared without speaking for a good thirty seconds, possibly the longest I'd seen him neither talking, smoking, nor engaged in useful work in the time I'd known him.

"What are you doing?" he asked finally.

"Sieving the dirt," I said, indicating the bagged detritus now covering a corner of the garage slab.

"Going down to bedrock?" The Chief was never judgmental; he just liked to know what he was dealing with.

"Just the topsoil," I said. "Eight inches."

"Lot of people would just cover it up."

"I know."

The Chief pursued the matter no further, no doubt thinking I was best left alone till my compulsions had run their course. They did, but not quickly. Damned if I didn't run pretty much all the dirt within ten feet of the house through the sieve over the course of a week or so, filling scores of plastic bags with the leavings. That done, I flattened the filtered earth with a roller, seeded and watered, and by September had (temporarily, as it turned out) grass. I don't claim it was the right way, just my way, and as anyone who has done similarly knows, you paid a price sometimes for the privilege of pursuing it. But the plus side was, you were free.

From that point on work proceeded sporadically. All the space in the house was now usable to some degree. Major projects remained, but we'd complete them as time and money permitted. In the meantime, we decided, we were going to return to the surface world.

21

This may not be the average person's idea of light recreation, and I won't say it was invariably mine, but not long after making the above resolution I took an afternoon off to hear the *New York Times* architecture critic Paul Goldberger give a talk to a local civic group entitled "Is There Still a Need for Cities?" Unshocking answer, given the speaker and audience: yes. I don't recall much of what he had to say, but toward the end he made a declaration along the lines of: *We who live in the city embrace diversity because, let's face it, in the city diversity is pretty much constantly in your face.* (I'm sure he phrased it more eloquently than that, but as I say, the details are vague.)

I was skeptical of this line of argument at the time. I was willing to believe it was true of New York, particularly the twenty-five-ring circus known as lower Manhattan, but it didn't seem all that obviously true of Chicago. The venue in which Mr. Goldberger had given his talk was a block or two from North Michigan Avenue, which, while undoubtedly one of the world's more imposing shopping streets, was no paragon of diversity. In the 1970s, Chicago had had the reputation of having two downtowns—State Street, the city's original retail district in the Loop, was for black people (it was the era of blaxploitation movies, which attracted a lot of teenagers), while North Michigan Avenue across the river was for whites. The division was never as stark as it was sometimes portrayed and had become less so over time; still, you saw a lot more minorities on State than you did on Michigan, and the idea that city life was inherently conducive to tolerance struck me as smug.

As time went on, though, I had occasion to reconsider. In 1996, the North Michigan Avenue business association asked me to edit a "vision" plan for their street, which had been the beneficiary of considerable vision already. Originally it had been a narrow residential thoroughfare called Pine in what was then a quiet (because inaccessible) part of town. The 1909 Burnham plan had proposed turning it into a grand ceremonial boulevard. This took quite a while. The major public improvements, including widening of the street and an ornate double-deck bridge over the Chicago River, were completed in the 1920s. Energetic private development ensued for a time, among other things producing a famous quartet of buildings flanking the Michigan Avenue bridge (Tribune Tower and the Wrigley Building are the best known) that the architectural historian Carl Condit, whose class at Northwestern I'd once taken, described as "the foremost skyscraper enclave in the world"—a large but not indefensible claim. Unfortunately, due to the Depression and World War II, large-scale commercial construction then pretty much stopped, with some lots remaining vacant or given over to marginal uses well into the 1960s. Development resumed in a big way with the construction of the one-hundred-story John Hancock Center, which was completed in 1969, and within another twenty-five years North Michigan Avenue had been largely built out. Now the street had become a tourist attraction and the business association was trying to deal with the usual problems attendant on success—crowding, insufficient parking, and so on.

The committee in charge of the vision plan had come up with a pretty good first draft, I thought. Among the factors contributing to Michigan Avenue's success they'd cited density, mixed uses, and a pedestrian-friendly environment—either they'd been reading their Jane Jacobs or had arrived at similar conclusions on their own, a good sign either way. The sad fact was that a previous generation of civic leaders in Chicago and elsewhere had been depressingly oblivious to the qualities that made cities citylike. In the Loop, for example, hundreds of street-level shops had been demolished in the 1960s and 1970s due largely to a crack-brained zoning code that encouraged the construction of office buildings with empty glass lobbies. No doubt the more enlightened view now prevailing among North Michigan Avenue business people derived from the observation that there was money in it—lively streets drew more shoppers. All the more reason to wonder what had been going through the minds of everybody else.

At times, though, Michigan Avenue could be a little too lively, or so some felt. One issue the plan attempted to grapple with was street performers. Sidewalk entertainment had been illegal in Chicago until 1983, the authorities having taken the view that only vagrants performed in public for pocket change. Dogged argument had been required to make the city understand that 90 percent of the industry worked on this basis. The law having been amended, musicians, dancers, and other artistic sorts doing their thing in the public way became considerably more plentiful. Some performers were amazingly good—Mary and I spent part of a charmed summer's evening at the Water Tower off Michigan Avenue in the 1980s listening to a talented a capella quartet that went on to a successful career in the clubs.

Other performers drew a more ambivalent response. Many of these fell into the category of what we might call inner-city entertainment—your robot dancers and so on. They tended to concentrate on the busiest corners, drawing large crowds and blocking store entrances, which annoyed merchants. A few sniffs may have felt a bunch of ghetto kids detracted from the ambience. But for most people the main issue—certainly this was true of the bucket boys—was noise.

The bucket boys were synchronized drummers. (They are now, anyway. The earliest drummers in my recollection had played solo; whether this had given way to the now-standard team approach by 1996 is lost in memory's fog.) Urban percussion, of course, has a long history. As far back as I could remember Chicago had had informal aggregations of conga players who performed in the parks during the warm months, often on the lakefront. The performances were hypnotic and went on for hours, commonly attracting hundreds of people. The drummers weren't in it for the money—I never saw a hat being passed, at any rate. One had the sense of eavesdropping on some ancient rite.

At some point, presumably after 1983, drum-centered ensembles began showing up on State Street and Michigan Avenue. Mostly they used professional-looking drum sets; once in a while they were joined by horn players and other musicians. In contrast to the conga sessions in the parks, these performances generally were intended as moneymaking ventures, with a conspicuously displayed receptacle containing some coins and bills.

The bucket boys hoped to make money, too, but their equipment was more basic—they played on upended five-gallon plastic buckets using drumsticks. I've heard this practice originated in New York, although it's not like the technology took a Stradivarius to perfect. If we neglect the annoyance factor, the bucket boys were actually pretty good, with precisely coordinated stick- and headwork and deft handoffs between soloists. The fact that a few of the guys were exceptionally buff and sometimes played shirtless no doubt added to the appeal amongst the frivolous. To me there's no question the lads had talent, though I concede there's a diversity of views on this subject. But there's also no doubt they were loud.

Cities are unavoidably noisy places, as anybody who lives in one knows. Much of the din you simply tuned out. Mary, for example, was genuinely surprised when I informed her one day that our favorite outdoor Mexican restaurant, which we'd patronized for years, was located perhaps fifty yards from an L line, where the trains clattering past made enough racket to loosen your teeth. She hadn't noticed—possibly because, what with the many buses, motorcycles, and beaters lacking mufflers regularly passing the location in question, nothing short of a pipe bomb would have really stood out.

Human noisemakers were more difficult to ignore. Anyone who worked in downtown Chicago during the 1980s, for example, remembers the fierce-looking giant who played saxophone near the Michigan Avenue bridge. He had his defenders, I realize, and possibly there was some late-period-Coltrane thing going on that I lacked the capacity to grasp, but whatever delights his work may have conveyed to those at the top of the food chain, it sure sounded like a car wreck to me.

The bucket boys weren't in that category, but the extreme decibel level they generated, plus the fact that they could go for twelve hours at a stretch, strained the patience of the most devoted music lover. Although they showed up periodically on State Street or at the ballparks and other popular venues, Michigan Avenue was the 100 percent location in Chicago crowd-wise, and that they favored most of all.

So there was simmering unhappiness, of which I thought I detected some trace in the vision plan. I was apprehensive—this was Chicago, after all. In the old days a controversy pitting highrise residents and prominent business interests against street kids would have been resolved in about ten seconds, and how different things were now I wasn't altogether sure. The North Michigan Avenue association had formerly had a reputation for archconservatism, and even now had a low tolerance for gaudy signage and other perceived breaches of propriety. The draft plan, it's true, offered the mild proposition that a committee be formed to study the matter; perhaps I was being paranoid, but I wondered if this were merely a placeholder for an argument yet to be joined, with advocates of a clampdown waiting for their moment. I dropped the mild suggestion into my new draft after some polishing, submitted the finished document to the review committee—not a bashful group, from what I'd seen—and braced for the reaction. Surely someone would demand sterner measures to deal with annoying street performers—more regulation, possibly a ban.

But no one did. The issue never came up that I heard about. The mild suggestion about a committee made it into the published plan unaltered.

I found this interesting. It's not that no one thought the issue important, as we'll shortly see. The review committee had been vocal about plenty of other subjects. But something had changed. I had a hard time putting my finger on what it was until I heard a comment at one of the committee's meetings. A businesswoman recalled how impressed she'd been by Michigan Avenue on her return to Chicago in the early 1990s after an extended absence: "It had matured," she said.

I was struck by this remark and thought about it a lot afterward. The woman had been speaking of the commercial district, but it seemed to me her comment applied to the city as a whole. Although people were only then beginning to realize it, the town had grown up.

Partly this was a matter of appearances—the city looked more finished, a matter to which I'll return. But it seemed to me the city's maturity involved more than just physical improvements. You could see it in people's attitudes. A good example of this, I thought, was the subsequent controversy over street performers, which as was to be expected didn't end with the formation of a committee. On the contrary, what we'd seen in 1996 was the beginning of a protracted and bitter dispute, of which I can give only a summary:

1. In 1999, a ban on street performers at certain times on certain downtown streets was proposed by Alderman Burton Natarus, who'd already joined the ranks of Chicago's legislative immortals for a vain attempt to get carriage operators to put diapers on their horses.

2. After impassioned arguments on both sides, a watered-down ordinance was passed that didn't ban performances but did limit them from ten a.m. till ten p.m. on weekends and nine p.m. on school nights.

3. Whatever may have been the case in 1996, after the turn of the millennium bucket ensembles became the rule, typically consisting of two to five players, although I have heard possibly apocryphal tales of groups as large as twenty.

4. One especially polished contingent of bucket boys came to the attention of talent agents and performed at Bulls basketball games and in a KFC commercial.

5. Notwithstanding commercial success, the increased volume generated by massed bucket drumming led to fresh demands for its suppression, impelling Alderman Natarus to introduce another ordinance in 2005 banning street performances of all types at certain Michigan Avenue locations.

6. During the ensuing debate numerous downtown (including Loop) residents were heard from, some no doubt sharing the low tolerance for urban distractions exemplified by the woman who complained that the bucket boys made it impossible to concentrate on her opera recordings, but others having on the face of it a legitimate beef, including one plaintively arguing in a blog that s/he could tolerate the L, fire trucks, ambulances,

honking taxi drivers, garbage trucks, the saxophone player in need of lessons, Christmas Muzak blaring from Daley Plaza, and the incessant preacher in front of Old Navy, but the sound of buckets being drummed on for hours at a time was an order of magnitude worse.

7. Even though the bucket boys and other street performers didn't make campaign contributions or constitute a sizable voting bloc, many politicians nonetheless spoke up in their behalf, including the mayor and some aldermen, although their expressions of support at times betrayed a certain ambivalence—for example, "Michigan Avenue belongs to all of us, and the music on the street I sometimes enjoy."

8. Lest I give the impression that the bucket boys constituted the entirety of the Chicago street-artist corps, you also had violinists, numerous guitarists, the aforementioned robot dancers in metallic body paint, the occasional mandolin player, Peruvian flautists in native costume, and bands of varying composition, with one ensemble consisting of six brothers in their late teens or early twenties who among them played two trombones, two trumpets, a tuba, and a French horn.

9. In the end street performances were banned on the four-block stretch of Michigan Avenue most densely thronged with tourists, plus one location near the Millennium Park concert pavilion about three-quarters of a mile south, but only when concerts were in progress.

10. Predictably, no one was happy with the outcome, with bucket-boy opponents claiming the ban didn't go far enough while supporters claimed Michigan Avenue was fast becoming a bland suburban mall.

None too edifying, you may think. I disagree. Whatever one's view of the solution *pro tempore* (I doubt we've heard the last word on the subject), it seemed to me just the sort of argument to be expected in a city come of age. Even during the city council debate, those doing most of the talking weren't the civic leaders who in earlier times would have dominated the discussion (if there had been a discussion at all), but rather the people most directly involved—the politicians saw themselves mostly as mediators or champions of their constituents' rights.

Moreover, if we ignore the thin-skinned sort, the attitude of bucket-boy opponents could be generally characterized as: *There's only so much urban irritation you can ask even city people to take.* Sure, nobody was entirely happy with how things had turned out, but in a way that was the point. City life had innumerable drawbacks—noise, congestion, crime. Some of the problems might ease over time but they never disappeared. What kept the city going was the collective calculation by those who lived or did business in it that the attractions outweighed the costs—and people would fight hard to keep the cost from getting too steep.

Arguments over street artists were by no means the only arena in which you saw this. I had some friends who were fixing up an old Victorian town house on the west side, on a street where homes in the mid-1990s sold for the then royal sum of $350,000. Their house faced a small park, on the other side of which was a sprawling low-rise public housing development. My friends weren't enthusiastic about this, speaking darkly of shots fired and visits by the police. But they put up with it—it was the price they paid to live in the city.[1]

So I think in that sense Paul Goldberger had been right. City people weren't necessarily more tolerant because they were naturally inclined that way, but because living in the city didn't give them much choice. I don't mean to suggest that their acceptance of the raucous urban scene was in all cases grudging; on the con-

[1]It was the price they paid then, anyway. The public housing development has since been torn down.

trary, whatever they might think of this or that detail, I think most found it one of the city's great charms. Nor would they put up with conditions they found intolerable. But they didn't feel powerless to change things. Unlike city dwellers fifty years earlier, they didn't just bail when things got tough; they waded in and duked it out.

In short, Chicago had matured. People were more invested in the city, in several senses of the term. There was more energy in the air, more shops and cafés, more people on the street. The city had always had its diehard fans, but now I sensed that for a great many Chicagoans the city was no longer just a place they were passing through, but rather the end of the line. That's easy to say, and city people have long been notorious for taking the rosy view, but an objective measure of the new attitude (or so it seemed to me) would arise soon enough.

22

Although the work no longer occupied our every waking moment, we wrapped up an impressive number of projects during the late 1990s. We painted the front hall, living room, and dining room; stripped and refinished the front staircase; stained and varnished the new oak woodwork in the front of the house; painted the poplar woodwork everywhere else; finished the downstairs bathroom by among other things mounting a mosaic-tile frieze depicting twining ivy, which I assure you was more winning in reality than it probably sounds on the page; hung closet doors; rerouted the upstairs ductwork yet again because, notwithstanding my ad-libbed improvements following the discovery of Pete's iceberg, the air handler had to work too hard and the compressor burned out; scraped the paint off the front porch deck twice because it kept peeling and the first time Henryk repainted with latex, as opposed to more durable oil, Henryk being the one worker who reminded us that devotion to the right way was a learned behavior, and not part of Polish DNA;

repaired an ominously seeping crack in an upstairs bathroom radiator, which required drilling out the fissure and filling it with epoxy, because I remembered the previous owner's sad experience with the failed radiator and the three inches of ice; plus numerous other small projects, the details of which it's not necessary to review.

In 1997 we finished the basement sufficiently for our purposes, which is to say we, or rather a squad of Polish workers hired for the purpose, painted the floor with epoxy and the walls and ceiling (more precisely, the joists and the underside of the floor planking) with white latex. As usual Tony and Jerry were the contractors, and as usual, from what I could gather, they barely made a dime, although for once the fault was only indirectly mine. They'd calculated that the ceiling would require twenty-five gallons of paint; in the event the antique timbers sucked up sixty-two. I coughed up some more cash unasked.

Painting the basement was one job I had no intention of doing myself, because I knew it likely involved a paint sprayer, the devil's instrument. As with much in my life throughout this period, it all started with the radiators. I loved radiators, I truly did, but they were a pain in the neck to work with, too heavy and always in the way, and in particular they were a nightmare to paint. From the outset I had known that I should have gotten the radiator painting done at an early stage of the project, before the house was closed up and life grew more complex, but at the decisive moment I had had no time and no money. For years thereafter the knowledge that I had merely postponed a task that would require baroque logistical arrangements under the best of circumstances filled me with the blackest dread. My fears along these lines had been confirmed during the finishing of the attic, when I had assigned the Chief to paint the two radiators appurtenant thereto. The job took him the better part of a week. The Chief could be meticulous to a fault, and at times with his small brush and exacting technique seemed bent on resurrecting pointillism à la Georges Seurat, but on investigation I could see such precision was necessitated by the intricate design of the radiator, a labyrinth of fins and rods and interior vanes. No fault could be found with the finished job, but I knew if we painted all the radiators at that pace we'd be at it till Jesus came back.

When the time came to paint the radiators in the basement, therefore, I was amenable to the Chief's suggestion that we buy a paint sprayer. Use of a sprayer presented several challenges. One was drips. If you lingered a millisecond too long when maneuvering the spray head, the paint would collect in a pendulous stratum recalling the fate of Dorian Gray. Another problem was overspray. If you were outdoors and some zephyr came along at a speed above half a knot, an alarming percentage of the paint wouldn't go where it was nominally aimed but instead would bedizen the rhododendrons. A third concern was asphyxiation, especially when painting indoors.

The last item was the major obstacle for us. Since the weather at the time was chilly—it was early spring, as I recall—and we had no hope of getting the radiators up the steps anyway, we painted them in the basement in a spray booth constructed of two-by-twos and sheet plastic and bearing an unpleasant resemblance to a gas chamber. I hooked up the shop vacuum in hopes of evacuating the most lethal fraction of fumes, and bought the most formidable breathing mask I could find, a complex piece of apparatus with multiple compartments for replaceable filter cartridges, which looked as though it would equip the wearer to survive a gas attack at Ypres. However, since the budget didn't permit piping in oxygen, you still had the problem that at an advanced point in the spraying process your input air supply consisted of three parts standard atmosphere to two parts paint. After working for any length of time I developed a throbbing headache and fogged vision, and had the sense of watching brain cells individually die. We finished the basement radiators after considerable suffering—I note with satisfaction that we had minimal drips—but I vowed that for future painting I'd hire someone else.

Thus the Polish workers. You may think it unseemly that I subcontracted my dirty work to third parties, but having inhaled my life's quota and then some of carcinogens, I thought it wise to farm out the balance, in which aim Tony and Jerry cooperated during this interval (though we didn't plan it that way) by never sending over the same crew twice. I was grateful for their assistance in any case, and I think anyone looking at my situation objectively would say I'd better be, for reasons it will be worthwhile to explore.

During the time we worked on the Barn House I was often struck by the similarities between the era when it had been built and the present day. Granted, high-button shoes had pretty much bitten the dust, and cars and computers had transformed the world in ways no one a century earlier could have foreseen, but from a socioeconomic perspective, as the professors might say, there were curious points of comparison.

The dependence on immigrant labor was the most obvious parallel. Chicago, and quite likely my house, had been built by immigrants in the latter part of the nineteenth century and largely rebuilt by them in the latter part of the twentieth. I counted up the workers who participated in some substantial way in the Barn House's protracted reconstruction; setting aside the amateurs who helped with demolition, the total came to more than a hundred, of whom two-thirds were foreign-born. The majority of these had been sent over by Tony and Jerry, but even the people we hired on our own were nonnatives more often than not.

Immigrants had always been a presence in Chicago, but by the 1990s they were more numerous than at any time in my experience. You encountered them everywhere. At the barbershop I got my hair cut by Almo from Albania or Luba from Uzbekistan. I quit mowing my own lawn when I found I could get a crew of

Mexicans to do it for twenty bucks a week. We employed au pairs from Germany, France, Spain, and Croatia in addition to Petra from Switzerland, all of whom admittedly returned home when their thirteen-month visas expired. (Petra wanted to stay but couldn't get a green card despite having lined up a job, no doubt because some bureaucrat decided: *those shiftless Swiss.*) There was Janos, the Hungarian college student we hired to drive the kids home from school after we quit using au pairs, a long line of Polish and Mexican cleaning people, the four Juans who painted the house (this was later), and just about every restaurant worker on the north side who wasn't an aspiring artist or musician from Wicker Park, not to mention the numerous parties from India, Hong Kong, Ireland, Nigeria, the UK, Brazil, Italy, the Middle East, Southeast Asia, and elsewhere that you bumped into in the course of daily life.

Granted, there weren't as many immigrants as there had been in 1890, when more than 40 percent of Chicagoans had been born in a foreign country. But the city had again become a major port of entry. During the 1990s, well over a half million immigrants flooded into the metropolitan area. As of 2000, more than a fifth of residents in the city proper were foreign-born, double the percentage thirty years earlier.

A second similarity between a century ago and today was … well, I recoiled at the thought that we had servants. But as a friend pointed out, "You have staff." We had full-time child care for eleven years, live-in help for five, and drivers for a few years after that. We had house cleaners and landscapers. The majority of these people were foreign-born. We didn't hire them so that we could lead a life of leisure; on the contrary, Mary and I both worked long hours at demanding jobs and needed help with things we couldn't manage on our own. Just the same, we had people on the payroll.

A third point of comparison, which could be deduced from the second, was the widening gap between the affluent and everybody else. Heavily in debt though Mary and I were, the fact was we made more money than most people, and our income rose just about every year, mainly due to Mary's contribution. Average take-home for most other folks, inflation having been accounted for, stayed basically flat. It would be an exaggeration to say the United States had returned to the extremes of a hundred years ago, when there hadn't been an income tax. But things were headed in that direction. In the late 1970s, the top 10 percent of taxpayers took home about a third of the national income. By 2005, it was nearly half.

I don't recall having heard the term globalization in the 1990s, but in retrospect it had a lot to do with these developments. In the broad sense globalization simply means the increasing integration of the world economy, a process under way since the time of Henry the Navigator. But nowadays Americans often conceive of it in gloomier terms: the loss of jobs to foreign countries, the consequent stagnation of middle- and lower-income wages in the United States, the increasing numbers of immigrants who may or may not have something to do with keeping wages down, and, in contrast to the so-so fortunes of everyone else, the rapidly growing affluence of the managerial and professional class that runs the whole show.

The implications of all this didn't fully sink in till years later, but I may as well state it plainly now: The revival of places like Chicago had been made possible by globalization's uneven effects, specifically the lopsided distribution of wealth and the influx of immigrants who did good work cheap. Arguably it wouldn't have happened—certainly not as fast—had the benefits been more evenly spread around. Our own situation demonstrated this. The rebuilding of the Barn House was terrifyingly expensive—Mary and I, despite what ought to have been a comfortable income and the fact that I did a lot of the work myself, were barely able to afford it. The task would have been out of the question for a couple of more modest means. As it was we were only able to swing it because of immigrants, who had come to Chicago in part because relatively well-heeled folk like us were around to employ them. Lots of other city-house rehabbers could tell comparable tales. I make no apologies; collectively we salvaged towns, or parts of towns, that were falling to pieces. But I can't deny we got a break most people didn't.

No doubt that accounted for the sharply divergent views of immigration evident then and since. Much of the country felt (and feels) threatened by immigration, but on the whole it was welcomed or at least tolerated in Chicago. (In the city proper, anyway. Possibly the yokel element in the suburbs got more agitated.) Partly that was a matter of tradition; the city historically had assimilated millions of immigrants and was set up for it, with existing ethnic neighborhoods, decent mass transit, and so on. But the main thing was, we could use the people.

I don't say the newcomers presented no challenges. You had the occasional problem of getting rear-ended at a stoplight by a woman with only a Mexican driver's license in a van with nonfunctional brakes, which caused no obvious damage in our case but did leave you wondering whether you ought to report the incident to the cops, a question I decided in the affirmative on the reasoning that (a) Chicago cops in my observation didn't think it was their job to find out if you were legal, and (b) I wasn't doing the world any favors to let somebody in a brakeless vehicle escape the notice of the law.

But that kind of thing was unusual. More often, especially if you had occasion to hire, you had the sense of participating in a classic American spectacle—immigrants making their way in a new country. That sounds rather dutiful, I suppose. Not a bit. I found it exhilarating—I think any city person would say the same. The thought of living in a homogenous society with a uniform language and culture gave me the shudders. How much better to reside in one of the great crossroads cities, where people came from all over the world, some for a day's business, some for the rest of their lives. The immigrants we encountered virtually without exception were a pleasure to deal with, hardworking and optimistic and happy to be here. Plus, no little thing, they did a beautiful job, and time after time went above and beyond the call.

We saw this now with the Polish workers detailed to finish the basement. I knew I wanted epoxy paint on the floor, because the stuff had the reputation, as it turned out well earned, of being virtually indestructible. But the paint was an industrial coating rather than a consumer product, and the manufacturer evidently assumed that if you were looking for something to rustproof your steam turbine, aesthetics were a minor concern. I'd hoped I'd picked the least objectionable of the dismal choice of colors at the paint store, but an hour after turning my purchase over to the workers they summoned me down to the basement for a look. They'd gotten perhaps a quarter of the floor painted when compelled by revulsion to stop. The stuff was the color of pureed vomit. The workers gave me to understand they'd paint the rest of the floor this appalling hue if I insisted, but they personally advised finding something else. A different paint maker proved to have a less obnoxious palette. Once the workers were finished (they'd sprayed the walls and ceiling earlier), I did a little touching up as always, and the whole thing wound up looking pretty sharp.

The following year I had Tom the finish carpenter install cornice moldings around the ceilings in the living and dining rooms. Mary initially thought these of secondary importance, but it seemed to me on studying the photographs in the home-decorating magazines that the more sumptuous effects had primarily been achieved not, as the obsessive enumeration of accessories in the back pages suggested, with furnishings purchased at Restoration Hardware and Pottery Barn and other such establishments (although I conceded these had their place), but rather with interior architectural detailing that the writers of the accompanying articles, presumably English majors all, assumed was automatically there—at any rate they never mentioned it.[1] It wasn't, of course—someone had to ask for it, someone else had to design it, and additional parties had to perform whatever construction work was required. We didn't have the budget for columns, pilasters, wainscoting (apart from a fairly basic application of bead board in spots), chair railings, mitered walnut floor inlays (although I thought about it, and in a moment of madness had discussed dragging in my brother John to help with the carpentry in order to pare the expense), entablatures of the more rococo sort, vaulted ceilings, and other extravagances. But I did want the rooms to have some jump.

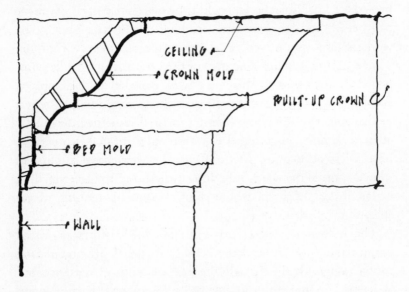

SECTION / ELEVATION of BUILT-UP CROWN MOLD

Here again Charlie the architect came to the rescue. Aware of both my taste for the finer things and my perennial shortage of funds, he devised an artful cornice consisting of a stock crown

[1] It's possible, and now that I think about it more likely, that the reason they never mentioned it was that the carpenters who installed such things didn't buy ads.

molding tacked to a strip of colonial doorstop, which, despite the suggestion of inherited wealth, was as plebeian as molding could get and could be obtained at any lumberyard. Tom offered no objection (I've since come to understand that assembling complex moldings out of simpler elements is a common architectural dodge), and proceeded to install the molding in the living room, dining room, and front hall. The result was all the more remarkable in light of the simplicity of the constituent parts. I don't claim the result would shame Monticello, but it didn't look half bad.

Next, after staring for far too long at the gashes in the drywall where mantelpieces would someday be, I contracted with a fireplace company, which sent over a mason named Cutty, a wiry fellow from Belize with a lilting Caribbean accent. As had been the case with the majority of tradesmen who'd walked through the door up to that point, Cutty was a member of the artisans' guild. He inspected the firebox I'd had built in the living room some years earlier. It was a reasonably competent job, but certain nuances of the mortarwork lacked the craftsman's touch. Cutty pursed his lips. Had the firebox been constructed by so-and-so, he asked, who worked for such-and-such company? I didn't remember the man's name, but he'd gotten the company right. "I knew it," said Cutty. I was impressed. To be a member of the Brotherhood of the Right Way was one thing, but to be able on the basis of forensic evidence to identify the shortcomings of your peers—that took matters to a new level entirely. Cutty and his helper spent a day or so building a couple of fireboxes, the more elaborate of which they proudly showed me with their names and the date neatly scratched in the drying mortar. As with so much in the Barn House, one hated to cover it up.

But of course that was the idea. Sometime earlier my neighbor Charlie[2] had offered to give me an old mantelpiece from an apart-

---

[2]Not to be confused with Charlie the architect. I realize that in this book Mikes and Toms are also far too plentiful. The next time I work on a house I plan to write about, I'll enlist males having a greater variety of names.

ment building he was renovating. I thought this kind and went over to have a look, my expectations low. To my surprise, the mantelpiece was magnificent, with well-proportioned pilasters rising on either side, the tops swooping out to support a couple of shelves, the intersection of the pilasters and shelves denoted with rosettes. I felt I was being given one of the lesser works of Rodin, but Charlie would take no money. Now I turned the mantelpiece over to Cutty. He'd also brought the makings of the new mantelpieces we proposed to construct in the living room and the front bedroom. It's here we get, at long last, to the subject of quartersawn oak.

Most oak planking sold nowadays is plainsawn, meaning that boards are sliced from the log with a succession of parallel cuts. Planks made in this way display great variation in grain, depending on the angle with which a particular cut intersects the log's growth rings. Some of the boards are fine-grained, while others show the coarse pattern I thought of as zebra striping. Most of the new flooring in the Barn House was plainsawn.

After we'd gotten the new oak flooring installed in the back of the house, we learned there was another way of cutting oak called quartersawing. This entailed slicing the log lengthwise into quarters, then sawing each quarter so that the cuts were roughly perpendicular to the growth rings.

The result was that all the boards were fine-grained. Many also exhibited what the wood experts called "medullary rays," also known as fleck or figure, which were stripes or splotches having to my eye a somewhat mica-like appearance running across the grain. Quartersawn oak was more expensive than plainsawn due to the extra labor and greater waste, but the effect was more elegant. Equally important, it had the useful ability to look instantly old. The new oak balusters milled to replace those missing from the fancy front staircase had been quartersawn (the stair guys had voluntarily provided them that way; we hadn't known to ask); once stained they were indistinguishable from the original except on minute inspection.

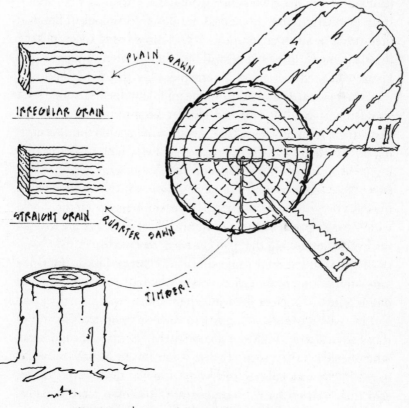

PLAIN-SAWN VS. QUARTER SAWN LUMBER

We couldn't afford quartersawn oak for the living and dining room floors. But with the fireplaces we had our chance.

Cutty and his helper spent most of a day installing three mantelpieces—the antique donated by Charlie plus two new ones of quartersawn oak. I busied myself in my office most of the day and spent little time inspecting the work in progress, having concluded that these were men who knew what they were about. In the late afternoon they called me down for a look. They had fires going in all three locations, a feat more easily accomplished than one might think, since we'd had the foresight to pipe in gas. I was charmed—the new mantelpiece in the living room, I thought, was particularly fine. In the middle of the horizontal span above the firebox the lads had glued a little ornamental carving depicting a stylized wicker basket with flowers and tendrils erupting out of it in a carefree symmetrical sprawl, which notwithstanding its being cornball was perfect for the spot. A few weeks would pass before I'd get around to applying stain, which would show off the oak's fleck to great advantage, but even then one felt the shock, which time's passage has only minimally diminished, of having uncovered something that had always been there.

Much of it was mere stage effects, of course. The artificial log sets—splits, they were called—were molded from some sort of dense poured concrete. Beneath them Cutty and his helper had spread a darkened gravel meant to suggest coals, and on top of this had scattered a fibrous material that became incandescent when heated, which is to say that when the gas flame ignited, it glowed. The resemblance to a wood fire was remarkable, except that there was no smoke, no need for kindling or constant fuss, and no ashes to haul out when done. While Charlie's mantelpiece was authentically old, the illusion of antiquity created by the quartersawn oak was a function solely of the angle used to cut the wood. The trick, in home renovation as in a good deal else, lay in the shrewd management of surfaces. No matter. Though it would be a long time before we could afford proper furniture, friends who visited the house were in awe.

Periodically we were reminded that we lived in the city. One late spring afternoon while working in my office I heard a popping sound that instinct suggested wasn't a firecracker. I looked out the window to see a tall man and a companion running down the sidewalk past the house. The tall man held what appeared to be a handgun—judging from the glimpse I had of it, possibly a target pistol (which, okay, is no Uzi, but still). Chasing him were two other men, one of whom was dressed in a uniform of some sort and waving what I took to be a revolver. The tall man was wearing black nylon pants and a fluorescent yellow shirt; he could scarcely have been more conspicuous if he'd been on fire. I called the police, expecting a brisk response, since Chicago cops in my observation generally responded to shots-fired calls with much spirited martial display; to my exasperation, five minutes elapsed before a lone cop in a squad car arrived, by which time the tall man and his pursuers were gone.

I briefly considered not telling Mary that armed men were racing past the lawn where our children sometimes played, then thought better of it—if ever there were a time to start holding out on unsettling information, this wasn't it. She muttered but said no more. When I inquired at the neighborhood police-beat meeting a couple weeks later, a cop told me in a conspiratorial tone that they knew who the shooter was, by which I gathered I was to understand: *We've got a handle on things.* One never knew what this meant. A cop in the neighborhood, regarded as something of a screwball ("soft" was the term a Chicago police detective I knew used to describe the force's flakier elements), had once confided to me his methods of suppressing crime, one of which was dangling a suspect upside down over the river by his feet. Whatever persuasive techniques may have been brought to bear in this instance, I saw no further guns brandished in daylight.

It took a while longer before things quieted down after dark. Mostly it was people playing loud *ranchera* music late at night in the building behind us, who would knock it off if I went out in the backyard and yelled; other times it was delinquents hot-rodding up and down the alley. One of these excursions concluded with a thunderous crash suggestive of rent metal and broken glass; after an interlude of ten or fifteen minutes, there commenced a series of clangs, which I assumed (it was maybe two a.m. and I was too groggy to investigate) was the vehicle's owner returned to the scene and now trying to pound out the dents. Once I was awakened by a loud noise I was certain was a gunshot and called the police; there was no one to be seen in the alley when I peered out a discreet interval later, but a neighbor later told me he found a large bloodstain on the pavement the next morning. Then there was the grizzled old geek often to be seen sitting near the *ranchera* building's alley entrance on a decrepit 1950s kitchenette chair; though no foul play was conjectured in my hearing, still it was disquieting to learn he'd been found in the basement dead.

Things like that became less frequent as the years passed, though. I'm not saying they stopped altogether. Violent crime on the north side was still twice that of the suburbs, in a typical south-side neighborhood ten times higher. Still, you could tell a corner had been turned. One sign was especially unmistakable: Property values, which had been drifting upward for a while, now began to spike.

23

Toward the end of 1999 the newspaper I wrote for asked me to contribute a year-in-review piece. The approach of the millennium seemed to demand something more momentous than usual, and almost immediately I thought of the perfect opening: "I knew the city had turned some kind of corner when I realized we would actually make money on our house."

This was true. Beginning in the mid-1990s, property values in our neighborhood had begun to rise sharply. In 1996 our neighbors Charlie and Vanessa had bought the house next door to us for a little over $400,000; they would sell it four years later for more than twice as much. Around 1998 a real estate developer purchased an old building a couple blocks away, tore it down (the likely fate of the Barn House had we not bought it, we realized), divided the fifty-foot-wide lot in two, and built two houses, both more attractive than one might have expected, given that they were basically oblong boxes built to the limits of the zoning envelope, as the real estate lawyers said. In 1999 one of the houses sold for $650,000, the other for $669,000. A few months later the same thing happened on the next street over—two houses replaced one. This time one sold for $750,000, the other for $802,000. We refinanced in 1999; the appraisal came in at $795,000. We thought that low, but no matter: The value of our house now substantially exceeded our total investment.

A residential construction boom had begun in the city. It was most evident downtown, where high-rise condo buildings sprouted on seemingly every block, but there was plenty of activity in the neighborhoods. Vacant lots filled up; dilapidated frame houses were pulled down and replaced with brick.

I called up the city's demographer, a patient and resourceful woman named Marie. (Some think a major league sports franchise is the mark of the urban big time, but I say it's when you've got your own demographer.) We spent an absorbing hour reviewing statistical arcana such as residential building permits—they now exceeded demolitions by a healthy margin, which may seem a modest achievement but hadn't always been the case. However, the most surprising fact to emerge was a development anyone could understand. Chicago's population, in decline since 1950, was now going back up—the 2000 census would eventually show that over the past decade the city's population had increased by 112,000.

It seemed clear that the city had passed an inflection point of some kind. Residential building permits had doubled in the mid-1990s and stayed high since, in some years exceeding the numbers reported in Sunbelt cities such as Los Angeles. L ridership, which had reached an eighty-seven-year low in 1992, had rebounded; the line serving the Barn House's neighborhood was now crush-loaded during rush hour, eventually necessitating a station expansion project to accommodate longer trains. The downtown population increased 40 percent during the decade, the fastest of any U.S. city. For years people in Chicago had believed the town was on the verge of turning the corner; now there was good evidence that it had.

In 2002, after completing various additional tasks to be enumerated shortly, we had my family over for Thanksgiving—we now routinely hosted this celebration at our house. Standing in the kitchen with a glass of wine, my father glanced around with as close to admiration as he was ever likely to get. "The place is finally getting a little finish," he said.

It was, and about damned time, considering we'd moved in eight years earlier. But there was no escaping the stubborn fact: For all the sweaty labor involved in the early going, the critical parts of the project didn't happen till late in the job. That was when you attained finish—the elusive state, familiar to all disciples of the right way, when everything came together and the whole exceeded the sum of the parts.

Finish was an entirely subjective concept. You might have toilets that flushed, lights that lit, a roof that kept you dry—but that didn't necessarily mean you had finish. You might appease the title company's every demand for lien waivers and W-9s, pass building inspection, and give the contractor his last check; as far as finish was concerned, these were necessary but not sufficient conditions. Woodwork, mantelpieces, even rugs and curtains . . . yes, of course, one wanted to cross these off the list. But finish was more than that. To put the matter scientifically, it was the point at which you walked into a room and said, or at least thought: *That's it. We're done.*

Finish usually took a while. There were a few masterminds, admittedly, who knew exactly what they wanted from the start and proceeded briskly to produce it, the foremost example in my mind being Frank Lloyd Wright, from whom fully realized designs were said to flow effortlessly whenever he felt like turning on the creative tap. True, Frank might overlook a few fine points, such as what was going to hold the building up, but these were details best left to the restoration committee.[1] More commonly you had our problem: We didn't have a clear vision of what it would take to finish this or that aspect of the house, except that we'd know it when we arrived.

A case in point was the kitchen and family room at the rear of the house. To be sure, with the help of Charlie the architect we'd done a good deal of planning at the outset, some of which didn't pay off till years later. The cherry kitchen cabinets, granite island countertop, and stainless steel ventilator hood over the cooktop—Mary knew she wanted those from the get-go, even though we didn't finish installing them till nearly two years out. We knew we wanted low built-in bookshelves along one wall in the family room, and to that end had had the windows there installed so that the sills were forty-nine inches above the floor rather than the thirty-two inches prevalent elsewhere, a difference visitors pointed out from time to time in case it were a discrepancy I'd overlooked. It was a relief to get Tom over in 2001, eight years after we bought the house, to build the shelves at last. Even then I had him construct a wide central tier that projected inexplicably into the room for another five years, since the big-screen TV I knew I'd put there took that long to drop in price.

The rest we made up as we went along. Cornice molding to echo the similar molding atop the cabinets seemed an obvious step, and looked very nice, but didn't finish the room. A backsplash for the kitchen counters—Mary came up with the idea of beadboard, and Tom suggested stainless steel behind the cooktop; these got us pretty close. But we could see in the end it would all come down to paint.

One would like to offer the thought that, where Mary and I

---

[1] Some feel this is unfair. I point to Fallingwater, the 1937 Pennsylvania house commonly considered Wright's greatest work, whose cantilevered floors sagged to the point that the building was thought to be in danger of collapse. Structural engineers discovered that a portion of the house was supported by the window mullions, the steel dividers between the panes of glass.

were concerned, paint did not to the marriage of true minds admit impediment and other sentiments of that nature. As one might deduce from the history of the project up to this point, it didn't happen. We fought like cats and dogs. Mary's chief argument was that I was color-blind. Maybe I was, I retorted, but I had outstanding grayscale discrimination. In addition, I had a plan. Mary had purchased more or less at random a couple paint samples from Martha Stewart's collection, which I conceded harmonized not only with each other but with the understated-but-definitely-not-white color we (okay, the Polish workers) had previously applied to the trim. I noted in addition that the two Martha Stewart colors came from the same paint-chip series, and by experiment determined that *any* color in this series would harmonize with all the other colors and with the aforesaid trim, and on this basis concluded that I had hit on a paint selection methodology that pretty much couldn't miss. Mary, on the other hand . . . well, we'll draw a veil over the lengthy and acrimonious process of negotiation that preceded the determination of the four colors used to paint the back half of the house. I'll merely say that, in concert as it were, they sang once the job was done.

We'd achieved finish. That's not to say we were *finished*, since we still had the second floor to do, which I didn't get to till additional years later with the assistance of the able Nick, a student at the Moody Bible Institute (regarding whom may I say that for reliability, resourcefulness, and all-round sunny nature a good evangelical Christian is hard to beat). But once you've achieved *some* finish, paradoxical as it may sound, the rest is a matter of time.

Much the same, I felt, could be said of the city. I realize this will strike some as an odd and possibly abhorrent thing to say, since the common view is that a dynamic metropolis is never finished and continually reinvents itself and so forth.[2] Maybe so,

[2]The history professor Thomas Bender makes this argument about New York in *The Unfinished City: New York and the Metropolitan Idea* (2002).

but it seems to me there's a difference in terms of physical appearance between a town having an urbane and settled air and one that looks like it was just unloaded off a truck. Chicago, I felt, had only now passed that critical threshold. Previously it had seemed a work in progress—even in neighborhoods not conspicuously blighted you saw vacant storefronts, temporary-looking buildings, fenced-off lots used for nothing much. Now, after decades of incremental improvement, the city had begun to fill in, the commercial streets especially. Michigan Avenue was the most conspicuous example, but in their own way less pretentious neighborhoods elsewhere in the city had arrived at a similar end state. To the extent such a thing could be said of a big urban center, sizable parts of Chicago were done.

Some of this was the doing of city hall, which had undertaken an energetic program of civic improvements involving wrought-iron fences, ornamental streetlamps, and whatnot. But ordinary folks had gotten into the act, too. Many neighborhoods were now well past the gunshots-and-rats stage of urban existence, allowing the residents to turn their attention to things like gardening. Quite a few streets were gorgeous. The preferred approach was what I'd come to think of as the forest-floor look, which eschewed the usual grass and petunias in favor of intricate layered arrangements of ivy and other greenery that, in combination with the venerable towering trees, produced scenes of such sylvan splendor you expected to see elves.

People weren't just fixing up their own property, either. The railroad embankment used by the commuter trains a couple blocks from our house had once been a scraggly waste; the neighbors had taken it upon themselves to weed, seed, and plant shrubs and flowers—now the narrow street paralleling the embankment had the appearance of a country lane. A woman I met at a community meeting had turned the vacant lot next to her house not far from us into a park for the neighborhood, complete with benches and landscaping. My own project, to which I'd returned once the Barn House ceased to monopolize my time, was working with a civic group to establish a recreational path along the banks of the neglected Chicago River.

My contribution set aside, that kind of thing seemed to me the hallmark of a mature city: Its citizens took collective responsibility for it. The timing in any case worked out nicely. We'd been busting our hump for a good ten years, and now it was time to relax.

24

By some point in the early twenty-first century—you'll forgive me if I don't recall exactly when—we'd acquired the following essential household items:

■ Wooden screen doors fore and aft. Screen doors of any type have become surprisingly rare in the United States, what with May-to-October air-conditioning having become pretty much de rigueur, but, at the risk of coming off like granola-eating radicals, we ran our air conditioner only when it was hot, letting the breeze blow through the house at other times during the temperate months. Mary was particularly adamant on this point, since she worked at a downtown corporate office run by men who evidently wore three-piece suits in July and in compensation caused the thermostat to be turned low enough to give the shivers to an Inuit. Naturally I was happy to accommodate her—God knows in Chicago from November through April you got plenty of refrigeration for free. Screen doors thus being advisable, since in our appreciation for things natural we drew the line at bugs, it seemed only reasonable to acquire the wooden kind, which produced that satisfying slam. However, there was more of a learning curve to the whole business than at first one might have thought. Initially I had Tom trick the doors out with simple spring-type closers not far removed from what one might have seen in 1956, which slammed the doors with a force measured in kilotons. While that hadn't adversely affected my father's screen doors that I'd ever noticed, it threatened to make ours fall apart, largely because whereas my father's doors were held together with steel angle plates and corrugated fasteners and other sturdy hardware, the effete version we had (I'd ordered them at the lumberyard) used staples, which required more delicate treatment. Accepting the reality of the situation—no way did I have time to make doors on my own—I replaced the springs with standard pneumatic closers, which I could calibrate to dampen the pounding while preserving the desired acoustic effect. That done, we painted the doors with a color we called burgundy when company was over, but it was always purple to me.

▪ A hammock suspended between two trees, as commonly depicted in the funny pages but seldom seen in real life, mainly because no American born since 1945 has the patience to plant two trees the right distance apart and then wait till they grow. We didn't either; we got lucky. But the opportunity having presented itself, we didn't need it to knock twice.

▪ A porch swing, a once-forlorn wooden contraption we'd spied in the Barn House's basement on our first visit and maybe eight years later gave a fresh coat of paint (purple again), then suspended from the porch ceiling by springs obtained at a Renaissance Faire in Wisconsin—not a venue known for quality home improvement products, but these were holding up a Colorado-type hanging chair that was sold at a booth and

presumably appealed to the Ren Faire demographic, and I figured would work just fine for me. I thought I had a discount
coming—the springs normally were sold singly whereas I
needed two, and I felt in light of the stiff price of the first I
deserved some consideration on the second. The sales varlet
didn't see it that way, and I have to concede that, in the big-
picture view, we were a little late in the project to start worrying about price.

You see what it adds up to. We'd had a house when we started;
now we had a home. Once I'd gotten the swing hung and my feet
up and had a moment to contemplate the passing scene, any
peevishness with respect to worldly woes vanished instantly away.
Our street was idyllic. We had a dogwood out there, courtesy of
the people in the town houses next to the Witnesses; a locust;
numerous maples; a dying but still majestic ash; what I deduced
from my tree-finder book to be a linden, and was pleased to be
told by a guy from the forestry department actually was; and of
course (let's be honest) my pathetic and embarrassing lawn, fortunately concealed by bushes from everyone's eyes but mine.
Against this bucolic backdrop there promenaded the adorable
neighbor kids and their hundred-square hopscotch game; virtuous dog walkers identifiable by their plastic bags, as opposed to
wicked ones without; my neighbor Joe's son Larry manicuring the
family's already enviable lawn; plus the usual parade of cyclists,
Nike-shod yuppies, and neighborhood characters intent on secret
errands. Perhaps I lacked ambition, but I wanted nothing more.
It was widely agreed among the neighbors who occasionally
stopped by to chat that the city had never looked better, and not
just downtown—once-seedy neighborhoods all over town had
been transformed. The Old Town School of Folk Music, a beloved local institution looking for larger quarters, moved into an
old library building in a neighborhood not far from us called
Lincoln Square; soon a thriving restaurant district developed to

serve the crowds attending concerts. It had a Starbucks like every other semigentrified community in America, but in addition had a handsome branch library (the replacement for the old one), one of the librarians in which for a time had been a guy who sat two rows over from me in fourth grade and used to get a swat once a week from the nun; a park with a bunch of baseball diamonds, which you expected to see in a Chicago park, but also a gazebo, which you didn't; a homeopathic drugstore established in 1875; an old movie theater (admittedly converted to multiple screens) where I had seen German movies—this was an ethnic neighborhood of long standing—while in high school language class in 1968; a classic toy store; numerous outdoor cafés; an excellent pastry shop and restaurant founded by a couple of local women in the early 1980s, when founding any kind of upscale business in most Chicago neighborhoods took nerve; an absurdly ornate but nonetheless delightful storefront that was the last commissioned work by the architect Louis Sullivan and couldn't have made economic sense even when opened in 1922; the inevitable L line with a nondescript modern station, snappy transit design in Chicago being a largely (and inexplicably) lost art;[1] a municipal parking lot where the city held farmer's markets periodically during the growing season; a small fountain surrounded by benches, the majority of which on most days were occupied by regular people, as opposed to comatose drunks; and ten or

---

[1] I confess this is a sore spot. There are a handful of well-designed transit stations of recent vintage in Chicago. One is the O'Hare terminal on the Blue Line, a gorgeous essay in backlit curvilinear glass block by the architect Helmut Jahn, who also designed the United Airlines terminal, which features a kinetic neon-lighted pedestrian tunnel owing a good deal to *Star Wars*. A number of the World War II–era subway stations downtown have also been nicely renovated under the supervision of Charlie's old firm. If you arrive at the United C terminal, take the Blue Line downtown, and disembark at one of these stations, you're likely to think Chicago's reputation as a design center is well deserved. However, if you get off pretty much anywhere else in the system, the impression will be short-lived.

twenty other points of interest that have momentarily slipped my mind. The street buzzed with life, and yet—important point—it was no South Beach, which is to say it wasn't a tourist attraction. It had only a handful of chain stores, Starbucks being one, all small. The average commercial building was three stories tall, the houses mainly two-flats. For the most part it was an ordinary city neighborhood, returned from the dead.

Chicago, I'm willing to believe, had once had many such thriving districts. At its nadir during the 1970s it had had maybe three. (I concede the precise count is open to debate.) Now vibrant communities were again numerous. Many were organized around a theme of some sort: Wrigleyville, a lively area around the Cubs' ballpark, hosted a sort of daylong Mardi Gras whenever the team was in town; Boystown on North Halsted Street was the principal gay nightlife strip; Roscoe Village had a vaguely retro, small-town-in-the-big-city feel and seemed to be overrun with parents pushing strollers and little kids on scooters—although children were pretty common all over.

Then there was Andersonville, called Girl's Town by some, owing to the supposed preponderance of lesbians. I was skeptical, since in my observation lesbians didn't congregate as conspicuously as gays, but one day Mary and I took the kids over to a well-known Andersonville shoe store—well known for being just that, a basic (if large) locally owned full-service shoe store, as opposed to the usual chain store or overpriced boutique—during the week of the city's Pride Parade, formerly (and still basically) the Gay Pride Parade, which was definitely a slice. On the day we were in the shoe store, it turned out, Andersonville had scheduled a satellite pride parade, informally known as the Dyke Hike. Among other things the parade featured several contingents of chesty topless maidens who concealed their nipples from casual view with shiny red cellophane tape. Naturally the transit of this picturesque aggregation brought sales activity in the shoe store to a temporary halt. The kids, along with everybody else in the store, watched with interest, then returned to business after the parade had passed. [2]

So okay, it wasn't the Chicago of the 1950s. Who would have wanted it to be? It was a real neighborhood in a real city nonetheless. We were content. We'd accomplished what we'd set out to do—fix up an old city house, raise a family, and lead, admittedly by a relaxed interpretation of the term, an ordinary middle-class life.

I don't mean to give the impression that all was perfect. Real estate developers seemed to be engaged in a long-running research project to see if it was possible to build a condo building so ugly no one would live in it. (Answer to date: no.) One innovation in the hideousness department, which caught on in a big way during the 1990s, was the substitution of concrete block for conventional common brick. Concrete block may be cheaper (it requires less hand labor), but it isn't beautiful and can't be rendered beautiful by any known technique. The only hope was to use as little as possible—we'd limited ourselves to four courses for the Barn House's foundation, thinking that concrete-block structures of larger scale were best confined to places where they'd have limited visibility, such as caves. But that wasn't what was done. On the contrary, developers took sinister delight in finding loopholes in the zoning laws that enabled them to build four-story concrete-block eyesores on sites the size of a bath mat. The front of the house had to be given some passably attractive treatment, lest the

[2]An indication of how Chicago has changed in this regard may be found in the views of Alderman Richard Mell, an old-school ward boss who was allied with the white city council faction opposed to Harold Washington, the city's first black mayor, during the Beirut-on-the-Lake era of the 1980s. Mell's daughter Deborah is openly lesbian. The alderman has famously remarked, "I'd like to slap the bastards [who reject their gay children]. . . . Come on! If your child comes to you and tells you this and you really have a problem with it and it becomes a real issue, you really don't deserve to call yourself a parent." Say what you will about his politics, a guy like that you can deal with.

neighbors revolt, but commonly the façade had the pasted-on appearance of an afterthought, which it's safe to say it was.

For all that, the new construction had the virtue of being essentially citylike, no trifling achievement. This was most evident on the city's commercial streets. Twenty-five years earlier the common practice in Chicago had been to build a row of one-story shops with a parking lot in front—a strip mall, the kind of thing one might find in the suburbs. Now this was less prevalent. More commonly one saw apartments stacked over stores, a building type common before World War II but little seen since. High-density mixed-use buildings didn't represent any great conceptual breakthrough on the part of real estate developers—Jane Jacobs had advocated them in 1961. The difference was that now people would live in them (and banks therefore would finance them)—in Chicago, at least, they were part of the urban deal.

Occupying the condos were phalanxes of kids in town for their first big jobs out of college. As was true the world over, this group's arrival didn't occasion universal applause, owing to the oblivious sense of entitlement some of its members displayed. The term for the female offenders in Chicago was "Trixies," who in the stereotypical view were airheaded blondes who whined about their wedding plans via cell phone on the bus; Ned once referred to their backward-baseball-cap-wearing male counterparts as Lincoln Park meatheads.

I don't wish to exaggerate the failings of this much-maligned subculture. True, we now had the problem that, while the *ranchera* music in the building behind us had by and large died down, some obnoxious yuppies moved into a renovated two-flat down the alley and threw parties on their deck (and why couldn't *that* one collapse?) that entailed playing loud music till two a.m. and necessitated my calling the cops. There was also the ponytailed ditz in the SUV who gunned around me on Sheffield Avenue— Sheffield is a narrow two-way street—because I was too slow pulling away from a stop sign for her taste and she couldn't spare the additional two seconds it would take to reach a parking spot up the block, which spot she then pulled into headfirst without looking, with the result that she clipped the car parked astern and had her right taillight erupt in a burst of red plastic shards. Here was an individual, one felt, who wasn't long for the city, and maybe not long for this earth.

More commonly, though, you met people like the young guy who lived in the condo building next to my buddy Joe's renovated two-flat in outer Bucktown, with whom we spent a pleasant summer afternoon discussing the local real estate prospects, not that either of *us* had a clue, because he thought old houses were cool and it'd be fun to fix one up, and who were we to disabuse him? Perhaps he'd come looking for a party, but the city had sucked him in.

We had many such conversations with friends and neighbors—the local real estate market fascinated us all. Property values had continued their extraordinary climb; by the early 2000s many of us were paper millionaires and a few were just millionaires. A couple several doors down moved out of their house and invested well over $300,000 in a gut rehab that took the better part of a year; they moved back but decided they wanted to cash in, believing the run-up in price was a bubble soon to pop, and sold for $1.14 million, which they found disappointingly low. The new owner promptly commenced another round of renovations that he intimated cost around a half million dollars, among other things necessitating the demolition of a brand-new kitchen equipped with stainless steel Sub-Zero fridge and granite countertops; only a few months after the work was completed his firm transferred him to London and he sold for $1.75 million. Three blocks away someone bought a house roughly the same age as ours for $980,000, then tore it down so he could build new. (I liked the old place well enough, but admit the new one, which plays off its neighbor across the street in terms of color and mass, is a cunning piece of art.) Our own house was appraised at $1.6 million, almost two and a half times what we'd put into it.

We were baffled by these staggering prices. We'd been reading for years about overheated property values in coastal cities, but in Chicago they were new. We wondered where all the tycoons had come from who could afford to spend millions on a house.

It wasn't until we took to vacationing in rural Michigan, of all places, that I got an inkling what was up. In 2000, we began sending our kids to a summer camp in the northwest corner of the state,[3] a classic midwestern landscape of dunes, water, and forest. After delivering the kids Mary and I spent a few days at a bed-and-breakfast in a hamlet called Beulah on the shore of Crystal Lake, which was separated by a narrow isthmus from Lake Michigan. Beulah, permanent population 367, was the archetypal upper midwestern beach town, consisting of sun-washed clapboard houses (on our street, anyway) with front porches overlooking the two-block-long downtown, a little park, and beyond that the beach. I thought it charming—possibly the least pretentious municipality I've ever encountered. [4] Only gradually did the realization steal upon us that it and the surrounding region were among the most beautiful places on earth.

[3]Native Michiganders from ancient custom don't express geographical matters in such terms, preferring instead to indicate a spot on the backs of their left hands, which the lower peninsula resembles. According to this system the kids' camp was situated at the first knuckle of the pinky.

[4]The following, which I found on a historical marker at the beach, gives some sense of the place:

> In 1873 an ambitious but ill-advised project was put through in an effort to connect Crystal Lake and Lake Michigan with a navigable channel. The original level of Crystal Lake was, at that time, much higher than its present level. The project was a complete failure in respect to accomplishing its purpose. [The canal's promoters had neglected to observe that Crystal Lake was several feet higher than Lake Michigan, so that when the channel was cut through, the smaller lake partially emptied into the larger with a roar that could be heard for miles.] The result was the lowering of the lake and exposing a wide stretch of beach around the entire lake and making possible the development of Crystal Lake as a resort and residential area as well as the village of Beulah.

A town like that you've got to love.

We were far from the first to realize this, we soon realized. Browsing around the area for a few days, we found not the Wisconsin Dells–type collection of T-shirt shops the vacations of our youth had taught us to expect, but rather a surprisingly urban level of amenities—good restaurants, bookstores, art galleries, and so on. Come lunchtime, for example, while I don't doubt we could have found a burger and fries if we'd tried, more commonly our sandwiches featured basil pesto and portobello mushrooms and other such stuff, none of which would be considered out of the ordinary in the city but was something of a surprise in the sticks. Upscale establishments of this sort, moreover, weren't confined to one or two towns; rather, there was an entire circuit, extending from, oh, Manistee up through Frankfort to Glen Arbor, and I guess if you were determined to take it that far, Charlevoix, Petoskey, and Mackinac Island. What's more, so far as I could tell, all this bustling enterprise had been accomplished without the intervention of national chain stores (the Starbucks nearest to Beulah of which I have definite knowledge was in Traverse City, forty miles away), marketing consultants, or—you'll excuse the hubris—us, by which I mean people from Chicago.

This requires a word of explanation. Chicago's influence extended a considerable distance into Michigan. The southwestern corner of the state, notably a string of Lake Michigan vacation towns that the real estate agents had succeeded in getting everyone to call "harbor country," was part of metropolitan Chicago for practical purposes; you could pick up a Sunday *Tribune* at the corner grocery as far north as Saugatuck. Crystal Lake, however, was a six-hour drive distant. At the breakfast table in our B&B in Beulah, the other guests were from places like Flint and Ann Arbor and Grand Rapids, or sometimes Toledo or Phoenix or Gillette, and while they enjoyed our tales of walking to Wrigley and fireworks on the lake, we were clearly visitors from a distant shore. That's not to say we felt like intruders or in any way unwelcome; on the contrary, we were delighted at having been invited to a party that had been organized by someone else.

What puzzled us for a long time was who had organized it. I had the naïve idea at the time that a prospering hinterland required a prospering city—but Chicago was too far away. Detroit . . . well, our companions at breakfast, or at any rate the Michiganders, generally spoke of Detroit as one would of the departed at a wake. We met quite a few people from Ann Arbor, which from all accounts was thriving, but it remained a town of modest scale. Grand Rapids was larger, but still seemed insufficient to support such a formidable economic superstructure.

The truth (or so it seemed to me) didn't dawn on us till we began talking to the proprietors of some of the little restaurants and bakeries we frequented. Mostly they were young and well-educated, having graduated from the state's big universities. Equally important, they were entrepreneurs, looking to start small businesses, and northern Michigan ("up north," in local parlance) was where they'd gone. My impression was that the decision had involved no close calculation of the prospect of X number of individuals with Y disposable dollars showing up. Mostly they just liked it there, opened a business, and hoped customers would show up. The young entrepreneurs were the product of an urban environment—you didn't learn about portobello mushrooms and snappy logo design kicking cowpies on the farm—and had taken a path that in principle wasn't far removed from that of an urban rehabber. The fact that they hadn't wound up in the city was irrelevant. They'd fallen under the spell of a place, made the choice to live there, and endured whatever hardships it entailed.

What I deduced from this was that a rural area could gentrify just as a city did. That in turn shed some light on real estate prices. When Mary and I browsed the vacation-home listings—strictly for amusement, since we could barely cover the mortgage on the house we had—we were struck by the enormous variation in pricing. A villa with a hundred feet of frontage on Crystal Lake might list for a million dollars, for example, while humbler dwellings not far away were going for relatively trifling amounts. Price disparities like that were common in the city, but we'd assumed they reflected differences in crime and poverty. Now we realized a simpler phenomenon was at work. People with money had set their sights on the limited number of properties they considered desirable—old houses on Chicago's north lakefront, lakeside cottages in Michigan—and had bid up the price.[5]

As for where all these people came from with a million dollars to throw around, well, that wasn't all that complicated either. We stayed one night at a bed-and-breakfast in an old Victorian mansion on a hillside overlooking Frankfort, Michigan, a pretty harbor town where lake ferries had once docked. The following year we were told the place had been sold to a wealthy businessman from Texas who meant to use it as a vacation home. How he'd found out about the area I have no idea. The point was, once a place achieved a certain cachet, the wealthy just showed up.

It seemed to me I now understood what was going on back home in Chicago. Property values naturally rose when an area became more desirable, and up to a point it was essential that they did; otherwise fixing up old houses and other properties to the level required made no economic sense. Eventually prices reached the point where new construction became viable—undoubtedly the city construction boom of the mid-1990s had begun partly because the potential selling prices home builders plugged into their spreadsheets reached the point that the minus signs on the bottom line disappeared. That in turn greatly simplified the problem of urban revival. At low moments during our work on the Barn House the chances of the city making a comeback seemed remote—no one with a choice would sign up for the grief we'd endured. Once rising prices attracted home builders back into the city, the problem solved itself. People who wanted

[5]I've learned this is the nub of the argument advanced in "Superstar Cities" (Working Paper 12355) by Joseph Gyourko, Christopher Mayer, and Todd Sinai, published by the National Bureau of Economic Research, July 2006.

to live in the city didn't need to fix up old houses; they simply bought new.

The downside was that the process didn't end with the initial run-up in property values—prices could continue rising for a long time. (In the sociological literature this is known as "super-gentrification.") Eventually supply and demand would come into equilibrium, but given increasing affluence nationwide, pent-up demand, and gentrification's inherently slow spread, prices could easily exceed the levels that ordinary people could afford.

That had happened in Chicago, we now recognized. My brother, transferred to Nashville ten years earlier, told me moving back to Chicago was now financially out of the question. We ourselves realized we couldn't afford to buy a house in our neighborhood. Property taxes jumped across broad swaths of the city, leading to protests. We were insulated from this for a time by the historic-preservation tax freeze we'd earned for fixing up the Barn House, but eventually that expired, and over a period of a few years our annual tax bill tripled. I appealed three years running, getting a reduction the first time and denials subsequently. After the latest round of reassessments I considered appealing yet again and printed out all the proposed assessments for the neighborhood from the assessor's online database, then walked up and down the streets hoping to suss out the Byzantine classification system. Finally I concluded that on a comparative basis my assessment was probably on the low end and I'd better just shut up. The state enacted a cap intended to limit the amount assessments could increase each year, but that just postponed the inevitable. In the end, most people recognized, none too happily, that their taxes would go up.

We recognized ruefully that we ourselves were only transitional figures in the neighborhood's transformation. The first wave had been the creative types and free spirits who preceded us, with good intentions but little cash. The second wave consisted of undercapitalized rehabbers like us, who could afford, barely, to undertake major renovations, although the work might take them years. The third wave consisted of those with sufficient resources (thank God) to buy the finished job.

That was the point the Barn House's neighborhood had now reached. The thought gave me pause—it does to any rehabber. We hadn't been poor, of course, and the house's appreciation had made us unexpectedly wealthy, at least on paper. The people who bought it from us, though—anybody who could afford $1.6 million for a house would have to be rich to start with. Already the neighborhood had seen a few people who dwelt on this lofty plane—an actress, a rock star, a wheel in the world of finance. No doubt there would be more as time went on.

We comforted ourselves with the thought that this was Chicago, and not an especially fashionable part of Chicago at that. We lived in an interior neighborhood, not on the lakefront; if nothing else the mix of housing, with big homes like ours on the same street as apartment buildings and town houses, meant the neighborhood wouldn't become an enclave of the superrich anytime soon. Sure, the more decrepit multifamily dwellings might eventually be renovated and rented to lawyers and bond salesmen. But for now we had a good mix.

All American parents, recalling their own rebellious youth, regard the looming adolescence of their children with unease, not merely because of the possibility of disasters involving inebriants, cars, and sex, but because of the prospect of clashes over basic values. God forbid you should invest countless hours in soccer games, owie patching, and homework help only to have your kids prefer Green Day to the Rolling Stones. Or in our case, discover they liked the broad lawns of suburbia better than good old urban grit.

We needn't have worried. The kids loved the city, without prompting or indoctrination from us. No doubt in large part this was because they went to grade school downtown, which was abrim with things to see and do, predisposing them to think the world was organized for their amusement and leading to disgruntlement when they realized large parts of it weren't. Mary and I first noticed this attitude on our annual spring car trips to visit friends in Atlanta, which involved frequent detours onto choice bits of two-lane Americana—my favorite was Route 135 in southern Indiana, a delightful landscape of remnant hardwood forest atop limestone hills. We might as well have been driving through the Gobi Desert as far as the kids were concerned. "What do people *do* around here?" they wailed as we cruised past this or that bucolic scene. They brightened up if we stopped somewhere sufficiently diverting to accord with their idea of civilization, but were always relieved when we got home.

Naturally, Mary and I made it our business to provide our children with urban survival skills. In addition to the usual look-both-ways-and-don't-talk-to-strangers lectures, we instructed them in such elementary procedures as riding the L home from school, which we decided we could hazard when Ryan entered seventh grade, by which time he was taller than me. (Ani could take the L, too, as long as she rode with her brother.) Mary, with maternal caution, bought Ryan a cell phone and suggested I follow the train in the car after the manner of Popeye Doyle in *French Connection.* I thought this excessive and said I would take all three kids on a dry run before school started.

First we took the L from our house to school, during which time I offered instruction on the rudiments—here are the signs, there are the maps, this is how you insert a fare card in the slot. I laid special emphasis on the necessity of changing trains at a station called Belmont. We rode down to the school uneventfully, then turned around and headed home. The kids ran ahead while I purposely hung back. They succeeded in negotiating the turnstiles, taking the stairs to the proper platform, and boarding the train. As we rumbled along, Ryan and Ani gazed out the window at the passing scene, oblivious to the fact that we were approaching the transfer point. When the train pulled into the station, Andrew, always a methodical child, got up and headed toward the door. "We have to get off here," he announced. Startled, Ryan and Ani scrambled up from their seats and out the door.

I chastised them on the platform as we waited to change trains. "Were you looking at the signs and listening to the announcements like I told you?" I asked Ryan.

"No," he said.

"Then how do you expect to know where to get off?"

"Social cues," he said.

I don't know if you can call it progress, but that isn't an excuse I'd have thought to give my old man. "Ryan," I said with as much sternness as I could muster, "you're going to be riding with total strangers. They're not all going to get off at the same stop as you. That's why you have to pay attention."

"Oh," said Ryan. He looked around. "What did you say the name of this station was?"

They got the hang of it eventually, although this entailed many adventures, the most frequent of which—even Andrew fell prey to it—was changing to the Purple Line by mistake, which also stopped at Belmont but then ran express five and a half miles to the city limits, where you had to get off and catch the next train back. The first time Ani did this she sounded so woebegone on the cell phone that I drove up to Howard Street to get her, but when she did the same thing a month later I said, "Honey, you're on your own," having first provided the necessary directions. She arrived home an hour later and never got on the wrong train again.[6]

Just living in the city was an education for the kids. Ryan, six

---

[6]This approach didn't always sit well with the kids. Years later, assigned to prepare an autobiography for school, Andrew wrote, "My dad works at home but I still have to take the train home every day. Unlike Matt, whose parents love him."

feet tall by the time he reached eighth grade, began playing basketball with a racially mixed travel team organized by a coach
from one of the public high schools. The team's home court was
a YMCA a few blocks up the street from Cabrini-Green, the notorious public housing project. While waiting for a game to start
during a holiday tournament I sat in the stands at the Y's gym
with another parent, an avid basketball fan and sometime coach.
"Uh-oh," he said when he noticed the opposing team filing in. "I
know these guys. They're from Washington Park. They've got
their own weight-training coach." Washington Park was in a
tough neighborhood on the south side. The weight training had
evidently paid off—three of the kids, presumably also eighth-
graders, were taller than Ryan and looked to be half again his
bulk.

The Washington Park team proceeded to trounce Ryan's squad.
At one point Ryan tried to block an opponent going in for a
layup, and in my estimation timed his leap pretty well; the other
kid passed the ball from his right hand to his left while airborne,
then tossed it over his shoulder for a basket. Ryan's team wound
up losing by 51 points. In the car on the way home I expected
him to be crushed. Not so. He was in good spirits—he'd learned a
few things, admittedly the hard way. "You see how the game is
played," he said.

Fact was, none of our fears had come to pass—raising a family
in the city had again become a mainstream choice. We signed the
kids up for soccer; I became a coach and later the organization's
webmaster. The old hands told me that in the space of a decade
the program had grown from a few hundred kids to twenty-five
hundred. (As I write it's three thousand.)

In 1995, the dismal Chicago public school system had been
taken over by the mayor and reforms instituted. By the time Ryan
was approaching the point where we had to think about such
things, the city had established a half dozen selective-enrollment
high schools, one of which, based on test scores, was the best in
the state. Ryan took the entrance exam for this school, Northside

College Prep, and was admitted. At freshman orientation, one parent unclear on the concept asked if scholarships were available. "This is a public school," the principal explained. "Tuition is free."

True, Northside was an elite school—but it was an elite *public* school, which in Chicago historically had been rare. The best high schools of my youth had mainly been Catholic, the public schools in those days being largely the preserve of greasers in baggy gray pants. Moreover, it was by no means an elite *rich* public school, a common enough thing in the suburbs but in the city completely unknown. Thirty-one percent of the students came from low-income families; three out of five were minorities. There were lots of Asians and girls in head scarves; the social center of gravity for my kids' friends (Ani followed Ryan in due course) seemed to be a handful of outlying neighborhoods that, due to residency requirements, were popular with firemen and cops.

I don't mean to exaggerate the extent to which things had improved. Northside and its peers were among the few bright spots in a public school system that the middle class had largely abandoned—some might say had never embraced. Eighty-six percent of Chicago public school students were poor; only 8 percent were white. During the 1990s, a period when poverty in the city as a whole declined slightly, the percentage of low-income students in the public schools had markedly increased. In many affluent parts of town, the students at the local elementary schools, quite a few of which, judging from test scores, were actually pretty good, were overwhelmingly poor. In our far-from-impoverished neighborhood, for example, the low-income rate at the local public elementary school exceeded 90 percent.

If the community was willing to make the effort, though, the local school could be turned around. We heard about a Wrigleyville elementary school where the community had managed it, mainly by persuading middle-class parents in the area to send their kids there. In ten years enrollment had increased by close to two hundred students while the low-income rate dropped from 90 to 35 percent—a figure still likely to leave suburbanites aghast, but which in the city you could live with. (Lest it be thought the change was accomplished by evicting all the minorities, white kids currently constitute just 38 percent of the student body, which nonetheless is two and a half times as many as were on hand in 1996.) A couple with a preschooler sent around a flyer trying to drum up some interest in our neighborhood school; Mary ran for a seat on the local council overseeing this school and won. We'll see what develops. But experience showed that the schools could be improved, slowly and mostly through local initiative, one at a time.

As for that bedrock educational mission, the transmission of life lessons to your kids—in my case, the principles of the right way and the love of manual labor—I confess the issue remains in doubt. The world conspires against you. The kids were too young to help with most of the house work, and the scale of the remaining projects—building a garage, for example—isn't likely to provide many opportunities for patient instruction. I thought I might at least familiarize them with tools by showing them a few simple auto repairs, but even that proved difficult. Several times I tried teaching Ryan to change the spark plugs in our ancient Corolla, but on every occasion the lesson was interrupted after we'd barely started—basketball practice, an overdue school project, and so on.

I remained determined till one day the auto repair shop called with an estimate for repairs on our van, a newer vehicle. We needed new spark plugs, the auto repair man informed me. Price: $300.

"Three hundred dollars?" I protested that changing plugs took twenty minutes and cost six bucks. The auto repair man said I obviously hadn't changed a newer car's plugs—they were platinum now, designed to last a hundred thousand miles, and replacement required major disassembly.

You see the problem. Forget spark plugs. Maybe I'll get the kids to help repaint the basement.

25

When I decided to write this book in 1994, I thought it would be a story about a house—which is to say, an opportunity to spin a good yarn, as books about houses mostly have been. It turned out to be more than that purely by luck. At the start of work on the Barn House, the revival of Chicago had a lot in common with the Second Coming or, to put the issue in terms likely to have greater local resonance, the Cubs winning the World Series—consummations devoutly wished for that few expected to see. When it actually occurred, no one was more surprised than us. Things had been building slowly for some time, but the climax was so sudden and unequivocal that it left many wondering why events had come to pass as they had. The details naturally are specific to Chicago, but broader lessons may be drawn.

One explanation I've seen proposed is that Chicago had evolved from a factory town into a global city, and the professional types who flocked to such places tended to like city life. I resist this explanation for three reasons: (1) If Chicago is a global city today—and hey, why not?—it was no less of one in 1893 or 1930; certainly no dramatic change in this respect occurred in the 1990s;[1] (2) the global-city argument to my mind implies that only cities bulking large on the world stage can aspire to urbanity, which I don't think is the case; and (3) most pertinently, it suggests we were borne along irresistibly by the historical tide, which sure isn't how it felt to us.

My own view is that Chicago didn't revive because it had become a global city, but rather that it became a global city (or acquired whatever enhanced stature it may have) because it had revived—although revived is the wrong word. As I've tried to explain, I think it's more accurate to say it had matured, by which I mean that it had become a city that people lived in because they wanted to, not because it was the best they could do at the time.

One important element in the maturing process, and we may as well speak plainly, was gentrification. The term has acquired a pejorative connotation in some quarters, leading many to resort to euphemisms, such as urban renaissance or neighborhood revitalization. I'm going to stick with gentrification, partly because it's a term everyone knows, and partly because it conveys with reasonable clarity what happens—the upper middle class establishes itself in some existing urban place and brings upper-middle-class money and habits with it. The process involves changes good

[1]The global-city argument was most explicitly expressed by R. C. Longworth, "The 2000 Census—Chicago Has Entered the Global Era," *Chicago Tribune*, August 25, 2002. For more on Chicago as a global city, see Abu-Lughod, Janet, *New York, Chicago, Los Angeles: America's Global Cities* (Minneapolis: University of Minnesota Press, 1999); Madigan, Charles, ed., *Global Chicago* (Urbana, Illinois: University of Illinois Press, 2004); and Taylor, Peter and Lang, Robert, "U.S. Cities in the 'World City Network,'" Brookings Institution—Survey Series, February 2005. In assessing the "global network connectivity" of U.S. cities, the Brookings report notes that while New York is in a class by itself, "Chicago and Los Angeles constitute a clear, second stratum[um]."

and bad. On the plus side, the neighborhood typically becomes safer, city services improve, more shops and restaurants open, and the area becomes physically more attractive due to increased investment and better maintenance. The downside varies with the city. In New York, London, and some other cities gentrification was accompanied by fears of displacement of lower-income residents;[2] in Chicago, as I've said, the more frequent complaint was sharply rising property taxes.[3] I don't wish to belittle such concerns, but to focus exclusively on them is to miss an essential point: gentrifiers choose to live in the city, often at considerable cost to themselves, in my observation usually making common cause with the city folk who were there to start with. That a healthy city requires an abundance of such people hardly needs argument. Far from being alien invaders, they're the city's heart and soul.

Or so one might think. The academy, however, on the whole prefers the alien-invaders take on matters. I have a recently published book that aspires to be the first textbook on gentrification, in which one finds the statement, "Gentrification is nothing more and nothing less than the neighborhood expression of class in-

[2]Whether these fears were well founded is a matter of debate—see, for example, Freeman, Lance, "Displacement or Succession? Residential Mobility in Gentrifying Neighborhoods," *Urban Affairs Review* 40 (2005), pp. 463–91. Freeman's analysis purportedly shows that while gentrification undeniably changes the socioeconomic makeup of a neighborhood over time, the turnover rate is no greater than occurs in nongentrifying neighborhoods. To use Freeman's terms, gentrifiers *succeed* the original residents but don't *displace* them. Freeman bases this conclusion on a national database, however, and it may be that abuses occurred in particular cities.

[3]I don't claim displacement isn't an issue; it has been a long-standing concern in neighborhoods like Uptown and Pilsen, and more recently in Bucktown, Wicker Park, and Logan Square. However, I'd say the attitude toward displacement in Chicago is generally pragmatic. Ron, a city guy I knew who had done some small-scale real estate development, put it this way: "Lower-income people should not be forced out of the neighborhood. But anybody who takes the place of a scum-sucking low-life dirtbag is all right by me."

equality."[4] This is a *textbook*, mind you. It goes on to note that "the gentrification literature is 'overwhelmingly critical,'" which from my admittedly cursory reading is indubitably true. Gentrification does have its scholarly defenders, but their work likewise has its problems, of which I'll speak later. Anyone attempting a popular treatment of the subject is thus in the uncomfortable position of having to explain (and defend, although in my opinion having to defend gentrification is like having to defend agriculture) a phenomenon on which, to be charitable, the apparatus of scholarly inquiry has yet to get a handle. The reader accordingly is cautioned that what follows was prepared without benefit of adequate research or professional qualifications other than possibly having a clue.

It seems clear enough to me that gentrification broadly speaking is a relatively old phenomenon, aspects of which were evident in the mid-nineteenth century;[5] that it's a common though by no means inevitable consequence of urbanization occurring throughout the world; that notwithstanding its being fundamentally a product of cities it can be found in rural as well as urban areas; that even in our hubba-hubba age it's a leisurely and complex process not easily started or stopped absent radical measures; and that—pivotal point—it isn't inherently good or bad except to the extent, and I assure you I say this without irony, that practical advantages accrue to stability and don't to catastrophic decline. While it would be foolish to claim a gentrified neighborhood will never deteriorate, it's much more likely in my view to manage

[4]Lees, Loretta, Tom Slater, and Elvin Wyly, *Gentrification* (New York: Routledge, 2008), p. 80.
[5]Bohemianism, the first stage of gentrification, was first noted (and named) in 1840s Paris. For a summary, see Lloyd, Richard, *Neo-Bohemia: Art and Commerce in the Postindustrial City* (New York: Routledge, 2006), pp. 50 *et seq*. Lloyd's main subject is the alternative arts culture that flourished in Chicago's Wicker Park neighborhood in the 1990s. Today the district is substantially gentrified and few artists can afford to live there.

urban challenges successfully than a community to which people have no attachment other than convenience. I'd go so far as to say that, in a dynamic society like the United States, a city will either gentrify or die.

The point is worth emphasizing. In their early days big cities and their neighborhoods follow a predictable arc—an initial boom, a period of prosperity, then (with rare exceptions) decline, typically in tandem with the expiration or departure of the industries that were the reason the community was built in the first place. In this last stage, the housing stock deteriorates, local problems mount, and flashier accommodations become available someplace else. Departing residents are replaced by progressively poorer ones, perhaps some newly arrived ethnic group. (I once heard a suburbanite say he was thinking of selling his house— Koreans were starting to move in.) If the process continues unchecked for a long time the community becomes a slum, and if things really tank the city empties out and the buildings crumble or are pulled down. Examples of towns that have reached this extreme state can be found throughout the world.

In some neighborhoods in some cities, though, the process of decline reverses. The impetus varies. In the imperial capitals of Europe, the bohemian element settled in districts offering access to prospective patrons. The housing stock, however dilapidated, may have some intrinsic charm. The neighborhood may have amenities, such as proximity to downtown or a body of water, or it may offer a pretty prospect. It may simply look urban—as I say, I'm convinced this was the determinant in much of Chicago. The main thing is, people come to feel that a place is special in some way and begin to invest in homes and businesses. Perhaps they're simply locals who've made some money; probably more often they're newcomers.[6] The result is the same either way: Eventually

---

[6]Some distinguish between neighborhood revitalization (accomplished by existing residents) and gentrification (done by outsiders). I don't think any

the neighborhood is perceived as more desirable (quaint, edgy, what have you), property values begin to rise, and—again, we need to be blunt—departing residents are replaced by more affluent ones. The neighborhood has begun to gentrify.

Gentrification is a block-by-block process. Maturation, in the sense that I use the term, operates at the level of the city (or at least the neighborhood) as a whole. It has two elements, one visible and one not, to both of which gentrification contributes. The visible element is urbanity—the city's beauty, vitality, and amenity. Gentrified neighborhoods are attractive, bustle with life, and offer the multitude of conveniences great and small that one expects to find in a fully realized urban place. The invisible element lies in the attitudes and expectations of those who live and work in the city. Some are there mainly because of circumstance—they were born there, that's where their job or family is, and so on. Others are simply consumers, taking advantage of what the city has to offer and giving little back—a good many affluent residents of gentrified neighborhoods fall into this category.

But some—these are the essential ones—are there because of the city itself. They make an emotional investment in it, and quite likely a financial and personal one as well. They fix up a house, plant a garden, raise a family, join a community organization, volunteer. Not all these people are gentrifiers, but a lot of them are. No great city can arise without a sizable core of this group, who enjoy urban life and are willing to put themselves to some trouble for its sake.

And cities always mean trouble. The giddy day may come when your chances of getting robbed, beaten, or killed aren't significantly greater in the city than in the suburbs, and poverty and homelessness are only unpleasant memories. Even then, though, cities will remain more crowded and unpredictable, filled with

---

sharp distinction exists. Improvement of the Barn House's neighborhood was a joint effort by older residents and newcomers.

people whose language you don't know and whose culture is different from your own. There will always be more dirt, more noise, more crazies, more congestion, more risk. For those of a certain sensibility cities also promise a richer life, but it comes at a price, and not all care to pay.

Some cities mature more quickly than others. A few so dominate the life of a wealthy nation that their emergence as metropolises is all but assured—New York and London are in this category. Others are blessed with spectacular sites, pleasant weather, or similar advantages. San Francisco, for example, whatever its economic ups and downs, has long been sustained by the conviction of its citizens that they live in one of the favored places of the earth.

Others—I expect this is true of most declining industrial cities—take longer to find their place. I think what sustains the city folk who live in these towns isn't so much the gritty reality that may then surround them as the *idea* of the city—what it might someday become. It's the equivalent of buying an old house because it has potential. Few share that vision in the early going. It's only in the final stages that the path seems easy, if things ever get to that point.

Chicago was in this last category. In its early years it was the classic American boomtown. Founded in 1833 and largely destroyed in the 1871 fire, it nonetheless had become the second-largest city in America by 1890, leading boosters to believe it was destined to become the preeminent city on the continent, and possibly the planet. The idea wasn't as off the wall as it now sounds. The "white city" created for the 1893 World's Columbian Exposition captured the imagination of the globe; during the 1920s the city would surpass Berlin to become the fourth largest city in the world.

The 1909 Burnham plan gave magnificent expression to these lofty ambitions. It's a remarkable document to read even now, proposing a sweeping program of civic improvements befitting a world capital—islands in the lake, wide boulevards, grand civic buildings. Okay, maybe it was delusional, but you can see why people got caught up in it. As depicted in Jules Guerin's glowing watercolors, Burnham's fantasies look tantalizingly real. It's easy to imagine the reaction among Chicago's civic elite: *This rocks. Let's do it all.*

Remarkably, the city came fairly close to doing just that. Although it would be a stretch to say Chicago was rebuilt as drawn, the plan's main features, particularly those having to do with the central business district and lakefront, are easily recognizable in a modern aerial photo of the city. Even more remarkably, the work was accomplished without the leadership of a dominant, long-lived personality comparable to New York's Robert Moses. Burnham died in 1912. Walter Moody, managing director of the Chicago Plan Commission and a tireless promoter whose *Wacker's Manual of the Plan of Chicago* was drilled into the city's school-children for years, died in 1920. It didn't matter. The work was taken up by others and pursued with minimal interruption for close to fifty years—a period marked by wars, gangland violence, municipal corruption, and prolonged economic depression. The last major portion of the lakefront park system—virtually all of it was built on landfill—was completed in 1958. The result was nearly twenty miles of beaches, harbors, and open space, plus numerous museums, monuments, concert venues, a zoo, and numerous other cultural and recreational facilities, an achievement unique among Great Lakes cities and not bad for any town anywhere.

Long before 1958, however, Chicago's larger hopes had faded. Sure, it was big and rich; following World War II the city was home to the largest concentration of heavy industry in the world—its factories and mills employed 668,000 people at their peak in 1947. But it hadn't become the world's or even the country's largest city—its population peaked in 1950 at 3.6 million, less than half that of New York. More important, it lacked a mature city's sense of itself. In a 1952 series of *New Yorker* essays that hung the city with the indelible nickname "the Second City," the journalist A. J. Liebling acidly described Chicago's shrunken ambitions: "The city . . . has the personality of man brought up in the expectation of a legacy who has learned in middle age that it will never be his." The lakefront parks and other great civic works concealed what Liebling described as "a boundless agglutination of streets, dramshops, and low buildings without urban character": "what [you] see is like a theatre backdrop with a city painted on it."

It took most of the twentieth century for Chicago to grow into its clothes. The process started earlier than most realize and was excruciatingly slow. The vanguard then as today was the now-familiar collection of artists, musicians, gays, bohemians, and the like who began congregating in down-at-heels neighborhoods with lots of character and cheap rent. On the north side gentrification arguably got under way in 1927 when the former Art Institute of Chicago students Sol Kogen and Edgar Miller began converting a decaying Victorian mansion at 155 W. Burton Place in Old Town into artists' studios. (The eccentric complex, one of a block of similar buildings recently nominated for the National Register of Historic Places, is a sight to see—suffice it to say it wouldn't have met the secretary of the interior's guidelines for historic preservation.[7]) This and a few other projects established Old Town as an artists' enclave, and things spread gradually from there. My father had done some plastering in the late 1950s for a couple renovating an old house on the near north side overlooking what was then known as Bughouse Square, famous for soapbox oratory by the Wobblies and such; my impression is that the

---

[7] I might add that the National Register nomination was filed by Vicki, my historic preservation consultant, and that one of the houses on the block is owned by Bob, the former publisher of my newspaper. The city-guy mafia in Chicago has its tentacles everywhere.

pace of gentrification in Chicago began to quicken around that time.

Other deteriorated north-side lakefront communities followed suit. In the mid-1970s—by my reckoning, close to fifty years after gentrification in Chicago began—the rehabbed portion of Lake View, which had a large gay population and was then called New Town, consisted of a corridor along the lakefront roughly three-quarters of a mile wide. By 1990, I calculated following the release of census data from that year, the gentrified portions of the city accounted for about twenty square miles, less than 10 percent of its total area, but evidently, in retrospect, close to the tipping point. Beginning in the mid-1990s, as we've seen, property values began to rise sharply, a construction boom began, and neighborhoods all over the city blossomed. In 1990, I think, even an optimist would have to say that Chicago had a ways to go. By 2005, in important respects, it had arrived.

In emphasizing the importance of individuals in the city's revival I don't ignore the fact that larger forces were at work. Most of these are well known. As manufacturing employment in Chicago evaporated (as of 2006 only 85,000 factory jobs remained in the city, an 87 percent decline), professional and other white-collar employment rose, and there's no denying that city life tends to be a yuppie predilection. Plenty of other demographic changes arguably also favored urban life—the increasing numbers of singles and childless couples, greater affluence, higher levels of educational attainment, and so on. The city's sheer size worked in its favor. Globalization unquestionably had some impact, especially if one understands the term to include increased immigration, which was the major driver behind the rise in population in Chicago and some other cities during the 1990s. The city had become an international trading hub specializing in exotic financial instruments; as in other global centers, wealthy traders and financial services executives pumped a lot of money into the local real estate market. A central-city housing boom began in the mid-

1990s and continued at least through 2006; although at first we thought this was limited to Chicago, in hindsight it was clearly a national phenomenon—Chicago, New York, Los Angeles and several other older big cities all built large numbers of new homes at roughly the same rate.[8]

But I don't think any of these things was decisive. The switch from a manufacturing to a services-based economy, for example, was a nationwide phenomenon, occurring in many ex-blue-collar towns, or at least in their metropolitan areas. Yet only a few came back. Likewise the housing boom, although it transformed Chi-

---

[8]The following chart, which shows residential building activity in the most densely populated U.S. cities, is adapted from F. Branconi and F. Heydarpour, "Building Boom Puts New York in Good Company," *Economic Notes* (Office of the New York City Comptroller), April 2007, with additional data from the U.S. Census Bureau:

CITY	DENSITY (pop./sq. mi.)	RESIDENTIAL BLDG. PERMITS (average annual units)		RATE OF CHANGE (percent)	NEW UNITS PER 100,000 POPULATION
		1997–99	2004–06		
New York	26,403	10,598	29,245	176	356
San Francisco	16,638	2,296	2,329	1	314
Chicago	12,752	4,000	10,354	159	364
Boston	12,169	718	1,551	116	260
Philadelphia	11,236	562	2,511	347	172
Washington, D.C.	9,316	376	2,112	462	363
Baltimore	8,057	92	2,087	2,168	328
Los Angeles	7,877	3,241	12,485	285	325
Detroit	6,852	312	603	93	88
Seattle	6,710	3,336	4,634	39	805
Milwaukee	6,212	395	777	97	135
Minneapolis/ St. Paul	5,864	820	2,671	226	412

Note that Los Angeles, by reputation the automobile city par excellence, has become one of the more densely populated cities in the United States. Most new residential construction in the city is multifamily; ridership on its rapid transit system has risen sharply since 2000. Although the belief persists in the scholarly literature that Los Angeles represents a new urban paradigm, the evidence suggests that its core is evolving along traditional urban lines.

cago and some other places, passed many cities by. Broad economic and social trends contributed to a rising tide that raised a lot of urban boats from the mid-1990s onward—but you had to have a boat that would float.

I think the main factor separating Chicago from less fortunate places was a purely local one—the city-guy mafia. I don't mean by that just the civic leaders and real estate developers who pushed various projects and initiatives along, although their role was obviously important.[9] I mean the depth and breadth of city people who desperately wanted to make the town work, and who were linked by a tangled net of relationships of whose extent few had any inkling and whose power astonished us all. A common observation in Chicago in those days was that it was the world's biggest small town, and that everyone knew everyone else (by which was meant, though the matter was never expressed in these terms, that all the city people knew each other)—as if this were a local peculiarity. My guess is that it wasn't, and that in fact it's a characteristic of mature or maturing cities everywhere. One might invent a more felicitous term than "city-guy mafia"— no doubt something along the lines of urban metanetwork would make more of an impression on the Ph.D. committee. But it's a real phenomenon whatever you call it. Without it, nothing is possible; with it, everything is.

Not that it'll be easy even so. The economist Richard Florida, one of the relative handful of gentrification advocates in academia, has made a name for himself in recent years writing about the "creative class," which he conceives of as the inheritor to the urban bohemian tradition, except that this crowd has ambition

[9]In particular I ought to acknowledge Chicago Mayor Richard M. Daley, who inaugurated an extensive program of civic improvements on taking office in 1989. Notwithstanding the contributions of his administration, few would dispute that the city's revival wouldn't have occurred without broad participation by ordinary citizens.

and will generate tomorrow's wealth.[10] The creative class, Professor Florida contends, is drawn to places having, among other things, historic architecture, diversity, and recreational amenities—qualities that broadly overlap with those of gentrifying cities. Declining towns hoping to restore their economic vitality, he argues, should try to attract the creative class by providing amenities, encouraging diversity, converting old buildings into artists' quarters, and so on. The state of Michigan has gone so far as to establish a "cool cities" program to foster such initiatives by its municipalities. Professor Florida's work has been much criticized—among other things, no close correlation has yet been demonstrated between concentrations of the creative class and economic growth. But I think he's right in intuiting that artists and other creative people play an important role in urban maturation. What's unfortunate is the implication in his work that government initiatives can coax a city to mature within some predictable period of time. Our experience in Chicago suggests the outcome is chancy even under the most favorable circumstances, and progress sure won't be fast.

Chicago wasn't the first and certainly won't be the last American city to mature, but I think it represents an important milestone in one respect: It was a city of unexceptional advantages by modern lights that succeeded by making the most of what it had. Let me put the matter bluntly—if you can make a great city out of Chicago, and I say this with all affection, you can make one out of anything. Here was an industrial town built on a muddy plain in an almost comically harsh climate, with neither an ocean nor mountains nor proximity to the great centers of population on either coast, which endured racial strife, political corruption,

[10]Professor Florida's books include *The Rise of the Creative Class, and How It's Transforming Work, Leisure, and Everyday Life* (New York: Basic Books, 2002); *Cities and the Creative Class* (New York: Routledge, 2005); and *The Flight of the Creative Class* (New York: HarperCollins, 2005).

and devastating losses of people and jobs—yet by dint of stubborn exertion over a span of generations turned itself into one of the foremost urban centers in the world. Surely there's a lesson in this for towns that still struggle. Rare is the American city lacking any spark whatsoever. One evening a while back my brother-in-law Joe, a college professor in Ohio, drove us through Public Square, the centerpiece of downtown Cleveland. By day Public Square is said to look a bit tattered; by night, different story. *Whoa,* I thought. *Cool.*

I n 2007, while concluding the writing of this book, I went back to visit James and Diane, the couple renovating the old house on Chicago's south side, whom I hadn't spoken to since the early 1990s. I purposely saved this task for the end, for I suspected their story—and that of their neighborhood—would be in many ways more remarkable than mine.

Any doubts about the extent of Chicago's having pulled itself together will dissolve after a tour of the city's south lakefront, which James was kind enough to provide. Admittedly things aren't quite as far along as on the north side. He and Diane still lived in their old house in North Kenwood/Oakland; just like ours, it still wasn't done. Their lives in the thirteen years since I'd seen them last hadn't been entirely easy. James, who'd quit his job as a high school teacher and become a contractor, had bought an old mansion on South Michigan Avenue some years previously and begun renovating it. Someone had broken in and stolen the house's nine carved wooden mantelpieces—"it was like somebody sticking a knife in your gut," he said. But burglary was the least of the neighborhood's troubling events. On a July evening in 2002, down the block from James and Diane's house, two local ne'er-do-wells drove through a stop sign in their van and crashed into a group of teenage girls sitting on the front stoop of a house. Three of the girls were injured and one later died. An infuriated mob of onlookers pulled the driver and his passenger out of the vehicle, grabbed pieces of the shattered steps, and beat the men to death.

On the whole, though, signs that the neighborhood was improving outnumbered those that it was getting worse. Purely from the standpoint of appearances the area had improved to a startling degree. The proximate cause of the change was the city's decision to raze more than eighteen thousand units of public housing, including virtually all the projects in North Kenwood/Oakland. In 1994, not long after writing about James and Diane, I'd gone to one such project a few blocks from their house to do an interview for another story. As was often the case in Chicago, the building was one of a mass of public housing developments built side by side, stretching along Pershing Road for half a mile. Most of the buildings were low and barracks-like—these were the Ida B. Wells Homes. At the end of the long rank stood four grim high-rises, Darrow Homes, in one of which the housing authority had established a satellite office, my destination. As I approached from the parking lot I noticed many windows in the four towers were boarded up with plywood, some with scorch marks on the bricks above. None of the high-rises had handles on the exterior doors—to enter, you had to knock and wait till a security guard admitted you. Once inside you passed through a dim hallway where silent figures watched out the windows. The offices upstairs were cheerful enough, but suspended in front of the windows were enormous sheets of half-inch Plexiglas, meant to shield the occupants from flying glass or worse should violence erupt outside, which I gathered it frequently did.

It seemed obvious on first sight that the housing authority couldn't continue like this, an impression that a review of its records and reports only deepened. Huge numbers of the dwellings under its nominal control were vacant and uninhabitable; repairing them would cost more than a billion dollars. The likelihood of obtaining that kind of money to restore the status quo was nil. It was time, I wrote, for the CHA to prepare for the inevitable downsizing to come. Pretty much everyone else felt the same way. A plan to replace most family public housing in Chicago with mixed-income developments was announced in 1999, and soon thereafter the first public-housing high-rises were razed.[11]

The housing market in North Kenwood/Oakland, long moribund, had been slowly coming to life in the 1990s, but once public housing began coming down, the process visibly accelerated. James spent the better part of the day driving me around the neighborhood to show me how much had been done. We began at the former public-housing site on Pershing Road. Power shovels were methodically demolishing what remained of the Ida B. Wells Homes. Darrow Homes was long gone, replaced by two- and three-story town houses and apartments laid out on a conventional street grid and comparable in appearance to what you'd see on the north side. Many of the homes were occupied; many others were still under construction. Piles of sewer pipe were spaced out at intervals across the newly cleared prairie where streets were to be built—the original streets had been ripped out decades earlier to create "superblocks" for public housing, a once-fashionable idea that had fallen into disfavor. But the city wasn't now trying to create some facsimile of suburbia. Rather, the neighborhood was being reconstructed roughly along the lines it had had when first built.

Notable though this sprawling construction project was, it had

---

[11]Some indication of life in high-rise public housing in Chicago may be found in a September 4, 1987 story by Steve Bogira in the *Chicago Reader* entitled "They Came In Through the Bathroom Mirror." It told of a mentally ill CHA high-rise resident murdered one evening when an intruder crawled through a pipe chase and shoved her bathroom medicine cabinet out from behind to gain entry to her apartment. The woman called the police; neighbors called a few minutes later reporting gunshots. The police on arrival found that no one would answer the door—at that point presumably the woman was dying or dead—and left without attempting to enter. The decaying corpse was discovered two days later. Two other people were murdered in unrelated incidents in the same complex two and five days later.

been set in motion by public money. More remarkable, I thought, was the frenetic building activity on the nearby streets—the neighborhood was in the midst of a housing boom, most of it privately financed. Next door to James and Diane's house there had once been an empty lot; now there was a newly completed four-story condo building—a large sign in front boasted of granite countertops and marble master baths with heated floors. Looking out their back porch thirteen years earlier I'd been able to see all the way to Drexel Boulevard, where the El Rukn temple had once stood. Now the view was blocked by a three-story condo building across the alley. Plans were afoot for a residential project to fill the larger of the remaining vacant lots on the street. James had paid $22,000 for his house in 1979; I asked what he thought it was worth now. He guessed $700,000.

The sweep of the work was astonishing—there was new construction on almost every block south of Oakwood Boulevard. I don't know how many condos were newly completed, under construction, or promised with billboards on the street corners, but the number was surely in the thousands. On blocks where most of the older structures had survived, new infill housing stood on once-vacant lots. Other blocks had been almost entirely rebuilt. In most cases an attempt had been made to replicate the general features of the original buildings in the neighborhood. Though a few buildings were as ugly as anything you'd find on the north side, on the whole the quality of design was high and the construction substantial.

James, to hear him talk, wasn't entirely happy about the changes in the neighborhood—his chief gripe was that some of the new housing wasn't sufficiently upscale for his taste. He pointed out a few modestly scaled subsidized housing developments salted in among the more extravagant homes. Other buildings had stylish brick façades facing the street but vinyl siding everywhere else. (Recalling my sister's house, I assured him this sort of thing wasn't unheard of among white folks.) James had been restoring a house not far from his home; now he'd gotten wind of a plan by the city to buy up the block and allow a developer to put up high-rises—the property offered unobstructed views of the lake.

Eventually we crossed 47th Street into the portion of Kenwood that had been under the protection of the University of Chicago. The day was sunny, and the trees and other plantings were unusually lush due to abundant summer rain, and that plus James's evident satisfaction and my own modest expectations may have prejudiced me—perhaps I shouldn't have been as dazzled as I was. But I think anyone would have been impressed.

Those on the north side of Chicago have the idea they reside in the plush part of town, and it's true you can find pockets of mansions and such; recent years, moreover, have seen the erection of numerous upscale apartment buildings, town houses, and single-family homes equipped with eurostyle cabinets, stainless steel appliances, and that kind of thing, and persons surrounded by such luxe appointments may conclude they're living pretty large. The fact remains that the north side as initially built had been the abode mostly of the middle and working classes, and even today consists in the main of apartments and houses of economical design on unpretentious streets.

The south lakefront, in contrast, had been built for the rich. Virtually the entire area east of State Street between the Loop and Hyde Park had been, at one point or another, and omitting the usual institutional, commercial, and (in later days) industrial uses, a dense stand of luxury housing in an era when luxury meant something. The most prestigious streets—Drexel Boulevard, Michigan Avenue, King Drive, and others—had been conceived of as pleasure drives with wide parkways lined with trees, walkways, and planting beds. The houses themselves were eye-poppingly ornate, the majority of them graystones, which in Chicago was the term for a multistory masonry home with a limestone façade, often of elaborate design. In the twentieth century arson, abandonment, vandalism, urban renewal, and other plagues had taken an appalling toll on the south side, but Kenwood south of 47th Street had had relatively few demolitions. Now it had been restored.

We drove around for quite a while; James knew the area well. On street after street we saw meticulously maintained mansions, row houses, and apartment blocks—for sheer breadth of opulence the north side had nothing to compare. James pointed out the mansion where Louis Farrakhan lived, another formerly owned by Muhammad Ali. Senator Barack Obama lives in the community; the headquarters of Jesse Jackson's Operation PUSH is located in a former synagogue at 50th street and Drexel Boulevard. Later I would look up the census numbers—the neighborhood, which is 70 percent African-American, has a median home price of close to $350,000, compared to $300,000 in our north-side community. The gentrified portion of Kenwood, in short, is wealthy and predominantly black. Few inner-city neighborhoods can be so described.

We continued into Hyde Park, which for fifty years has been Chicago's only stable, substantially integrated neighborhood (it's 40 percent black). It too was now mostly gentrified.[12] We stopped for a few minutes at Robie House, the celebrated Frank Lloyd Wright–designed mansion on the University of Chicago campus, now largely restored. I asked James what he thought about what he and Diane had gone through. "It's not something the average person can endure," he said. "You have to be a little bit crazy to do what we did. Was it worth it? Absolutely. Would I do it again? No." Still, he thought, "growing up in the country"—he'd been raised in Arkansas—"coming to the city, looking at the architecture . . . it inspired me. This is the fulfillment of a dream."

I was curious to see what kind of people were moving into the

[12]Some object that Hyde Park never became badly deteriorated and so can't be described as gentrified. Be that as it may, the community today is affluent and in excellent physical condition.

new homes on the south lakefront, so a few weeks after my tour with James I went to see Kendall, a fellow parent at FXW School whom I'd worked with on the annual fund-raiser. She'd recently moved with her family into a condo two blocks from James and Diane's house. On her street as elsewhere in North Kenwood/Oakland the signs of old and new were incongruously juxtaposed. The air was filled with the sound of hammering and heavy equipment; down the street a power shovel was digging up an old foundation. A sign on the corner offered directions to the sales office for a new condo development. Directly across from Kendall's condo, on the other hand, was an empty courtyard apartment building with boarded-up windows surrounded by a chain-link fence. Orange stickers on the gate read NOTICE OF WATER SERVICE TERMINATION for nonpayment of $42,000. They were dated six weeks before.

Kendall, I learned, had grown up in a high-rise on Riverside Drive in Manhattan—David Dinkins, the first black mayor of New York, had lived across the hall. She'd gone to prep school (Horace Mann, of which I confess I knew little before she mentioned it, but I gather is quite the place) and graduated from Princeton University, where she'd met her husband, Chris, a New Jersey native who was the son of a nurse and one of the first black neurologists in the country. She'd never been to Chicago before flying out for a job interview with Leo Burnett, the advertising agency. "I fell in love with the city instantaneously," she said. "You get the big-city experience but at the same time you have beaches. I thought, this is as good as it gets." She got the Burnett job but left after a year to become director of development for a not-for-profit agency founded by Chicagoan John Rogers, Jr., another Princeton grad who had founded Ariel Capital Management, the largest black-owned investment firm in the United States, with $16 billion under management. There she worked with Arne Duncan, who would go on to become chief executive officer of the Chicago public school system.

Years later they established a charter school in North Kenwood, Ariel Community Academy; one of the people they interviewed to become principal of this school was Mary Ellen Caron, the principal of FXW. Although Mary Ellen didn't take the job, six years after she left FXW and became commissioner of the city's Department of Children & Youth Services, she hired Chris, a lawyer, to become executive director of her department's newly established Juvenile Intervention Center, which provided services for youth at risk of becoming part of the juvenile justice system.

I go into all this detail to make three points. First, Kendall was a city person; second, she was a member in good standing of the city-guy mafia—hell, she made me feel like a hermit; and third, she didn't have to live in North Kenwood if she didn't want to, yet here she was. She offered numerous reasons why the community was a smart place to invest, all of which at a certain level of abstraction made sense: the community was close to the lake—indeed, a new beach at 40th Street and other lakefront recreational facilities were then under construction; it was convenient to the Loop and transportation; the upside potential, as the real estate people say, was terrific. With most of the high-rise public housing gone, property values were spiraling upward; two $1.7 million homes were nearing completion down the block. The fact remained—and I hate to belabor the point, but come on—she, her husband, and their three small children were living a short walk from the spot where five years before two men had been beaten to death with rocks.

I asked Kendall about that. "I couldn't have done this even three years ago," she said. "But it's a different world now. I could see all the building going on. At the end of the day I have kids and I'm not going to put them at risk, but I'm comfortable enough about the direction of the neighborhood to think they'll be safe.

"I think this is an exciting experiment, for lack of a better term, in what this city can do. Chicago is so segregated.[13] I went to prep school my entire life—I got tired of being one of the only African-Americans. I want to be around a great mix of people, and I think there will be more of that here than on the north side. Our neighbors are predominantly African-American, but I'm seeing more Caucasians and other races moving in. My hope is that it will be more like Hyde Park."

I mentioned a book I'd read about North Kenwood/Oakland pointing out that the improvements in the neighborhood didn't benefit all residents equally.[14] The book said schools like Ariel Community Academy mainly served the middle class, which was better equipped to negotiate the complex admissions process; students from poor families generally had to make do with the older schools, which were among the worst in the city. The Chicago Housing Authority had promised the residents of public housing projects in North Kenwood/Oakland slated for demolition that they'd have first claim on replacement housing, but a federal judge had thrown out the agreement. While fears that white people would take over the community seemed overblown, it wasn't so hard to believe that affluent black people might supplant a lot of the poor ones.

"I struggle with that," Kendall said. "I don't see enough disadvantaged and well-off African-Americans mixing—there's little common ground. Socioeconomic status divides way more than race ever will. Some African-Americans don't want to be around

[13]Not to be in any way defensive about this, but while Chicago is segregated, it's not the most segregated city in the United States, as is widely believed. For the record, Chicago as of 2000 was the ninth most segregated of forty-three major metropolitan areas in the United States having a significant number of black residents. Source: U.S. Census Bureau, Housing and Household Economic Statistics Division, "Racial and Ethnic Residential Segregation in the United States: 1980–2000," Table 5-4; available at www.census.gov/hhes/www/housing/resseg/tab5-4.html; accessed October 18, 2007.

[14]Pattillo, Mary, *Black on the Block: The Politics of Race and Class in the City* (Chicago: University of Chicago Press, 2007).

people with the same skin color as theirs just because they don't have the same income or they don't speak as well. Some people don't have a problem with that. I do. I don't want it to be all wealthy African-Americans. To me being successful is being able to deal with all kinds of people in all situations. You want a balance, but at the same time you don't want to displace people. I don't know how you solve that problem.

"For Christopher and me social justice is very important. We believe we were called to do what we do. We African-Americans who have more advantages tend to look out for ourselves and don't give back as much as we should. That's a big part of why our people as a whole are in the state that we are. Some of our African-American neighbors make a lot of money, and I want my kids to see that. But I also want them to see a socioeconomic and racial mix. I want my kids to be citified—when I take them to the playground I want them to see all kinds of people and hear all kinds of languages. The richness of having grown up in a major city is irreplaceable."

I knew what she meant. For city people, diversity wasn't something you put up with; it was an essential part of the draw. You got to see the whole human circus. Sure, in the suburbs you might have better luck finding a parking spot. But in the city you felt more alive.

There are other arguments to be made for cities, I realize. We stand at the brink of an age in which resources will become increasingly scarce, and some believe dense older towns are better adapted to the coming economic realities than newer ones built around the automobile. That may be so, although the analysis is more complicated than might be supposed (I won't get into it now), and in any case few make lifestyle choices based on altruism. The argument for me was simpler: I found the city offered a more satisfying life. Others, I knew, had contrary opinions and were welcome to them. The main thing was, now you had a choice.

There was another attraction to urban living as well, one that was peculiar to a gentrifying as opposed to a gentrified town, and I think any city person who has had the experience will own up to it—the sense of participating in a grand adventure. Many of us who had lived a long time in Chicago felt it with particular acuteness—we'd seen a mature city emerge during our lifetimes, and perhaps felt we had contributed ourselves in some small way. There was something noble about it, I think. Here was one of the great human projects, in which generations long forgotten had invested their lives, for a time seemingly destined for the scrap heap. We had restored it to the main current of history. How much longer our little piece of it would endure was impossible to say, but craftsmanship had gotten Mrs. Carr's house this far; perhaps our modest contribution would get it a little further.

Granted, the larger job was far from complete. Many who followed us in Chicago would try to salvage neighborhoods in worse shape than the ones we called home. In one important respect, though—and you'll forgive me if I boast in saying so—they'd have an advantage an earlier generation didn't. They wouldn't have merely the idea of the city before them; they'd have the thing itself.

Epilogue

The Barn House was one of the last home renovation projects Tony and Jerry worked on. Reasoning that there had to be an easier way to make money, they began bidding on commercial jobs, and eventually found a profitable niche rehabilitating hotels and motels—a business that lent itself to production-line economies, since once you'd figured out an efficient way to renovate the first room, you merely repeated the process for every room thereafter. They moved their office to the suburbs and Jerry relocated to Florida. Eddie remained in Chicago, and I hired him for several additional projects at the Barn House—among other things, his guys rebuilt in cedar the porch steps I'd been foolish enough to have made out of pine initially. As always the work was exquisite.

I spoke with Tom the trumpet player on the phone a few times after he departed the Barn House; for a time I believe he was working for a small ad agency downtown. We made tentative arrangements to get together a couple of times but for one reason or another these fell through. He had no permanent phone number and I was never able to call him. I haven't spoken to him in years.

I referred Lee to some friends who were looking for an electrician to do some wiring in their two-flat in Lincoln Square. They were delighted with his work but scandalized that he charged so little and occasionally pressed more money on him. I got an e-mail from them some time later: they'd called to ask him about another project but were told that he was dead.

The Chief and I see less of each other than we used to but still make a point of getting together around the holidays to have dinner. Having long had the idea that the Chief was barely scraping by financially, I pressed him finally and established that he made his living trading securities and such on his own account. His shrewdest investment was buying a seat on the Chicago Board of Trade in anticipation of its going public. His net worth today is in excess of $2 million.

Mary and I are still together, although I'd have to say working on the house permanently strained our relationship—it would have strained any couple's. The job had been interminable. The house was under construction continuously for more than three years, with major projects for nine years after that. I didn't paint over the carpenters' pencil marks in the upstairs bathrooms until 2005, twelve years after we'd bought the house. We're not done even now. Was it worth it? My answer is much the same as James's: I'm happy to have done it once. The kids have been a great joy to us—Ryan is preparing to enter college as I write—and because of them I'd say, yes, the long struggle was worthwhile. But nothing could make either of us go through it again. I think anyone who has endured a project like ours would agree the cost was far higher than planned, in ways you didn't expect. I'll tell you one thing, though—after all these years Mary's still a knockout.

One spring morning not so long ago my doorbell rang—it was my neighbor George. He'd been out walking his dog and noticed Ned's front door was open, which struck him as odd. He wasn't foolish to worry. Earlier there had been an incident a few blocks away in which (as we heard the story) a fellow pretending to deliver flyers tried the front door of each house he passed till he found one that was unlocked. On entering, presumably bent on robbery, he surprised an elderly man, whom he bludgeoned to death.

I phoned Ned's house; there was no answer. We called the police. On arriving, one cop went around the back while the other drew his revolver and entered the front door. After some minutes the cops returned; they'd found no one inside and nothing amiss. Later that day I got a call from Ned, who was at work. He had left the door open for the exterminators, who had neglected to shut it on departing. "Thanks, neighbor," he said. *No problem*, I replied, feeling moderately virtuous, but knowing I could just as easily have been calling him and saying I saw smoke.

APPENDICES

Appendix A

The two ways to wire a three-way switch, or anyway the two I know, are shown opposite. (The purpose of a three-way switch, for those who have never paid attention to such things, is to allow you to turn the lights on at one location and off somewhere else, as when walking down a hall.) The second way isn't recommended, and may violate modern electrical codes for reasons I'm not about to go into. But it'll work, and if it's what you've got in your old house and you don't feel like redoing the wiring when replacing the switch, it beats sitting in the dark.

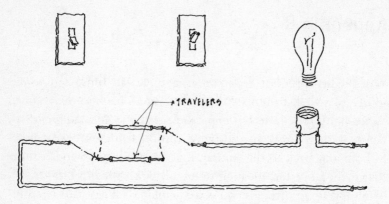

CONVENTIONAL THREE-WAY SWITCH

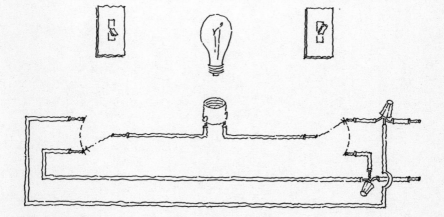

THREE-WAY SWITCH IN ED'S PARENTS' HOUSE

Appendix B

When lights are connected in series, a single wire runs from power source to switch to bulb #1 to bulb #2 and back to the source. When lights are connected in parallel, each is connected independently to the source, with the wire running from source to switch to bulb and back to the source. It seemed pretty obvious to me that if the juice ran through one bulb you'd get full brightness, whereas if it ran through two you'd get half. It sure wasn't obvious to my old man, but then again he didn't have Charlie's illustrations as an explanatory aid.

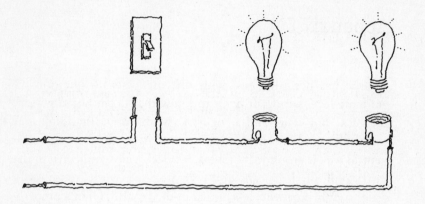

LIGHTS WIRED IN SERIES (HALF-BRIGHTNESS)

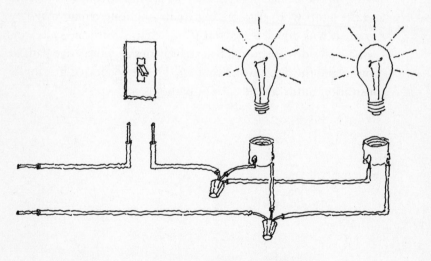

LIGHTS WIRED IN PARALLEL (FULL BRIGHTNESS)

Appendix C

Charlie has done his best with this one, but no question it's graduate-level wiring. It helps to know that (a) in house wiring, there's a "hot" wire and a "neutral" wire, notwithstanding that we're talking about alternating current here; (b) for safety, the neutral wire is grounded—that is, it's electrically connected to the earth, typically by means of a wire attached to the house's cold water supply pipe, which is buried in the ground; (c) in a properly wired house, the metal housing of a fluorescent light fixture is also grounded, either by conduit (in Chicago) or a separate ground wire (most other places); (d) many old fluorescent light fixtures had a ballast that sometimes melted and shorted to the metal housing; (e) in a correctly wired lighting circuit—that is, with the switch on the hot side—a shorted ballast trips the circuit breaker and the lights won't turn on; but (f) in a lighting circuit wired by a goof such as myself at age fourteen—that is, with the switch on the neutral side—a shorted ballast provides an alternative path to ground and the lights won't shut *off.* The heavy dotted line in the illustration indicates the current path.

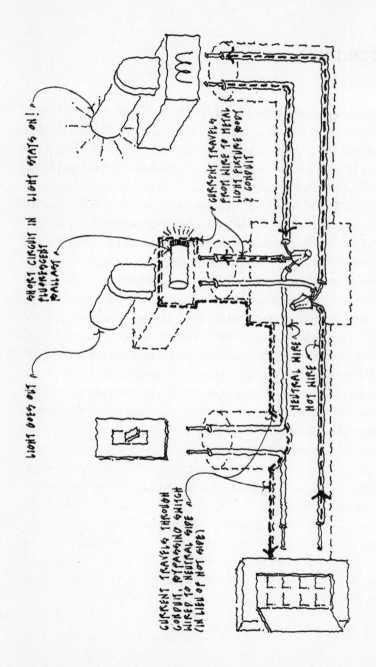

Appendix D

The drawing below depicts one of the subtleties to which the Chief and I were introduced by Lee the electrician, which had to do with wiring a string of outlets. This will make little sense unless you know that: (a) outlets typically have two screws on either side, to which the wires are attached (many outlets also have push-in wiring terminals, in case you're in too much of a hurry to use the screws, but these don't change the argument); (b) in ancient days, it was customary when wiring a string of outlets to attach the wire from the upstream outlet to one screw and the wire from the downstream outlet to the other screw, to save a minute or two of installation time; (c) this was perfectly safe provided the two screws were connected by a fat metal strip, as was the case for many years; (d) however, at some point—I'm chagrined to say it was probably around the time I was born—manufacturers quit using a fat metal strip in favor of a thin metal bridge, which could easily be broken off in case you wanted to separate the two sockets electrically; (e) from then on, daisy-chaining outlets together by connecting the wires to the screws was unwise, because the full current load was carried by the thin metal bridge, and if the load was unusually heavy—for example, if you had a toaster at the far end, as shown in Charlie's illustration—the bridge might overheat or melt, overheating being the more serious problem due to the danger of fire. The correct procedure is shown on the left side of the illustration—connect the two wires directly with a short lead to the outlet. I ought to have learned this in year one of my electrical studies rather than year twenty-eight, but at least I learned it.

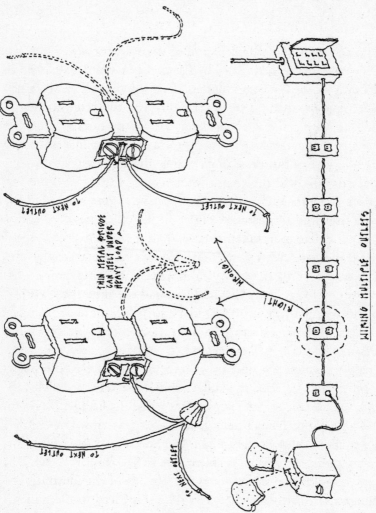

Photo by Patrick O'Neil

ED ZOTTI is a longtime journalist and editor of the syndicated "Straight Dope" newspaper column by Cecil Adams. His articles and book reviews on subjects ranging from architecture to pigeon racing have appeared in such publications as the *Wall Street Journal* and the *New York Times*. He has published six books and is the recipient of a Citation for Excellence in Urban Design from the American Institute of Architects. Ed lives in Chicago with his wife, Mary Lubben, and his kids, Ryan, Ani, and Andrew.

If you'd like to comment on this book, visit Ed Zotti's blog at www.edzotti.com.